China Urbanizes

China Urbanizes
Consequences, Strategies, and Policies

Shahid Yusuf
Tony Saich

THE WORLD BANK
Washington, D.C.

1818 H Street NW
Washington DC 20433
Telephone: 202-473-1000
Internet: www.worldbank.org
E-mail: feedback@worldbank.org

ISBN: 978-0-8213-7211-1
eISBN: 978-0-8213-7212-8
DOI: 10.1596/978-0-8213-7211-1

Library of Congress Cataloging-in-Publication Data
China urbanizes : consequences, strategies, and policies / edited by Shahid Yusuf and Anthony Saich.
    p. cm.
    ISBN 978-0-8213-7211-1 — ISBN 978-0-8213-7212-8 (electronic)

    1. City planning—China. 2. Urbanization—China. 3. China—Population. 4. China—Economic conditions—2000- I. Yusuf, Shahid, 1949- II. Saich, Tony.
    HT169.C6C474 2007
    307.1'2160951—dc22   2007032196

Cover photo: Corbis
Cover design: Naylor Design, Washington, D.C.

Contents

Preface

Urbanization and urban development will leave a deep imprint on structural, social, and economic change in China for decades to come. In 2007 the urban share of China's population was almost 44 percent, and the urban economy accounted for nearly 80 percent of domestic output. Both these percentages will be rising, the first steeply, the second much more gently, because the urban sector is already the dominant economic force.

Given these changes, the urban dimension figures prominently in China's 11th Five-Year Plan. Urban issues were also central to the World Bank's study, *China's Development Priorities*, by Shahid Yusuf and Kaoru Nabeshima, prepared in close consultation with China's National Development and Reform Commission (NDRC). The chapters in this volume were initially prepared for that study. They were subsequently revised and updated in order to incorporate feedback received in seminars and discussions in China and to reflect the latest research.

The chapters, all written by leading specialists on China, examine key facets of the urbanization process, highlighting both the challenges for and options open to policy makers. By stitching together the implications of migration, poverty, urban financing, governance, energy use, and water consumption, the chapters provide an integrated perspective on the recent past and the medium-term outlook for urban change in China.

We are deeply grateful to the U. K. Department for International Development (DfID) and the Asia Programs at Harvard University for generous financial support, without which the preparation and publication of this volume would not have been possible. We thank David Dollar, Bert Hofman, the staff of the NDRC, Jianqing Chen, and Julian Chang for the support they provided throughout this study. We also greatly appreciate the efforts of Marinella Yadao and Rebecca Sugui in helping us prepare the manuscript; our editors Stuart Tucker and Patricia Katayama; and our production manager Mary Fisk. Finally, we thank the contributors to this volume for their patience and perseverance in revising their chapters, and Kaoru Nabeshima, who helped us shepherd the study since its inception and who contributed substantively to the volume's structure and content.

Contributors

C. **Cindy Fan** is Professor, Department of Geography and Department of Asian American Studies, University of California—Los Angeles.

Patrick Honohan is Professor of International Financial Economics and Development, Department of Economics and Institute for International Economic Studies, Trinity College, Dublin.

Kaoru Nabeshima is a Consultant, Development Research Group, World Bank.

Albert Park is Reader in the Economy of China, Department of Economics and School for Interdisciplinary Area Studies, University of Oxford.

Tony Saich is Daewoo Professor of International Affairs, Kennedy School of Government, and Director, Harvard University, Asia Center.

Zmarak Shalizi is former Senior Research Manager, Development Research Group, World Bank.

Edward S. Steinfeld is Associate Professor, Department of Political Science, Massachusetts Institute of Technology.

John G. Taylor is Professor of Politics, Director of MSc Development Studies Programme, London South Bank University.

Shahid Yusuf is Economic Adviser, Development Research Group, World Bank.

Abbreviations

ADB	Asian Development Bank
APERC	Asia Pacific Energy Research Centre
CASS	Chinese Academy of Social Sciences
CBO	Congressional Budget Office
CCP	Chinese Communist Party
COD	chemical oxygen demand
CPI	consumer price index
CULS	China Urban Labor Survey
DfID	Department for International Development
EIA	Energy Information Administration
FAO	Food and Agriculture Organization
FDI	foreign direct investment
GDP	gross domestic product
GNP	gross national product
GW	gigawatts
HGF	Housing Guarantee Fund
HPF	Housing Provident Fund
IEA	International Energy Agency
IT	information technology
LP	legal person

MLSS	Minimum Living Security Standard
MOCA	Ministry of Civil Affairs
Mtoe	million tons of oil equivalent
MWR	Ministry of Water Resources
NBS	National Bureau of Statistics
NDRC	National Development and Reform Commission
NGO	nongovernmental organization
PADO	Poverty Alleviation and Development Office
PPA	power purchase agreement
PSB	Public Security Bureau
OECD	Organisation for Economic Co-operation and Development
OPEC	Organization of the Petroleum-Exporting Countries
RCC	rural credit cooperative
R&D	research and development
RPI	retail price index
SEPA	State Environmental Protection Administration
SME	small- and medium-size enterprises
SOE	state-owned enterprise
toe	tons of oil equivalent
TVE	town and village enterprises
UDIC	urban development investment corporation
UNDP	United Nations Development Programme
UNESCO	United Nations Educational, Scientific and Cultural Organization
USDA	U. S. Department of Agriculture
WHO	World Health Organization
WTO	World Trade Organization

CHAPTER 1

Optimizing Urban Development

Shahid Yusuf and Kaoru Nabeshima

China's outward-oriented industrialization, spearheaded by the coastal provinces, led to a quickening of urbanization from the start of reforms in the early 1980s. In 1980 China, with an urbanization rate of 19.6 percent, was less urbanized than Indonesia (22.1 percent), India (23.1 percent), or Pakistan (28.1 percent) (table 1.1). By 2005, 42.9 percent of China's population lived in urban areas, still somewhat below the global average of 50 percent but close to the average for East Asia (41 percent) and well in excess of India's 28.7 percent rate.[1]

Between 1980 and 2000, 268 million Chinese entered into the urban domain, mainly through migration from rural areas. This figure was almost twice as large as the increase of the urban population in the rest of East Asia (table 1.2). By 2020, urbanization could pass the 60 percent mark, with 200 million or more rural dwellers joining the ranks of the urban population. The scale of urbanization in China will dwarf that occurring elsewhere in East Asia.

This shift in the demographic center of gravity has seismic implications for China and major spillover effects for the rest of the world. It will be a driver of economic growth. The urban economy should generate enough jobs to absorb the additions to the urban workforce at steadily

---

1 The classification of the urban population has changed overtime (see Fang 1990; Zhou and Ma 2003).

1

Table 1.1. Percentage of Population Living in Urban Areas in Selected Asian Countries, 1980–2005

Country	1980	1985	1990	1995	2000	2005
China	19.6	23.0	27.4	31.4	35.8	42.9
India	23.1	24.3	25.5	26.6	27.7	28.7
Indonesia	22.1	26.1	30.6	35.6	42	48.1
Pakistan	28.1	29.3	30.6	31.8	33.1	34.9

Source: NBS 2006; World Bank 2006.

Table 1.2. Urban Population in China and East Asia, 1960–2005
(millions)

Year	China	East Asia
1960	130.7	86.2
1970	144.2	125.2
1980	191.4	177.6
1990	302.0	241.1
2000	459.1	314.2
2005	562.1	352.4

Source: Data for East Asia are from World Bank 2006. Data for China are from Fang 1990, Pannell 2003, and NBS 2006.
Note: East Asia includes Hong Kong (China), Indonesia, Japan, the Republic of Korea, Malaysia, the Philippines, Singapore, Thailand, and Vietnam.

rising wages if the economy continues to grow at least 8 percent a year (feasible given the elastic labor supply); capital accumulation is sustained; and the scope for enhancing technological capabilities increases.[2,3] Meeting these conditions is crucial for urban residents, because urban employment opportunities and the median urban wage will determine living standards in cities (see chapter 8). These conditions will have a bearing on whether the influx of people leads to the formation of slums, as it has in many Latin American cities. They will also affect income distribution,[4]

---

2 Bosworth and Collins (2007) estimate that total factor productivity rose by 4 percent a year between 1993 and 2004 and that its contribution to overall growth was only a little less than that of capital. He and Kuijs (2007) estimate that TFP grew by 2.8 percent per annum during 1993–2005.

3 New York's real manufacturing wages kept rising in the second half of the 19th century, even though a significant number of immigrants came to New York. In the early part of the 20th century, when immigration to the United States increased dramatically, real wages in New York (the entry point of many immigrants) started to fall (Glaeser 2005b).

4 Because of the widening gap between rural and urban incomes and interprovincial disparities, China's income distribution, as reflected by the Gini coefficient, has risen rapidly, from 0.33 in 1980 to 0.49 in 2005 ("China's Income Gap" 2006). Other estimates of the Gini coefficient in 2005 are slightly lower. The distribution of net wealth in urban areas, which is strongly influenced by property ownership, is also becoming more skewed, although it remains relatively equal (Wu 2004; Gustafsson, Shi, and Zhong 2006; Saich 2006).

overall energy and water consumption, and the quality of life in cities. A rising median wage rate and a relatively egalitarian income distribution would be broadly advantageous, but they would also push up per capita resource consumption. Chinese cities would become larger users of local and global resources, including global public goods. At the same time, prosperity and technological capability would provide the means to contain the resource costs and externalities associated with growth. A slow-growth scenario or a scenario in which average income rises but incomes become more unequal might lead to somewhat lower resource consumption, perhaps more than counterbalanced by sociopolitical tensions, which could jeopardize economic performance.

A host of policies will collectively determine growth, income distribution, resource use, and the quality of life. From an urban perspective, five sets of policies are especially noteworthy:

• Policies affecting rural-to-urban migration and intersectoral differences in average household incomes
• Policies affecting the size distribution of cities and the relative concentration of people in major metropolitan centers
• Policies affecting the development of urban infrastructure
• Policies that impinge on the availability of and access to public services and social safety nets
• Policies and institutions that regulate energy and water use in cities and help control urban pollution.[5]

These policies are the primary focus of this volume.

The rest of this chapter is divided into five sections. The first section briefly reviews the history of urbanization since ancient times. The second section describes some of the positive and negative consequences of migration to cities. The third section explores factors that will define China's urban development strategy. The fourth section examines the policies that will guide urban change. The fifth section provides some concluding observations.

Urbanization in China since Ancient Times

Urbanization in China began almost 4,000 years ago, although Neolithic villages had begun sprouting in river valleys as early as 5000 BC

---

5 China's plans with regard to energy-use pricing, efficiency, technology, and regulation are presented in NDRC (2007). Rosen and Houser (2007) assess the demand and supply situation and the implications of China's consumption on global markets. Shalizi (2007) provides an assessment based on a comprehensive modeling framework.

(Ebrey 1996). Ho Ping–ti writes of the "large urban centers" that arose in Shang times (circa 1700–1100 BC) and of the high walls of packed earth that surrounded many settlements, including most notably, the cities near Cheng-chou and An-yang in Hunan (Ho 1975; Friedman 2005). The number of cities proliferated during the Zhou dynasty (1122—221 BC). Created primarily to fulfill military and administrative roles, these cities also took on other functions (Zhao 1994).

The curve tilts ever so gently upward as urban populations began to grow during the Qin (221–206 BC) and Han dynasties (202 BC–AD 220). By the time of the Southern Song dynasty (12th century), 10–13 percent of the Chinese population lived in cities, with Kaifeng, the capital of the Song, having a population of almost 1 million people (Bairoch 1991).[6] Mote (1999) surmises that the number of urban dwellers in China during the middle years of the Song dynasty equaled those in the rest of the world at that time.

For a few hundred years thereafter, the curve remains fairly flat. However, the scale of cities such as Hangzhou on the West Lake impressed Marco Polo, who had seen no comparable center in Europe ("the most splendid city in the world . . . [with] 13,000 bridges mostly of stone") (Polo 1958: 213). By the time the Ming dynasty was entering its twilight years in the 16th century, the curve of urbanization had inched up a notch to 11–14 percent (Bairoch 1991). Major centers such as Beijing and Nanjing housed almost 1 million people, a handful of cities had populations of half a million or more, and "scores of urban places" had populations of 100,000. "Urban life was rich, comfortable, and elegant . . . varied and lively [in the larger cities]" (Mote 1999: 763).

By the late 19th century, the urban share of China's population had fallen to 6.0–7.5 percent, although the absolute number of urban dwellers rose, because population growth accelerated in the 18th and early 19th centuries (Bairoch 1991; Zhao 1994). By this time, the industrializing countries of Europe had pulled ahead, with urbanization rates of 61 percent in Britain and 29 percent in Europe as a whole. This gap between China and Western Europe had widened further by 1949, when the communist regime took hold of the reins of government.

Initially, the new government allowed cities to grow. Since the 1960s, however, China has sought to tightly manage the course of urbanization (see Kwok 1981; Fang 1990). The intersectoral movement of people and, from the 1970s, fertility rates were controlled with considerable

---

6 Zhao (1994) cites a much higher figure of 22 percent for the urban population under the Song dynasty.

success through the combined efforts of the Communist Party and the government bureaucracy.[7]

The main instrument used to regulate movement is the *hukou* system, which assigns every person in China a residence in a specific locality.[8] This system distinguishes urban from rural residents, with urban households enjoying far more benefits and privileges than rural ones (see Friedman 2005). The one-child policy—which is still enforced, albeit more flexibly than it once was—meanwhile checked population growth, pushing fertility down from 5.9 in 1970 and 2.9 in 1979 to 1.7 in 2004 (Hesketh, Lu, and Xing 2005). Urban fertility was 1.3 in 2005, while the rate in rural areas was a little less than 2 (Hesketh, Lu, and Xing 2005). By 2005 China's population was growing at 0.59 percent a year (NBS 2006).

Together these two policies slowed the increase in the urban share of China's population to a crawl until well into the 1980s (Fang 1990). Migration between sectors was not brought to a complete halt, but the *hukou* system reduced it to a trickle, by making it difficult to find housing or gain access to essential services outside of one's official place of residence. Changing one's residence and, most important, obtaining an urban *hukou* required and still requires hard-to-obtain official approval, especially in larger cities.

Once industrial and trade reforms gathered momentum in the 1980s, demand for workers from urban enterprises began drawing more migrants to the cities, increasing the pressure on municipal authorities to relax *hukou* rules. Initially, many cities resisted these pressures, preferring a very gradual easing of the restrictions for fear that anything more would attract an unmanageable flood of migrants. This change in policy stimulated the multiplication of industry in small towns and villages in rural areas, which by 1990 employed 93 million workers (see chapter 2) and was responsible for 17 percent of China's exports of manufactures.[9] By

---

7 China's efforts to regulate population growth gathered momentum after the Cultural Revolution in the late 1960s. Fertility was already declining in the 1970s before the announcement and subsequent implementation of the one-child policy in 1979 (Baochang and others 2007). See Hesketh, Lu, and Xing (2005) regarding the impact of the policy over a quarter century.

8 During the second half of the 1960s and in the 1970s, the government also "sent down" urban youth to rural areas and redeployed millions of urban workers to interior southwestern provinces in order to disperse industrial capabilities and reduce China's vulnerability to attacks from abroad. On these rustication and Third Front inland industry development programs, see Gardner (1971), Bernstein (1977), Naughton (1988), Fang (1990), and Demurger and others (2002).

9 The government encouraged these former "commune and brigade" enterprises, because they raised rural incomes and stemmed migration (Zhu 2000; Wu 2005).

1996 township and village enterprises (TVEs) employed 135 million and accounted for 46 percent of exports (Li 2006).[10] Rural industrialization drew on an unforeseen reservoir of entrepreneurship and was aided by fiscal decentralization that encouraged lower-level cadres to take the lead in developing industry (Oi 1992; Qian 1999).

By the mid-1980s, attitudes toward urbanization began to shift, with cities coming to be viewed as "growth poles" and the "city as leading the country." Some Chinese researchers argued that "growth poles should be scattered through the country, each sending waves of economic growth in its hinterland" (Fan 1997: 630). In order to accelerate industrialization and meet the needs of construction and other services, cities had to absorb more migrants. Moreover, the small towns that had become important foci for industrial development grew to become substantial urban centers with concentrations of industry and were reclassified as cities, a process known as *in situ* urbanization.[11]

China retained the *hukou* system, but by the mid-1990s the inevitability of rising urbanization was widely accepted, only its speed remained an issue. Differing views came to determine the enforcement of *hukou* requirements. Viewing migration as a means of expanding their industrial bases and using the fiscal revenue generated to build urban infrastructure, small- and medium-size cities began to welcome the flow of labor from the rural sector. In contrast, many larger cities, especially in coastal areas, remained wary. They absorbed large numbers of temporary migrants to satisfy their for industrial and construction workers needs[12] but continued to use *hukou* to limit permanent migration.[13]

Benefits and Challenges of Urban Migration

Urbanization is now perceived as intrinsic to the process of growth and modernization, and the role of rural migration in diversifying sources of rural incomes and narrowing intersectoral disparities in household incomes is better understood (Knight and Song 2003). But

---

10 Employment in TVEs declined thereafter but has since recovered, reaching 143 million in 2005 (NBS 2006).
11 Zhu (2000) describes this process in Jinjiang county, Fujian Province. See also chapter 2.
12 Pannell (2003) describes the regional pattern of urbanization in China and the demographic structure of the urban population.
13 In some cities, particularly in Guangdong and Fujian (for example, Dongguan), non-residents account for up to half of the population.

the desire to manage migration and contain the costs of urban housing and social benefits provided to residents means that there is an unwillingness to dismantle the *hukou* system, although Beijing has allowed local governments much greater discretion regarding how it is applied and enforced.

Per capita annual income disparities of 1:2.4 between rural and urban areas and vastly greater job opportunities in cities make it highly attractive for rural people to migrate.[14] The result is that migration is adding to the numbers of registered urban residents and swelling the ranks of the so-called "floating population," made up of people with rural *hukou* who are temporarily living and working in cities (see chapter 3). The size of this transient (inter- and intracounty) population was almost 148 million in 2005 (see chapter 3); they are most numerous in eastern metropolitan centers, such as Beijing, Guangzhou, Shanghai, and Shenzhen, which have plentiful jobs and the "bright lights" that draw migrants.[15]

The influx of migrants, permanent or floating, has had a number of positive and negative effects. The migration of mainly young people to cities drawn from the better-educated rural cohorts has promoted growth by enhancing the labor supply and by injecting an additional dose of entrepreneurship and dynamism into the urban labor market (Bloom and Williamson 1997).[16] The remittances migrants send to their villages have significantly bolstered rural household consumption, in some cases contributing as much as 40 percent of annual household incomes (the average is closer to 20 percent). Migrants have helped bring living standards in some of the poorest rural areas closer to urban levels. These and other positive outcomes outweigh some of the problems associated with migration.

---

14 The unadjusted differential in rural and urban incomes is 1:3.5. See chapter 2 and tables 10.8 and 10.18 in the *China Statistical Yearbook* (NBS 2006). The rural and urban income divide is the main cause of income inequality in China (Sicular and others 2007). Tsui (2007) shows that inequality among provinces has arisen from the allocation over time of capital and FDI and the influence that allocation has had on total factory productivity across provinces.

15 The provinces and cities that have attracted the largest number of migrants are Guangdong, Zhejiang, Jiangsu, Shandong, Beijing, Shanghai, and Guangzhou. About 15–20 million migrants work in Guangdong ("Delta Dreams" 2006), the destination of migrants from Hunan, Jiangxi, Sichuan, Guangxi, and Hainan. Shandong has attracted migrants from Heilongjiang and Liaoning (see chapter 3; Fan 2005).

16 Bloom and Williamson (1997) find that demographic shift, which affected labor force growth, age structure, domestic savings, and domestic investment, was responsible for 1.4–1.9 percent of the annual growth in GDP in East Asia between 1965 and 1990.

Perhaps the most serious concern centers on the risk migrants run of becoming part of the urban poor.[17] Temporary migrants have limited access to health and education services. Their age makes them healthier than older people but leaves them more vulnerable to accidents and childbirth. Migrants are less likely to visit a doctor when sick and more likely to self-medicate. The cost of sending their children to school can be a major burden. Some live in crowded conditions, although the evidence on this problem is equivocal.[18]

While migrants' income net of remittances can be meager, migrants are less likely than elderly or disabled urban residents to fall below the poverty line. The evidence reported in chapters 2, 3, and 4 suggests that only a small percentage of urban migrants can, strictly speaking, be classified as poor.[19]

There are worries that the departure of many young educated workers will denude the countryside of skills, know-how, and entrepreneurship. This is unlikely for some time to come, if ever. China's farm population exceeds the numbers needed; many workers return to their villages after a stint in the cities and invest their earnings in farming or other rural activities. Moreover, the most educated are less likely to migrate (see chapter 3; Murphy 2002).[20]

The increase in China's urban population from 191 million in 1980 to 562 million in 2005 has called for massive investment in urban housing and infrastructure. Amazingly, China has been able to absorb more than 370 million people in its cities without the proliferation of urban slums, although sewerage and waste disposal services have struggled to keep up with demand. Between 1990 and 2000, 130 million new urban dwellers were provided access to improved sanitation facilities;

---

17 Townspeople have traditionally displayed antipathy toward rural migrants, finding it difficult to comprehend their dialects, complaining about their lack of culture, and blaming them for bringing crime and disease to urban areas. Some of this antipathy persists and is responsible for the continuing resistance to migration (Zhang 2001). According to Ravallion, Chen, and Sangraula (2007), urban poverty is just 4 percent of the rural rate, and it has remained low since the mid-1990s, even in the face of heavy migration to the cities.

18 Wu (2002) finds that about a third of all migrants in Shanghai live in dormitories provided by employers and about half rent their accommodations. Overall, migrants in some of the larger coastal cities appear to be living in housing equivalent to that of urban residents at similar levels of income (Jiang 2006).

19 The exclusion of dependants could introduce some bias.

20 Murphy's (2002) study of counties in Jiangxi describes the proactive approach taken by officials to entice back migrants who have accumulated capital and skills while in cities. Returning migrants are responsible for establishing numerous businesses in their home towns and villages.

nearly a third of the urban population still lacks these services, however (Mohan 2006).

Old workplaces, their housing compounds, and concentrations of small businesses contribute to urban dilapidation in inner-city areas. On the fringes of major cities such as Beijing, migrants have created small enclaves, where housing quality can be variable. In Beijing's Zhejiang village, for example, living standards are relatively high, because migrants work in small businesses that produce clothing and footwear. Migrants from Henan who collect rubbish are much poorer (Wu 2004).

The relative smoothness of the urban transition has been made possible by the availability of investment funds intermediated by the banking system, the remarkable strides made by the construction sector, and acceptable growth in regulatory capacity in urban centers. But the role of capital generated through high domestic savings has been paramount.

Urban investment started from a modest base in the mid-1980s and accelerated throughout 1990s, although growth slowed in 1999 and 2000. Beginning in 2001, urban investment picked up the pace again, registering double-digit growth, especially in 2003, when it rose 20 percent, and 2004, when it rose 31 percent. For 2004 the share of housing expenditure is estimated to have been 10 percent of GDP, with total infrastructure spending estimated at almost 20 percent of GDP (Yusuf and Nabeshima 2006b).

This investment has made an enormous difference, visible to any visitor. More important, it has enabled China to accommodate a far-reaching geographic and intersectoral distribution of the population. Might the resources have been allocated more efficiently and through more-varied financial channels? Chapter 5 indicates how the allocative process has been distorted by the need to sustain state-owned enterprises and by the actions of local authorities, who are able to influence banks' lending decisions. But the fact remains that no country has matched the scale of China's achievement in mobilizing financial resources using the banking system to funnel capital to urban development. This financial widening is signified by the high rates of M3—a definition of the money supply that includes currency, demand deposits, savings and time deposits, ODs, money market accounts, eurodollar deposits, and REPOS and the ratio of loans to GDP, which compare favorably with those of Japan and exceed those of Brazil, the Republic of Korea, and Mexico. However, the low ratios of bonds and market capitalization of listed companies to GDP indicate a good deal of room for enhancing financial depth (figure 1.1).

Figure 1.1. Financial Development in Selected Countries, 2005

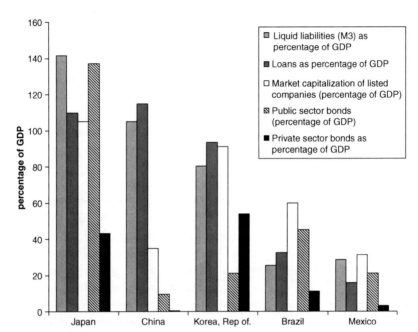

Source: Data on M3 and market capitalization are from World Bank 2006; data on public and private sector bonds as a percentage of GDP are from the World Bank's internal financial data base; data on loans as percentage of GDP are from International Fiancial Statistics (IFS) Chinese bond data are from Mu 2005.

Urban residents consume far more energy than their rural counterparts.[21] The energy is used for transport, heating, cooling, for generating electricity, and industry. In 2005, agriculture, forestry, and fishery consumed only 3.6 percent of total commercial energy. Urban households consumed 3.63 times more commercial energy than their rural counterparts.[22] As more of China's population locates in cities, commercial energy use per capita is bound to rise significantly.

Other factors also contribute to the energy intensity of the urban economy. They include motorization, space heating and cooling, and the proliferation of energy-using appliances, all of which have high-income elasticities. As urban households become more affluent, their demand for

---

21 For energy production in China from renewable and nonrenewable sources between 1980 and 2002, see Chen and Chen (2007a, 2007b).
22 This does not include energy consumption by rural enterprises or use of energy from biomass (Pan 2002).

all three will continue to push up energy consumption.[23] In 2005, industry accounted for 70 percent, transport for 7 percent, and households for 10 percent of energy consumed (NBS 2006).[24] The share of transport is sure to rise substantially, propelled by the trend toward private vehicle use.[25] Household consumption of electricity will also rise (see chapter 6).

Energy consumption creates negative externalities, in the form of carbon dioxide pollutants, and acid rain. In 2006, China became the leading emitter of carbon dioxide into the atmosphere (6.2 billion tons as against 5.8 billion tons by the United States). Release of sulfur dioxide and particulates, particularly in the northern parts of the country, is exacerbated by the shortage of water. As a result, only a very small fraction of the coal used can be washed to rid it of sulfur, ash, and impurities (Roumasset, Wang, and Burnett 2006).[26] As energy use climbs, air pollution in Chinese cities from nitrogen oxide, sulfur dioxide, and particulates—already among the most severe in the world—could become even more intense.[27] Of the 20 cities with the worst air pollution in the world, 16 are in China (Wu 2006; Ho and Nielsen 2007).[28]

China's energy demand mirrors the unusually dynamic growth of its urban economy. The increasing use of energy is a sign of economic vigor and rising incomes. Between 2000 and 2005, the elasticity of consumption averaged 0.93; in 2005, 69 percent of energy derived from coal and 21 percent from oil. Of the energy derived from petroleum, net imports accounted for

---

23 Although shifts in consumption that increase the share of services will reduce energy consumption, the Economist Intelligence Unit estimates that China's energy consumption relative to that of the United States will rise from 39 percent in 2000 to 86 percent in 2011 ("The Health of a Nation" 2007).

24 Industry and transport absorb 80 percent of petroleum consumed, mostly in the form of middle distillates (CBO 2006).

25 Ownership of passenger vehicles increased from 9.9 million vehicles in 2001 to 21 million in 2005, propelled by an easing of consumer credit (Roumasset, Wang, and Burnett 2006; China Statistical Yearbook 2006). Some cities, such as Suzhou, are taking a lead in improving air quality by encouraging the use of motorbikes that use battery power. But even in this "beautifully preserved" and "well-tended city," the air is "almost unbreathable" and the "canals are filled with black bubbling water" (Cheng 2006: 1859).

26 The impurities present in the coal being shipped increases the burden on China's railway system, which devotes 40 percent of its capacity to the transport of coal ("Free Flow" 2005). Washing coal is not without complication, because the sludge and wastewater must be treated to avoid localized pollution.

27 The severity of air and water population was already evident in the early 1970s. In response, a national conference was held in 1973 and a basic environmental law passed in 1979 (Kojima 1987). Acid rain falls on one-third of China; emissions from Chinese industry and power plants also contribute to acid rain in Japan and the Republic of Korea (Roumasset, Wang, and Burnett 2006).

28 The world's most polluted city is Linzen, in Shanxi, which produces coke. Lanzhou, the capital of Gansu, is also among the top 10 ("Lanzhou to Walk" 2007).

44 percent, and the share is rising (CBO 2006; NBS 2006). Given the depletion of petroleum resources and the threat of climate change induced by greenhouse gases (which could also contribute to a significant reduction in national crop fields by mid-century) the implications of China's urbanization are disconcerting in the medium term and troubling over the longer run. Limiting the energy intensity of urban development will be a struggle, but it is one that policy makers will find impossible to sidestep.

While fossil fuels can be imported, water in the quantities required cannot. Desalinating seawater consumes energy; pumping the water inland adds to the energy costs. Looking ahead, urban development in the drier regions of China is likely to be circumscribed by the availability of usable water. Currently, two-thirds of China's cities are faced with water scarcity, caused by the uneven geographical distribution of water supplies, the diversion of water for agricultural purposes, and pollution from industrial sources (especially organic material), which renders up to 70 percent of the water from five of China's seven largest rivers unfit for consumption. Research on the Pearl River delta area shows that urban river water is far more polluted than water in rural counties (Ouyang, Zhu, and Kuang 2006). At great cost, China is diverting water from the Yangtze to the northeastern part of the country to meet the needs of the increasingly water-stressed 3-H region (the basins of the Huai, Hai, and Huang [Yellow] Rivers). Once completed, this effort will provide some relief, though for how long is uncertain, as are the ecological consequences for the Yangtze basin and the receiving region.

Per capita water availability in 2005 was just 2,152 cubic meters, only 12 percent of which was used for household purposes. Urban per capita water consumption in China is relatively modest compared with Japan and the United States (see chapter 7). But water is inefficiently utilized, because it remains underpriced. China uses 6 times more water per unit of GDP than the Republic of Korea and 10 times more than Japan. For this reason, underground water is also being pumped at unsustainable rates, causing the water table to fall, increasing the mineral content of water, and resulting in the subsidence of the land in cities and the infiltration of brackish water into subterranean aquifers.[29]

---

29 The North China Plain derives close to 60 percent of its water supplies from groundwater, and according to some projects, the aquifers could be largely depleted in 30 years ("Beneath Booming Cities 2007; Evans and Merz 2007). Groundwater tables have dropped by as much as 90 meters in the Hai plains and by 100–300 meters in Beijing; they are also dropping in Shanghai and Shijiazhuang, where many wells must be dug to a depth of 200 meters to find clean water (see chapter 7). See Pielou (1998) on the problems caused by the unsustainable extraction of groundwater.

More than 680 million Chinese live in the drier northern region (which has just one-sixth of the per capita water supply available in the south and one-tenth of the world's average), more than half of them are urban dwellers. As this ratio climbs to 60 percent in the next 15 years and per capita urban consumption rises, as is likely, the intersectoral allocation of water and the management of water use will require strategic thinking on the cultivation of water-intensive cereals such as corn and wheat, the course and shape of urban development and the effective coordination of basin-wide water management both surface and subterranean (see chapter 7). The policies described below will have to be applied with considerable force, as there are no substitutes for water.

Urban development is a complex, multifaceted process; farsighted and entrepreneurial management is a key to success. The sheer pace at which Chinese cities are expanding and the decentralized structure of government puts a particularly high premium on the planning and managerial skills of local authorities. Cities in China have coped more effectively with rapid urbanization, the mobilization of resources, the building of infrastructure, and the wooing of industry than cities in other middle- and lower-middle-income countries. Moreover, the country's larger cities are better governed than its smaller ones (see chapter 8). So far, most cities have been able to arrest the spread of slums (Flavin and Gardner 2006; Jiang 2006) and contain the spread of crime. Chinese cities are cleaner than average, and in the majority of cases, the combined efforts of Street Offices and higher-level municipal departments ensure that policies are competently executed. This is a considerable achievement, and the fact that citizen satisfaction levels rose between 2003 and 2005 is a good sign (see chapter 8). On average, other large countries, such as Brazil, India, and Indonesia, lag well behind China in terms of effective municipal functioning.

However, according to the World Values survey conducted in 2006, Chinese have much more confidence in their government than Americans, with 97 percent of Chinese and just 37 percent of Americans expressing confidence. Moreover, 84 percent of Chinese but just 37 percent of Americans believe that the government is not in the grip of special interest groups (Shiller 2006).[30] The findings reported in chapter 8 indicate that urban Chinese place less trust in their local governments (67 percent) than in the central government (84 percent).

---

30 A Lichtman/Zogby poll conducted in late 2006 found that only 3 percent of Americans surveyed had trust in the U.S. Congress ("The Way We Were" 2006).

The dissatisfaction of China's urban dwellers with local governments derives from four sources. First, corruption is a major concern. As in other countries, it is associated with land deals, construction projects, bank lending, social security funds, and other activities.[31] Transparency International ranked China 70th of 163 countries in 2006, but this type of index provides only a partial perspective (Transparency International http://www.transparency.org/).

Second, there is dissatisfaction with the provision of health services, more so than with education.[32] Even for privileged urban residents, health services are becoming less accessible and costlier. More and more people have to pay out of pocket for health care and medications, and the shift to curative care is shortchanging more cost-effective preventive medicine.[33]

Third, as cities expand into periurban areas, the confiscation and sale of farm land to developers is being strongly condemned, especially by displaced farmers, who receive limited compensation and face difficulty finding employment in the urban labor market. Others view these sales as evidence of corrupt dealings and inept fiscal management, because current expenditures are being offset by the proceeds from these sales rather than being aligned with revenues appropriately augmented by intergovernmental transfers.

Fourth, the urban safety net for the poor—a mix of the widowed elderly, the disabled, laid-off state enterprise workers lacking marketable skills, people working in the informal sector, and migrants—is inadequate (Wu 2004). *Di Bao*—a means-tested transfer that offers minimal assistance to urban residents who satisfy the poverty criteria—is a bare-bones scheme that deserves to be augmented or supplemented by additional assistance. Beyond this, there is growing concern regarding unemployment compensation for laid-off workers and the adequacy of pension benefits.[34]

These are not minor complaints, and they are rising in volume, despite the efforts of the central government to root out corruption with frequent inspection tours by the Communist Party's Central Commission for

---

31 In September 2006 a number of officials from the Shanghai administration, including the mayor, were implicated in the misappropriation of US$400 million from the municipal pension fund ("Anti-Graft Campaign" 2006; "Shanghaied" 2006).

32 Gan and Gong (2007) show how periods of morbidity before the age of 21 significantly reduce an individual's education status.

33 Medical expenses account for 11.8 percent of household consumption, more than education or transport ("China's Income Gap" 2006).

34 Wu (2005) provides a detailed account of how China has developed the elements of a social security system (pensions, medical insurance, and unemployment compensation) and reviews current reform options. Other proposale for reforming the pension system are presented by Dunaway and Arora (2007).

Discipline Inspection, which meted out harsh punishments. Wu (2006) cites an official report indicating that 42,000 public officials were investigated for corrupt practices each year between 2002 and 2005 and that action was taken against 30,000 every year.[35] He notes that corruption was largely responsible for losses by the banking system equal to 6.25 percent of GDP between 1999 and 2001 and fraudulent public expenditures amounting to 2.4 percent of GDP. Reforms of the bureaucratic structure and incentives, the health system, local taxation, revenue sharing with the central government, transfers from the central government to cover the costs of unfunded expenditure assignments, and social security are all ongoing, but they barely keep up with the problems. As a result, the clamor about urban governance is not subsiding; as China's urban middle class grows and becomes more aware, protests could become more widespread.[36]

Governance issues may be easier to resolve, if partially, in China than elsewhere, because unlike many other countries, it has a vibrant urban economy that is generating jobs and constantly adding to the pool of resources. China does not face entrenched problems of slums, urban decay, an impoverished underclass, or low fiscal buoyancy, and so far it has been able to absorb migrant flows (Flavin and Gardner 2006). China's cities have performed relatively well, and many are governed by able and energetic leaders who are eager to improve economic circumstances and living conditions.

Crafting an Urban Development Strategy

Like many other countries, China is seeking a development path that tends to equalize rural and urban per capita incomes over time.[37] This objective, emphasized in the 11th Plan, calls for comparable growth rates across sectors (see Yusuf and Nabeshima 2006a). Barring that, rough parity between sectors can be maintained only by a decline in the population of

---

35 By redoubling its efforts in 2006 and firing four high-level officials, the government has made some headway ("China's Crackdown" 2006).

36 The number of protests rose tenfold between 1993 and 2005, to 87,000 ("In Face of Rural Unrest" 2006; Wu 2006). The spike in protests appeared after 1996, when the reform of state-owned enterprises began to add to the ranks of the urban unemployed. Many of those complaining are former state enterprise employees and displaced farmers. Some of these and other protests fall into the category of "rightful resistance," in which protestors frame "their claims with reference to protections implied in ideologies or conferred by policymakers" (O'Brien and Li 2006: 3).

37 Per capita rural incomes were below the national average in 21 of 31 provincial-level units in 2005. Rural per capita incomes were 20 percent below the national average in Sichuan and Chongaing and 40 percent below in Gansu and Guizhou ("China: Does the Countryside?" 2007).

Table 1.3. Rice, Wheat, and Maize Yields in Selected Countries and Regions, 1997–2002
(tons per hectare)

Rice (2002)		Wheat (1998–2000)		Maize (1997–99)	
Country	Yield	Country	Yield	Country	Yield
United States	7.4	China	3.8	United States	8.3
Japan	6.6	United States	2.9	Brazil	5.3
China	6.3	Argentina	2.5	China	4.9
Vietnam	4.6	Canada	2.4	Mexico	2.7
Thailand	2.6	Russian Federation	1.6	Argentina	2.4
Asia	4.0	East Asia	3.8	East Asia	4.8
World	3.9	World	2.7	World	4.3

Source: Pingali 2001; Ekboir 2002; data on rice are from World Rice Statistics (http://www.irri.org/science/ricestat/).

the slower-growing sector or income transfers from the higher-income sector to the lower-income sector.

Narrowing Rural–Urban Gaps

Crop yields in China are high relative to China's main comparators (table 1.3), leaving little scope for more than a very modest annual increase. Rice yields are close to those of Japan and the United States and well above those of Vietnam. Yields of wheat match those of the United States. These high yields are achieved through the use of improved seeds, the heavy application of fertilizers, and in the north through increasing reliance on groundwater. Farmers in China use 228 kilograms of plant nutrients per hectare—far more than the world average of 90 kilograms in 2002 (FAO 2003). By using agricultural extension services effectively, Chinese farmers have introduced new varietals and exploited biogenetic technologies, bringing themselves close to the technological frontier for food grains (Jin and others 2002), especially in rice production.[38] The gap between potential and actual yield is only 15 percent. This gap is much larger in India (58 percent) and the Philippines (65 percent)

---

38 Genetically modified crops are being widely researched and planted in China. China began research on genetically modified crops in the early 1980s and is now one of the leading countries in this field (Falkner 2006). Bt cotton is a transgenic strain of cotton that incorporates the genes of a soil-dwelling bacterium, *bacillus thuringiensis*, hence the name. The added genes induce the cotton plant to secrete toxins, which reduces the depradations of certain caterpillars, beetles, and flies that feed on the plant and can destroy it. Bt cotton was approved in 1997, and 3.7 million hectares were planted in 2004. Genetically modified varieties of rice, wheat, soybean, potato, rapeseed, cabbage, and tomatoes are under development or being introduced (Huang and others 2007).

(Jin and others 2002). According to Liu and Wang (2005), between 1991 and 1999, technological advances were responsible for more than half of growth in agricultural productivity in China.

A continuing shift toward animal husbandry, horticulture, and off-farm activities should gradually raise farm incomes, but substantial gains through a large increase in the prices of major grains, for example, would incur heavy fiscal costs, face resistance from urban interests, and be subject to restrictions by the World Trade Organization (WTO). The possibility of widening the scale of off-farm activities exists, but TVEs have passed their high-water mark, and industry thrives more in urban and periurban locations than in rural ones.

Rural development has been the objective of a succession of government programs, including, most notably, the 8–7 program, which spanned much of the 1990s.[39] Other programs are building infrastructure and attempting to improve the delivery of social services. Recently, the government has taken steps to raise the disposable incomes of agricultural households by eliminating the agricultural income tax. Despite these measures, bringing rural incomes closer to the urban average is proving to be an uphill task.

The challenge of narrowing income gaps is similar to that experienced in more-advanced countries. In Japan, for example, income differentials between sectors narrowed only as a result of migration, which sharply reduced rural populations; generous agricultural price support programs; and the increase in off-farm employment opportunities. In 2003 per capita incomes in the leading rice-producing prefectures, such as Niigata and Akita, were close to those in Osaka and 70 percent of per capita income in Tokyo (Japan Statistics Bureau 2005).

A mix of policies will be needed in China, but a significant narrowing will depend mainly on migration plus remittances. Other policies will also play roles, however. These include (a) continuing efforts to strengthen agricultural productivity through diversification into higher-value activities; (b) technological advances that raise yields and conserve land, water, and other inputs; (c) investment in rural infrastructure in areas where returns over the longer term are high; (d) provision of secure, longer-term property rights over farmland;[40] (e) provision of better social services for

---

39 The program, announced in 1993, provided subsidized loans, supported public works, and offered budgetary grants (Park, Wang, and Wu 2002).

40 The recently passed property law strengthens ownership rights and allows farmers to renew land leases ("Caught between Right and Left" 2007).

rural households; (f) rural credit schemes; and (g) to the extent feasible, resource transfers via the price mechanism or fiscal channels.

From the perspective of a development strategy that seeks to maintain high aggregate growth and bring rural incomes closer to urban levels, a multistranded approach is warranted. In conjunction with pricing policies, efforts to raise agricultural yields, conserve water, promote diversification, and strengthen the transport and marketing infrastructure can increase rural incomes and temper the incentives to migrate to cities. Creation of infrastructure should focus on areas with long-term potential, however; other kinds of transfer and income support are better suited for rural communities in which the land is infertile and water scarce. Encouraging people to move out of fragile areas is the most-sensible approach from both economic and ecological perspectives.[41] Attempting to improve their livelihoods through costly investments is likely to have a modest payoff and only delay by a few years an exodus from these areas. Regional policies—in Brazil, Italy, and other parts of the European Union—have a poor record (Sinn and Westermann 2001).

Directing Migrant Flows and Managing Urban Growth

Migration should be to where jobs are going to be; it should support growth in urban regions with the greatest longer-term promise. Directing migrants to high-growth areas would ensure that they are absorbed by urban labor markets and increase their chances of being assimilated into urban society. It is when migrants enter slow-growing or stagnating urban economies that problems of unemployment lead to social problems and the flaring of tensions between newcomers and longtime residents.

Geographical location and city size have the greatest effect on whether urban migration can contribute to a virtuous urban growth spiral. Migrating to a coastal location or a location on a major transport artery was favored in the past and remains advantageous, even though great advances in surface and air transport should have diminished the relative attraction of such locations.[42] Coastal cities in particular exert an unusually strong pull, which is linked to the quality of their physical environment and their milder climate. With sea levels set to rise, some coastal cities might be endangered

---

41 Current policies are helping shape such a trend: by the end of 2005, 23 million hectares of low-quality farmland had been converted to woodland or grassland ("Saying 'No'" 2006).

42 See Liu (1993) on the location of Chinese cities.

three and four decades from now, but for the moment, the pull they exert is undiminished.[43]

The availability of fresh water is emerging as an additional determinant of urban growth and livability, as cities grow very large and become voracious consumers of water.[44] A location along a waterway can help lessen water-supply constraints, and waterfront development can enhance the quality of urban life.

The size of cities is also important.[45] Economies of scale and agglomeration increase growth rates as cities expand (see, for example, Yusuf and others 2003; Rosenthal and Strange 2004). Agglomeration contributes by deepening labor markets, inducing technological spillovers, and encouraging a wide mix of activities. It enables firms and consumers to more easily access inputs and services and allows networked clusters of firms to emerge. Agglomeration also supports innovation—sometimes at the intersection of two or more activities or scientific disciplines—and the diversification of goods and services (Bettencour, Lobo, and Strumsky 2007; Carlino, Chatterjee, and Hunt 2007). Such diversification is often the principal avenue for increasing sales in national or world markets. In a globalizing economy, agglomeration economies are a safety valve permitting urban industry to expand in new directions and to maintain both a diversified portfolio of outputs and the potential for adding new activities as some existing ones die out.[46]

A large urban center also provides an environment in which firms have an easier time achieving scale economies, because local markets are large and enable firms to move down the cost curve before venturing

---

43 The likelihood that some coastal areas will be submerged as seawaters rise might call for planning with regard to the development of coastal cities ("Cities Should Plan" 2005). The experience of the Dutch will become more and more relevant. Among China's megacities, Shanghai confronts the greatest challenge, because of its limited elevation above the current sea level and low-lying terrain; subsidence caused by groundwater depletion; scouring of coastline by strong currents; the presence of wetlands and flood-prone areas; and susceptibility to typhoons (Sherbinin, Schiller, and Pulsipher 2007).

44 China is home to 22 percent of the world's population but just 8 percent of global fresh water supplies (Flavin and Gardner 2006).

45 China has three megacities with populations of more than 10 million: Beijing, Shanghai, and Chongqing. A fourth, Shenzhen, probably falls into this category if the nonresident population is included.

46 Although China's exports to the United States increasingly overlap with those from OECD countries, these exports sell at a discount, because their quality and technological sophistication are lower (Schott 2006). Hummels and Klenow (2005) and Hausmann and Klinger (2006) suggest that the growth of export revenues depends on diversification into new products (many in product categories that are close to those of current exports) and or improvements in quality as incomes rise.

into overseas markets.[47] Large cities are more likely to offer environments that are contestable, if not competitive, with low barriers to the entry and exit of firms and greater incentives for firms to be innovative.

Little in the empirical literature suggests that cities are subject to diminishing returns to scale, but poorly planned and managed cities can confront serious issues of congestion, pollution, and high living expenses, particularly as a result of increasing rents. These problems can also affect medium-size cities. Cross-country experience shows that good land planning, regulation, and coordination by bureaucracies as well as administrative subdivisions can enable cities to reap the benefits of size and avoid most of the pitfalls. In fact, as survey evidence presented in chapter 8 suggests, that larger Chinese cities tend to be better managed than smaller cities.

Polycentric spatial development (which prevents the congestion arising from a single downtown focus with the help of zoning regulations and the use of floor area ratios to vary population densities and create multiple foci) and a well-designed transport system are key to making large cities livable. Also important are land-use policies that conserve land through densification and mixed use without sacrificing essential green spaces and recreational amenities conducive to livability. Legislating rules is one key step; enforcing them firmly, but when needed, flexibly, is another. Cities often fail to follow through with policies governing the use of automobiles. As a result, they end up with severe congestion; urban sprawl, which increases energy consumption; and air and noise pollution.[48] The capacity to implement policy is thus a hallmark of the successful metropolitan area.

Large cities can encounter difficulties if they do not mobilize sufficient revenues to defray current expenditures or fail the test of creditworthiness, which makes it hard for them to raise capital from capital markets for long-lived investments. This problem is not limited to large cities, although the bigger centers are more likely to be burdened with fiscal expenditures.

In summary, size is a plus. In a more-open and competitive global economy, a large city gains an edge from agglomeration and urbanization

---

47 Pannell (1992) reviews the history of Chinese cities through the early postreform period. He finds that large cities were more efficient than smaller ones.

48 Sprawl is a particular problem for secondary cities in China. Because of the lack of infrastructure financing, new urban development tends to take place along existing highways or trunk roads, without much planning. This contributes to sprawl and increases commute time, congestion, the cost of providing energy, water, and sanitation infrastructure, and pollution.

economies that impart industrial flexibility. Major urban centers also enjoy the advantages of global transport connections and are more likely to be hooked into the international business networks for manufacturing, producer services, and research. These international links are sources of trade, capital, and ideas, the oxygen that gives life to urban dynamism.

Financing Urban Development

Urban development is not possible on the cheap. Huge volumes of funds have to be raised and committed to projects that can take many years to come to fruition and the effective life of which can span decades or even centuries.

Cities faced with the prospects of substantial in-migration can become caught in low-level traps if they fail to pour capital into such investments in a fairly short period of time. A "big-push" investment strategy has obvious merits for putting in place axial transport, housing, commercial, energy and water, and sewerage infrastructures.

Building ahead of demand makes sense, so that industry is not hamstrung by capacity constraints and urban physical plant can accommodate the influx of people without congestion and the creation of slums. An example is New York City, which was designed for 1 million residents when the population was barely 100,000. Central Park was created 150 years ago, and the subway system was built 100 years ago, well ahead of demand ("The New New York" 2006).[49] Planning for long-term growth smoothed the expansion of Tokyo in the postwar period.[50]

Several Chinese cities have followed this route. Throughout the 1980s, Shanghai spent 5–8 percent of its GDP on urban infrastructure investment. In the 1990s it spent 11–14 percent of GDP, in a big push to redevelop the city, including developing Pudong (figure 1.2); this effort is now winding down. Both Beijing and Tianjin spend more than 10 percent of their GDP on urban infrastructure (Yusuf and Nabeshima 2006b). To cope with the rising demand for electricity and to eliminate brownouts, China commissioned 80 gigawatts of generating capacity in 2006 and will put an estimated 75 gigawatts on line in 2007 ("What Shortage?" 2006).

---

49 Omnibus services began in the 1820s (Glaeser 2005b).
50 Until the 1960s, fewer than 100,000 housing units were constructed in Tokyo. Beginning in the 1970s, in line with the rapid increase of population in Tokyo, the construction of new housing units accelerated dramatically, reaching more than 900,000 units by 1990.

Figure 1.2. Investment in Urban Infrastructure in Shanghai, as Percentage of GDP, 1985–2004

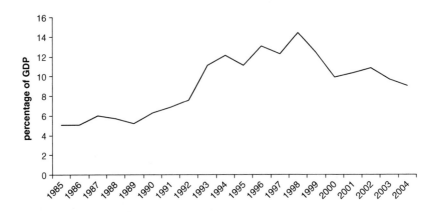

Source: Shanghai Municipal Statistical Bureau 2005.

Where cities have approached infrastructure development piecemeal and lagged behind demand—Lagos, Lima, Karachi, and Mumbai are prime examples—the urban environment has deteriorated.[51] As population pressures have mounted, industry has struggled to grow, fewer jobs have been created, and cities have entered into a low-level growth syndrome in which poverty, slums, and crime have become firmly entrenched.[52]

Conventional wisdom has resisted the big-push strategy, conflating it with lumpy investments. But experience with migration-led urbanization suggests that a high level of investment in industry and infrastructure has multiplier and accelerator effects, which can stoke prolonged virtuous spirals that generate not just growth and employment but also the urban facilities and housing needed to accommodate a rising population.

Urban development—especially when it is driven by a big-push strategy—requires capital, lots of it. Although the global integration of capital markets has created channels for the circulation of capital, much of this capital must come from domestic saving and financial entities

---

51 In 1950 fewer than 300,000 people lived in Lagos. The city's population rose by an average rate of 6 percent a year in the second half of the 20th century. Every year more than 600,000 people migrated to Lagos from West Africa. If current trends continue, by 2015 Lagos will have 23 million people, making it the third-largest city in the world after Tokyo and Mumbai ("The Megacity" 2006).

52 Informal transactions account for at least 60 percent of economic activity in Lagos ("The Megacity" 2006).

(Feldstein and Horioka 1980; Feldstein 2005). Rapid urban development that can keep pace with large intersectoral transfers of workers demands rising domestic savings and mechanisms for investing the resources. To be creditworthy enough to gain access to these resources, cities must be well managed financially. Financial deepening can facilitate the process, but it takes time to build institutions; train people; and create sophisticated instruments, risk-assessment skills, rating and monitoring agencies, and regulatory capabilities (Yusuf 2007). Late-starting countries that must cope with urbanization rates of 3–5 percent a year or more have to rely on banks initially, but they need to move quickly to establish mortgage and bond markets; institutions for both securitizing instruments such as mortgages and regulating the intermediates involved; and avenues for the secondary trading of securities.[53]

Local-currency bond markets make it possible to diversify lending away from banks and to match long-term assets with debt of equivalent maturity. They generate yields for a range of maturities and permit the hedging of exposures. Well-functioning bond markets not only lower borrowing costs, they also impart greater stability to financial markets.[54]

If urbanization is to avoid the many pitfalls that lie in wait, it needs to be supported by resource mobilization and fiscal transfers commensurate with the desired rate of development. When cities are not "bankable"—that is, when resource mobilization is weak or insufficient capital finds its way into urban projects because public and private channels are inadequate or transaction costs are too high—urbanization cannot be matched by the requisite urban development. The lack of financial depth and sophistication has not initially proven to be the binding constraint. It is the feeble supply of domestic capital for the urban sector (because the instruments, skills, and channels have not been created) and inept municipal financial management that are frequently associated with weak economic growth.

---

53 By the end of 2005, China's mortgage market, which started in 1998, had grown to US$227 billion (Y 1,777 billion), larger than the market in the Republic of Korea (US$200 billon). China's market represents just 10 percent of GDP, however, while the market in the Republic of Korea represents 27 percent of that country's GDP ("Mortgage Industry" 2006).

54 By abolishing a quota that limited the annual issuance of corporate bonds to Y 100 billion (US$13.2 billion), the Chinese authorities have encouraged listed companies to raise funds by issuing bonds and to use the funds to pay off higher-interest bank debts. Doing so is particularly appealing to companies engaged in urban real estate, infrastructure, and urban development ("Chinese Companies" 2007).

Providing Urban Social Services

In addition to physical infrastructure, people require social services. Vulnerable people need a safety net to avoid sliding into poverty as they age, become unemployed, or are affected by accidents or loss of property.[55] From social as well as private perspectives, the most needed services and the ones with the highest returns are health care and education. These services build human capital, contribute to individual well-being, provide a measure of insurance against poverty, and produce positive externalities (see chapters 2 and 3; Yusuf, Nabeshima, and Ha 2007a, 2007b).

Adequate access to health and education services for the entire urban population should be a central objective of urban development. It is an objective that is often not given the priority it deserves. The shortfall is most serious during the critical stage when urban populations are exploding. By making inadequate provisions for services, cities fail to augment a resource that over the longer term is vital for growth, industrial diversification, and the quality of the business climate. By focusing on physical infrastructure, governments at both the national and subnational levels defer essential and complementary investments in human capital, which builds manufacturing and technological capabilities. Investing in human capital is also the best insurance against unemployment and urban crime. Rather than waiting until shortages become glaringly apparent—by which time it is often too late to mobilize sufficient resources—cities should view services as intrinsic to their big-push urban development strategies.

Health and education services also permit the gradual phasing in of an old-age safety net and unemployment insurance schemes. These schemes are expensive. They need to be backstopped by supporting institutions and to evolve together with the financial sector.

Limiting Increases in Urban Energy Consumption

The lifeblood of the urban economy is energy (see chapter 6). Urban transport, industry, and households dominate energy consumption in all middle- and high-income countries. Energy use fuels growth and enhances livability, but it is also the principal source of air pollution and carbon emissions. For the foreseeable future, urban development will remain dependent on ample supplies of energy, with transport depending on petroleum and households relying mainly on electricity

---

55 On the problems posed by shocks for individual households and the options for insuring against them, see Baeza and Packard (2006).

and gas. Barring an incident that leads to an interruption of supplies, there is no imminent shortage of petroleum in the near term.

The warning signs of tightening petroleum supplies are everywhere, however. The more-accessible major sources of petroleum are being rapidly exploited, and even if new reserves are found offshore, production costs will be much higher, because the extraction must be from great depths. Thus, if economic growth rates worldwide remain healthy, the relative prices of energy could increase significantly.

Given the likely increase in energy prices and the deleterious effect of the consumption of fossil fuels on the environment, reducing the energy coefficient of urban development is essential. Especially for countries at a relatively early stage of urbanization, with a great deal of long-lived invest-ment in urban infrastructure and buildings ahead, measures that can cut energy use and energy losses have a high payback. Among the measures with the greatest consequences, the design of urban transport is the most significant, because it determines the physical characteristics of the city[56]— how much it sprawls and encroaches into the surrounding agricultural land—and the reliance on automobiles for intra- and intercity travel. Appropriate incentives can lead to the efficient utilization of public transit in large cities, which are much more energy efficient than other locales.[57]

Enforcing strict standards and codes are two additional measures that can limit the increase in electricity consumption for air conditioning and appliances, even as urban populations and urban incomes continue their upward march. Another approach would be to install "smart" meters, which can assess variable charges based on the time of day to encourage energy conservation, especially at peak load times ("Going Metric" 2006). Encouraging the adoption of "green" technologies and eco-friendly designs can also reduce energy use (see Yusuf and Nabeshima 2006a and the numerous practical suggestions in Steffen 2006).[58]

An efficient energy-conserving big-push strategy that is also eco-friendly needs to incorporate the construction industry. The quality

---

56 The spatial characteristics of a city, the occupational activities there, and the degree to which people depend on cars for mobility profoundly influence the incidence of chronic diseases associated with obesity, such as diabetes and cardiovascular disease, according to Frumkin, Frank, and Jackson (2004) and Monda and others (2006).

57 Phang (2000) describes Singapore's techniques for controlling the ownership and use of cars.

58 In projecting the energy intensity of China's economy, Wei and others (2006) find that incomes are the principal source of rising utilization and technological change the main mitigating factor.

and design of construction and the incorporation of new energy- and materials-conserving technologies will determine how much energy is saved, directly and indirectly (Fernandez 2007). The design, construction, and maintenance of infrastructure also influence energy use by the transport, water, and sanitation sectors. Among all of the industries contributing to urban development and local multiplier effects, construction is far and away the most important. Enhancing the productivity and technological capabilities of this industry should be a critical part of any urban development strategy.

Dealing with the Scarcity of Water

Full recognition of the trend in water scarcity is long overdue. For some cities, a crisis looms not too far in the future. Many others are likely to confront severe shortages within a few decades. For late urbanizers, there is a clear opportunity to design the water supply, wastewater collection, and sanitation systems so that they maximize the potential for recycling water, supplying water of different grades for different purposes, and minimizing the loss of water from leaking pipes.

As with energy, standards for appliances and sanitary systems can also reduce the amount of water and restrict the use of drinking-quality water for some purposes only. Standards for the purity of water released by commercial and industrial establishments can increase recycling and minimize pollution of water courses and aquifers.

Regulation, physical design, and technology are three strands of an urban water strategy. Pricing is a fourth. It complements the others and is critical to the success of any longer-term strategy to ensure that an urbanizing world will not run short of water.

Managing Urbanization

Urbanization, development, and a rising quality of life are difficult to combine without sound planning and regulation and the implementation of a host of policies. Small cities and large ones must be well managed for benefits to be fully realized and diseconomies kept in check. Achieving good management—and governance—is subject to many factors. These include the autonomy to conduct policy and raise revenue; the quality of local leadership; and planning and administrative capacities. They also include the availability of policy instruments; the existence of institutions for mediating and implementing policies (such as private–public partnerships and the legal system); and the efficacy of interjurisdictional coordination, where this counts. But urban development is arguably most affected by the design and efficiency of regulations that incentivize industry; by land-use and transport policies; by fiscal management and how it is reflected in credit ratings, as well as the provision of public services; and by environmental policies that intersect with and reinforce those impinging on land use and urban transport (see chapter 8 on the dynamics of decision making at the local level).

From Strategy to Policy

Given the pace of urbanization and the numbers of people involved, the decision makers responsible for guiding China's urban development have their hands full. Fortunately, they are better placed than their counterparts in other countries to achieve successful urban development, for several reasons:

- China is generating the resources to finance an urban big-push and to date has been able to channel these resources into urban industry and infrastructure, through the fiscal system, the banks, and new financial instruments.
- Because China is a relatively late starter and much building and renewal of urban physical capital lies in the future, there is unparalleled scope for designing efficient and livable cities.
- Chinese municipalities have the autonomy and the authority to introduce and implement regulations governing land use, the transport system, and the urban environment.
- The *hukou* system enables municipalities to exercise some control over the flow of permanent migrants. Industrial growth virtually throughout China is such that manufacturing, construction, and services are largely able to absorb inflows of migrants.
- Although many Chinese cities must cope with a backlog of air and water pollution, the slums and endemic poverty that have taken root in other countries are largely absent from Chinese cities thus far.
- As a late starter, China can draw on the experience of other countries with respect to urban design, the effects of private vehicle use, and pollution. At the same time, it can exploit advances in a host of technologies that will conserve energy and water and curtail harmful emissions.

This is not to say that urban development will be trouble free. For China, however, the enormous intersectoral transfer of people can be a less-daunting process than it was and is for other countries.

The chapters in this volume delineate a number of policies that can promote rapid urban development within a framework of a national strategy that seeks to achieve a balanced increase in incomes. From the range of policies presented, seven stand out.

Increase Human Capital

In both urban and rural sectors, education and health care policies that increase human capital can stimulate growth of agricultural and industrial activities and reduce the risks of unemployment (Glaeser and Saiz 2003; Berry and Glaeser 2005; Glaeser 2005a; Glaeser and Berry 2006). Greater access to these services can raise the incomes of rural households, which facilitates migration. Making these services available to urban migrants deepens the resource base in cities, promotes equity, and helps combat poverty. From the standpoint of both growth and welfare, health policies should focus on preventive and primary care, and education policies should seek to enhance the quality and raise the level of education.

Manage the Flow of Migration

Although the *hukou* system should be dismantled over the longer run, it remains a useful tool for directing and managing the flow of migrants. It should be used to achieve two objectives. One is to try to contain the number of migrants individual cities absorb as permanent residents. To the extent that the *hukou* system can achieve this, migration can match the supply of affordable housing, infrastructure, social services and jobs in cities. A second is to try to direct migrant flows from areas with declining agricultural potential and water shortages to urban areas with better growth possibilities, in order to realize economies of agglomeration and scale.[59] This matching needs to be combined with the planning and design of megacities in a way that achieves compactness and polycentricity. The coastal cities in the Yangtze delta and the south are likely to continue to attract migrants. These cities may need to extend urban *hukou* privileges to some of these migrants and to invest in infrastructure and services to accommodate them.

Deepen Financial Markets

To finance urban development, China needs financial markets that allocate resources more efficiently. It also needs a wider range of instruments, in order to meet the needs of different kinds of borrowers and offer the spread of maturities required by investors. The reliance on banks for financing and

---

59 China's WTO membership is likely to negatively affect wheat- and corn-growing farmers in the northeast, as noted in chapter 2.

the use of urban development investment corporations (UDICs) (created by municipal authorities as semiautonomous vehicles that borrow from the banks) have advantages but also some risks (Su and Zhao 2007). Municipalities can limit their fiscal commitments to urban development and instead tap the banks. But the UDIC–banking nexus increases banks' exposure on long-lived investments through organizational channels that might create problems in the future.[60] Changing the legal, tax, and accounting rules to permit the emergence of secondary bond and mortgage markets would be a step forward. Other measures include adoption of rules that encourage securitization of mortgages; strengthening of mortgage insurance; issuance of general financial bonds; and trading, including forward transactions, in the interbank bond market. Financial innovations and institutional developments, including refinancing arrangements and loan guarantees, would also facilitate urbanization.

Improve Cities' Fiscal Efforts
Many Chinese cities have been balancing their books by selling or leasing land or charging off-budget fees. The income from such transactions accounts for almost 25 percent of municipal revenues. Sooner or later, this process will come to an end. Urban governments need to create a durable fiscal system that can meet future and current capital needs, taking account of the anticipated growth rates of urban economies and populations. Doing so entails revenue-sharing and transfer agreements with the central authorities and an elastic base for local revenues with a few robust tax instruments to satisfy local needs. It also calls for a firm agreement with the central government on expenditure assignments that are equitable and sustainable given the anticipated flows of revenue from all sources.[61]

Contain Energy Costs
Ensuring that urban development is not constrained by rising energy costs will depend on four factors. Arguably the most important are pricing policies (especially of power) that accurately communicate information on relative scarcities and induce efficient utilization (see chapter 6).

---

60 Chinese banks have a history of loan portfolio problems. Although reforms have reduced the scale of the problem, weak risk-assessment skills and poor governance remain sources of vulnerability (Podpiera 2006).

61 See, for instance, World Bank (2003a, 2003b); Dabla-Norris (2005); and Su and Zhao (2007).

A second factor is how China proceeds with its motorization strategy within the context of urbanization.[62] One part of this strategy relates to the incentives for the automobile industry to produce fuel-efficient cars and to redouble efforts to innovate. Another part has to do with demand for cars, which will be a function of policies on taxes on cars, gasoline, licensing and registration fees, and road user charges; car financing; research and development; urban land use; investment in road building; and public transport. Currently, many Chinese cities are subject to so-called "ribbon development" alongside major highways and floor area ratios are still quite low. This type of development saves developers and local governments from investing in secondary feeder and access roads, but it leads to much greater sprawl and raises the energy- and infrastructure-related costs of urbanization.

A third factor is advances in home-grown technology and technology transfer from abroad. The degree to which policy accelerates these advances will influence the efficiency with which fossil fuels are utilized as well as the diversification into renewable sources.[63]

A fourth factor is the raft of regulatory policies, including environmental and land use policies and policies defining building codes and standards for consumer appliances. In conjunction with the perfecting of mechanisms for enforcement, these policies will play a significant part in determining energy demand.

Manage Water Resources
Pricing, regulatory, technology, sewage treatment, and wastewater recycling policies will also be decisive with respect to the utilization of water.[64] Given the distribution of water, its low per capita availability,

---

62 Between 1991 and 2005, the number of cars per 1,000 people in China rose from less than 2 to 10.

63 Considerable progress is being made in developing clean-coal technologies that China could tap. These include supercritical boilers (which heat steam to 600°C beyond the critical boiling point and therefore need 17 percent less coal than conventional coal-fired plants); integrated gasification combined cycles (which convert coal to gas); and techniques for capturing carbon ("Big Effort" 2006). An earmarked tax on electricity consumption now finances the development of renewable energy. The government is also investing in nuclear power and ethanol. China has 9 operating nuclear reactors supplying electricity, 2 more under construction, and another 20 planned (Flavin and Gardner 2006; Hunt and Sawin 2006; "Saying 'No'" 2006). Currently, among renewable sources of energy, only onshore wind turbines in certain locations are generally profitable. Solar energy, offshore wind turbines, and tidal power are still relatively costly ("On the Verge" 2006).

64 A little more than half of urban sewage is currently treated before being discharged into water bodies, which party accounts for the low quality of the lake and river water ("Saying 'No'" 2006).

and its deteriorating quality, the problem of water availability needs to be tackled immediately. As noted in this chapter and in chapter 7, the geography of future urbanization and the degree to which it is concentrated in the relatively water-abundant parts of the country could play an important role in providing a solution to the problem.

A massive transfer of water could be a costly solution, on a number of counts. The distribution of water resources, the implications of impending climate change on future supplies, and policies affecting the production of grain in the northeast should all be factored into the urbanization strategy. Ongoing climate change makes it desirable to take account of water availability across the country when making long-term plans for urban development.

Reduce Pollution

Policies on the conservation and consumption of water and energy resources will affect environmental pollution, which is a drag on GDP growth and degrades the quality of life. There are various estimates of the costs of indoor and outdoor pollution to the economy, ranging from 3 to 6 percent of GDP. A redoubling of efforts by the government and industry would appear to be desirable ("Green GDP" 2007; Ho and Nielsen 2007; "China's Green Accounting" 2007).

Concluding Observations

This chapter raises but a few of the issues and policies that will guide urbanization and urban development in China, but they are likely to be among the most crucial. More than half of China's population lives in rural areas; decades of urbanization lie ahead. Almost three-quarters of Brazil's population live in urban areas, and an even higher percentage of the population of the United States is urban (World Bank 2006). Possibly by the middle of this century, China could be approaching these levels of urbanization. Between now and then, decisions will be made that will affect the geographical distribution of the population and the building of the urban, transport, and water supply infrastructure to house and support urban inhabitants. Enormous amounts of capital will be committed if the big-push approach is continued.

With so much at stake, it is essential that decisions be closer to the optimal in the long-term sense. Markets alone cannot achieve the outcomes desired, but efficient financial, energy, and water markets, for example, can help achieve good outcomes. Taking the institutional and policy steps to make markets work more efficiently should be a priority. Successful markets will need to be backed by good government planning and policies based on careful analysis, using the best information available. Factoring in the systems of urban design and construction, as well as innovation, could increase the likelihood that urban development achieves multiple objectives. The approaches to urbanization, urban/ design and urban innovation systems will play major roles, especially when it comes to making longer-term decisions about the distribution of people geographically and across cities of different sizes.

The Chinese authorities have some instruments with which to influence both of these outcomes, namely, the *hukou* system and the government's role in allocating investment. These instruments are two among a number of factors that determine the flows of people and capital. The design of policies and the application of these instruments depend on complex negotiations by several levels of government as well as other players, such as the banks. Such interactions among the various stakeholders are useful, because many points of view and a broad range of information can be factored in; the process also diminishes the risk of egregious mistakes. By the same token, the negotiated approach increases the degree of policy slippage and delays in implementation. Policy slippages and the likelihood of delays are unavoidable, but urbanization will not wait. China must move forward with policies to contain the costs of rapid growth, narrow the gap between rural and urban incomes, raise the quality life, and minimize negative externalities. To do so, urbanization and urban development should remain at the top of policy makers' agendas until the pressing issues are resolved.

The potential gains to China from urbanization are substantial. So, too, are the costs. Striking the right balance between the two will be the greatest challenge for Chinese policy makers over the next quarter century and more.

References

"Anti-Graft Campaign Intensifies." 2006. *Business Asia*, October 30.

Baeza, Cristian C., and Truman G. Packard. 2006. *Beyond Survival*. Stanford, CA: Stanford University Press.

Bairoch, Paul. 1991. *Cities and Economic Development: from the Dawn of History to the Present*. Chicago: University of Chicago Press.

Baochang, Gu, Wang Feng, Guo Zhigang, and Zhang Erli. 2007. "China's Local and National Fertility Policies at the End of the Twentieth Century." *Population and Development Review* 33 (1): 129–47.

"Beneath Booming Cities, China's Future Is Drying Up." 2007. *New York Times*, September 28.

Bernstein, Thomas P. 1977. *Up to the Mountains and down to the Villages: The Transfer of Youth from Urban to Rural China*. New Haven, CT: Yale University Press.

Berry, Christopher, and Edward Glaeser. 2005. "The Divergence of Human Capital Levels Across Cities." NBER Working Paper 11617, National Bureau of Economic Research, Cambridge, MA.

Bettencourt, Luis, M. A., Jose Lobo, and Deborah Strumsky. 2007. "Intervention in the City: Increasing Returns to Patenting as a Scaling Function of Metropolitan Size." *Research Policy* 36: 107–120.

"Big Effort to Scrub Up a Dirty Image." 2006. *Financial Times*, October 20.

Bloom, David E., and Jeffrey G. Williamson. 1997. "Demographic Transitions and Economic Miracles in Emerging Asia." NBER Working Paper 6268, National Bureau of Economic Research, Cambridge, MA.

Bosworth, Barry P., and Susan M. Collins. 2007. "Accounting for Growth: Comparing China and India." NBER Working Paper 12943, National Bureau of Economic Research, Cambridge, MA.

Carlino, Gerald A., Satyajit Chatterjee, and Robert M. Hunt. 2007. "Urban Density and the Rate of Innovation." *Journal of Urban Economics* 61: 389–419.

"Caught between Right and Left, Town and Country." 2007. *Economist*, March 8.

CBO (Congressional Budget Office). 2006. *China's Growing Demand for Oil and Its Impact on U.S. Petroleum Markets*. Washington, DC.

Chen, B., and G. Q. Chen. 2007a. "Resource Analysis of the Chinese Society 1980–2002 Based on Energy. Part 2: Renewable Energy Sources and Forest." *Energy Policy* 35 (4): 2051–64.

Chen, G. Q., and B. Chen. 2007b. "Resource Analysis of the Chinese Society 1980–2002 Based on Energy. Part 1: Fossil Fuels and Energy Minerals." *Energy Policy* 35 (4): 2038–50.

Cheng, Margaret Harris. 2006. "China's Cities Get a Little Healthier." *Lancet* 368 (9550): 1859–60.

"China: Does the Countryside Hold the Seeds of Crisis?" 2007. *Oxford Analytica*, Global Strategic Analysis, May 30.

"China's Crackdown on Corruption Still Largely Secret." 2006. *Washington Post*, December 31.

"China's Green Accounting System on Shaky Ground." 2007. *Nature* 448: 518–19. August 2.

"China's Income Gap Grows despite Pledges." 2006. *Financial Times*, December 27.

"Chinese Companies Rush to Issue Bonds under Relaxed Regulations." 2007. *Financial Times*, August 18.

"Cities Should Plan Now for Effects of Global Warming on Infrastructure." February 25, 2005. http://www.newsdesk.umd.edu.

Dabla-Norris, Era. 2005. "Issues in Intergovernmental Fiscal Relations in China." IMF Working Paper WP/05/30, International Monetary Fund, Washington, DC.

"Delta Dreams." 2006. *Business China*, April 24.

Demurger, Sylvie, Jeffrey D. Sachs, Wing Thye Woo, Shuming Bao, Gene Chang, and Andrew Mellinger. 2002. "Geography, Economic Policy, and Regional Development in China." *Asian Economic Papers* 1 (1): 146–97.

Dunaway, Steven, and Vivek Arora. 2007. "Pension Reform in China: The Need for a New Approach." IMF Working Paper WP/07/109. IMF, Washington, DC.

Ebrey, Patricia. 1996. *China.* Cambridge, U.K.: Cambridge University Press.

Ekboir, J. ed. 2002. *CIMMYT 2000–2001 World Wheat Overview and Outlook: Developing No-Till Packages for Small-Scale Farmers.* International Maize and Wheat Improvement Center (CIMMYT), Mexico City.

Evans, Richard, and Sinclair K. Knight. 2007. "Groundwater Resource Management Challenges in North China." National Academy of Sciences. Arthur M. Sackler Colloquia, Washington, DC.

Falkner, Robert. 2006. "International Sources of Environmental Policy Change in China: The Case of Genetically Modified Food." *Pacific Review* 19 (4): 473–94.

Fan, C. Cindy. 1997. "Uneven Development and Beyond: Regional Development theory in Post-Mao China." *International Journal of Urban and Regional Research* 21 (4): 620–39.

———. 2005. "Modeling Interprovincial Migration in China." *Eurasian Geography and Economics* 46 (3): 165–84.

Fang, Shan. 1990. "Urbanization in Mainland China." *Issues & Studies* 26 (2): 118–33.

FAO (Food and Agricultural Organization). 2003. *Selected Indicators of Food and Agriculture Development in Asia-Pacific Region: 1992–2002.* Regional Office for Asia and the Pacific, Bangkok.

Feldstein, Martin. 2005. "Monetary Policy in a Changing International Environment: The Role of Global Capital Flows." NBER Working Paper 11856, National Bureau of Economic Research, Cambridge, MA.

Feldstein, Martin, and Charles Horioka. 1980. "Domestic Saving and International Capital Flows." *Economic Journal* 90 (358): 314–29.

Fernandez, John E. 2007. "Materials for Aesthetic, Energy-Efficient, and Self-Diagnostic Buildings." *Science* 315 (5820): 1807–10.

Flavin, Christopher, and Gary Gardner. 2006. "China, India, and the New World Order." In *State of the World 2006*, ed. Worldwatch Institute. New York: W. W. Norton.

"Free Flow: Big Challenge for Beijing: Moving Coal." 2005. *International Herald Tribune*, August 18.

Friedman, John. 2005. *China's Urban Transition.* Minneapolis: University of Minnesota Press.

Frumkin, Howard, Lawrence Frank, and Richard Joseph Jackson, 2004. *Urban Sprawl and Public Health: Designing, Planning, and Building for Healthy Communities.* Washington, DC: Island Press.

Gan, Li, and Guan Gong. 2007. "Estimating Interdependence between Health and Education in a Dynamic Model." NBER Working Paper 12830, National Bureau of Economic Research, Cambridge, MA.

Gardner, John. 1971. "Educated Youth and Urban-Rural Inequalities, 1958–66." In *The City in Communist China*, ed. John W. Lewis. Stanford, CA: Stanford University Press.

Glaeser, Edward L. 2005a. "Reinventing Boston: 1640–2003." *Journal of Economic Geography* 5 (2): 119–153.

————. 2005b. "Urban Colossus: Why Is New York America's Largest City?" NBER Working Paper 11398, National Bureau of Economic Research, Cambridge, MA.

Glaeser, Edward L., and Christopher Berry. 2006. "Why Are Smarter Places Getting Smarter?" Policy Briefs PB-2006-2, Department of Economics, Harvard University, Cambridge, MA.

Glaeser, Edward L., and Albert Saiz. 2003. "The Rise of the Skilled City." NBER Working Paper 10191, National Bureau of Economic Research, Cambridge, MA.

"Going Metric" 2006. *Economist*, December 13.

"Green GDP Will Be Expanded to Entire Mainland." 2007. *China Daily,* January 18.

Gustafsson, Bjorn, Li Shi, and Wei Zhong. 2006. "The Distribution of Wealth in Urban China and in China as a Whole in 1995." *Review of Income and Wealth* 52 (2): 173–88.

Hausmann, Ricardo, and Bailey Klinger. 2006. "Structural Transformation and Patterns of Comparative Advantage in the Product Space." Center for International Development, Harvard University, Cambridge, MA.

"The Health of a Nation." 2007. *Economist*, February 26.

He, Jianwu, and Louis Kuijs. 2007. "Rebalancing China's Economy—Modeling a Policy Package." Beijing PRC. World Bank China Research Paper No. 7.

Hesketh, Therese, Li Lu, and Zhu Wei Xing. 2005. "The Effect of China's One-Child Family Policy after 25 Years." *New England Journal of Medicine* 353 (11): 1171–76.

Ho, Mun S., and Chris Nielsen. 2007. *Clearing the Air: the Health and Economic Damages of Air Pollution in China.* Cambridge, Mass.: MIT Press.

Ho, Ping-ti. 1975. *The Cradle of the East.* Hong Kong (China): Chinese University of Hong Kong Press.

Huang, Jikun, Ruifa Hu, Scott Rozelle, and Carl Pray. 2007. "China: Emerging Public Sector Model for GM Crop Development." In *Gene Revolution: GM Crops and Unequal Development*, ed. Sakiko Fukuda-Parr. London: Earthscan, 130–55.

Hummels, David, and Peter J. Klenow. 2005. "The Variety and Quality of a Nation's Exports." *American Economic Review* 95 (3): 704–23.

Hunt, Suzanne C., and Janet L. Sawin, with Peter Stair. 2006. "Cultivating Renewable Alternative to Oil." In *State of the World 2006*, ed. Worldwatch Institute. New York: W. W. Norton.

"In Face of Rural Unrest, China Rolls Out Reforms" 2006. *Washington Post*, January 28.

Japan Statistics Bureau. 2005. *Japan Statistical Yearbook 2005*. Ministry of Internal Affairs and Communications, Tokyo.

Jiang, Leiwen. 2006. "Living Conditions of the Floating Population in Urban China." *Housing Studies* 21 (5): 719–44.

Jin, Songqing, Jikun Huang, Ruifa Hu, and Scott Rozelle. 2002. "The Creation and Spread of Technology and Total Factor Productivity in China's Agriculture." *American Journal of Agricultural Economics* 84 (4): 916–30.

Knight, John, and Lina Song. 2003. "Chinese Peasant Choices: Migration, Rural Industry or Farming." *Oxford Development Studies* 31 (2): 123–47.

Kojima, Reeitsu. 1987. "Urbanization and Urban Problems in China." IDE Occasional Paper 22, Institute for Developing Economies, Tokyo.

Kwok, Yin-Wang. 1981. "Trends of Urban Planning and Development in China." In *Urban Development in Modern China*, ed. Laurence J. C. Ma and Edward W. Hanten. Boulder, CO: Westview Press.

"Lanzhou to Walk Off Pollution." 2007. *China Daily*, January 17.

Li, Peter Ping. 2006. "The Puzzle of China's Township-Village Enterprises: The Paradox of Local Corporatism in a Dual-Track Economic Transition." *Management and Organization Review* 1 (2): 197–224.

Liu, Haiyan. 1993. "The Past and Future of Urban Histories Examining China's Modern Period (1840–1949)." *Social Sciences in China* 14 (Winter): 115–27.

Liu, Yunhua, and Xiaobing Wang. 2005. "Technological Progress and Chinese Agricultural Growth in the 1990s." *China Economic Review* 16 (4): 419–40.

"The Megacity." 2006. *The New Yorker,* November 13.

Mohan, Rakesh. 2006. "Asia's Urban Century: Emerging Trends." Paper presented at the conference "Land Policies for Urban Development," Cambridge, MA, June 5.

Monda, Keri L., Penny Gordon-Larsen, June Stevens, and Barry M. Popkin. 2006. "China's Transition: The Effect of Rapid Urbanization on Adult Occupational Physical Activity." *Social Science & Medicine* 64 (4): 858–70.

"Mortgage Industry Untapped, Says BIS." 2006. *Shanghai Daily,* December 11.

Mote, Frederick W. 1999. *Imperial China: 900–1800.* Cambridge, MA: Harvard University Press.

Mu, Huaipeng. 2005. "China's Bond Market: Innovation and Development." Paper presented at the Second Annual Asia Pacific Bond Congress, Hong Kong (China), June 16.

Murphy, Rachel 2002. *How Migrant Labor Is Changing Rural China.* Cambridge, U.K.: Cambridge University Press.

NBS (National Bureau of Statistics). 2002. *China Statistical Yearbook 2001.* Beijing: China Statistics Press.

———. 2006. *China Statistical Yearbook 2001.* Beijing: China Statistics Press.

Naughton, Barry. 1988. "The Third Front: Defense Industrialization in the Chinese Interior." *China Quarterly* 115: 351–86.

NDRC (National Development and Reform Commission). 2007. "11th Five-Year Plan on Energy Development." Beijing.

"The New New York." 2006. *Economist,* December 13.

O'Brien, Kevin J., and Lianjiang Li. 2006. *Rightful Resistance in Rural China.* Cambridge: Cambridge University Press.

Oi, J. C. 1992. "Fiscal Reform and the Economic Foundations of Local State Corporatism in China." *World Politics* 45 (1): 99–126.

"On the Verge of Viability." 2006. *Financial Times,* October 20.

Ouyang, Tingping, Zhaoyu Zhu, and Yaoqiu Kuang. 2006. "Assessing Impact of Urbanization on River Water Quality in the Pearl River Delta Economic Zone, China." *Environmental Monitoring and Assessment* 120 (1–3): 313–25.

Pan, Jiahua. 2002. "Rural Energy Patterns in China: A Preliminary Assessment from Available Data Sources." Program on Energy and Sustainable Development Working Paper 12, Stanford University, Stanford, CA.

Pannell, Clifton W. 1992. "The Role of Great Cities in China." In *Urbanizing China,* ed. Gregory Eliyu Guldin. New York: Greenwood Press.

———. 2003. "China's Demographic and Urban Trends for the 21st Century." *Eurasian Geography and Economics* 44 (7): 479–96.

Park, Albert, Sangui Wang, and Guobao Wu. 2002. "Regional Poverty Targeting in China." *Journal of Public Economics* 86 (1): 123–53.

Phang, Sock-Yong. 2000. "How Singapore Regulates Urban Transportation and Land Use." In Local Dynamics in An Era of Globalization, ed. Shahid Yusuf, Weiping Wu, and Simon Evenett, 159–63. New York: Oxford University Press.

Pielou, E. C. 1998. *Fresh Water.* Chicago: University of Chicago Press.

Pingali, P. L., ed. 2001. *CIMMYT 1999–2000 World Maize Facts and Trends: Meeting World Maize Needs: Technological Opportunities and Priorities for the Public Sector.* International Maize and Wheat Improvement Center (CIMMYT), Mexico City.

Podpiera, Richard. 2006. "Progress in China's Banking Sector Reform: Has Bank Behavior Changed?" IMF Working Paper WP/06/71, International Monetary Fund, Washington, DC.

Polo, Marco. 1958. *The Travels of Marco Polo.* Translated by Ronald E. Latham. New York: Penguin Classics.

Qian, Yingyi. 1999. "The Institutional Foundations of China's Market Transition." Paper presented at the Annual World Bank Conference on Development Economics, Washington, DC, April 29.

Ravallion, Martin, Shaohua Chen, and Prem Sangraula. 2007. "The Urbanization of Global Poverty." World Bank Background Paper 2008, Washington, DC.

Rosen, Daniel H., and Trevor Houser. 2007. "China Energy: A Guide for the Perplexed." Peterson Institute for International Economics, Washington, DC.

Rosenthal, Stuart S., and William C. Strange. 2004. "Evidence on the Nature and Sources of Agglomeration Economics." In *Handbook of Regional and Urban Economics,* ed. J. Vernon Henderson and Jacques-François Thisse, 2119–71. North Holland.

Roumasset, James, Hua Wang, and Kimberly Burnett. 2006. "Environmental Resources and Economic Growth." World Bank, Washington, DC.

Saich, Tony. 2006. "Hu's in Charge." *Asian Survey* 46 (1): 37–48.

"Saying 'No' to Growing Filthy Rich." 2006. *Business China,* November 20.

Schott, Peter K. 2006. "The Relative Sophistication of Chinese Exports." NBER Working Paper 12173, National Bureau of Economic Research, Cambridge, MA.

Shalizi, Zmarak. 2007. "Energy and Emissions: Local and Global Effects of the Giants' Rise." In *Dancing with Giants,* ed. L. Alan Winters and Shahid Yusuf. Washington, DC: World Bank.

Shanghai Municipal Statistical Bureau. 2005. *Shanghai Statistical Yearbook 2005*. Beijing.

"Shanghaied." 2006. *Economist*, September 30.

Sherbinin, Alex de, Andrew Schiller, and Alex Pulsipher. 2007. "The Vulnerability of Global Cities to Climate Hazards." *Environment & Urbanization* 19 (1): 39–64.

Shiller, Robert J. 2006. "Thrifty China, Spendthrift America." Project Syndicate. http://www.project-syndicate.org/commentary/shiller40.

Sicular, Terry, Yue Ximing, Bjorn Gustafsson, and Li Shi. 2007. "The Urban–Rural Income Gap and Inequality in China." *Review of Income and Wealth* 53 (1): 93–126.

Sinn, Hans-Werner, and Frank Westermann. 2001. "Two Mezzogiornos." NBER Working Paper 8125, National Bureau of Economic Research, Cambridge, MA.

Steffen, Alex, ed. 2006. *Worldchanging: A User's Guide for the 21st Century*. New York: Harry N. Abrams, Inc.

Su, Ming, and Quanhou Zhao. 2007. "China: Fiscal Framework and Urban Infrastructure Finance." In *Financing Cities: Fiscal Responsibility and Urban Infrastructure in Brazil, China, India, Poland and South Africa*, ed. George E. Peterson and Patricia Clarke Annez. London: Sage Publications.

Tsui, Kai-yuen. 2007. "Forces Shaping China's Interprovincial Inequality." *Review of Income and Wealth* 53 (1): 60–92.

"The Way We Were in 2006." 2006. *The Week*, December 29.

Wei, Yi-Ming, Qiao-Mei Linag, Ying Fan, Norio Okada, and Hsien-Tang Tsai. 2006. "A Scenario Analysis of Energy Requirements and Energy Intensity for China's Rapidly Developing Society in the Year 2020." *Technological Forecasting & Social Change* 73 (4): 405–21.

"What Shortage?" 2006. *Business Asia*, November 13.

World Bank. 2003a. *China: Promoting Growth with Equity*. Report 24169–CHA, Washington, DC.

———. 2003b. "Public Finance Reform and Macroeconomic Management." World Bank Policy Note, Washington, DC.

———. 2006. *World Development Indicators*. Washington, DC: World Bank.

Wu, Friedrich. 2006. "What Could Brake China's Rapid Ascent in the World Economy?" *World Economics* 7 (3): 63–87.

Wu, Fulong. 2004. "Urban Poverty and Marginalization under Market Transition: The Case of Chinese Cities." *International Journal of Urban and Regional Research* 28 (2): 401–23.

Wu, Jinglian. 2005. *Understanding and Interpreting Chinese Economic Reform*. Mason, OH: South-Western College Publishing.

Wu, Weiping. 2002. "Temporary Migrants in Shanghai: Housing and Settlement Patterns." In *The New Chinese City: Globalization and Market Reform*, ed. John R. Logan, 212–26. Oxford: Blackwell.

Yixing, Zhou, and Laurence J. C. Ma. 2003. "China's Urbanization Levels: Reconstructing a Baseline from the Fifth Population Census." *China Quarterly* (173): 176–96.

Yusuf, Shahid. 2007. "About Urban Mega Regions: Knowns and Unknowns." World Bank Policy Research Working Paper 4252, Washington, DC.

Yusuf, Shahid, M. Anjum Altaf, Barry Eichengreen, Sudarshan Gooptu, Kaoru Nabeshima, Charles Kenny, Dwight H. Perkins, and Marc Shotten. 2003. *Innovative East Asia: The Future of Growth*. New York: Oxford University Press.

Yusuf, Shahid, and Kaoru Nabeshima. 2006a. *China's Development Priorities*. Washington, DC: World Bank.

———. 2006b. *Post Industrial East Asian Cities*. Stanford, CA: Stanford University Press.

Yusuf, Shahid, Kaoru Nabeshima, and Wei Ha. 2007a. "Income and Health in Cities: The Messages from Stylized Facts." *Journal of Urban Health* 84 (S1): 35–41.

———. 2007b. "What Makes Cities Healthy?" World Bank Policy Research Working Paper 4107, Washington, DC.

Zhang, Li 2001. *Strangers in the City: Reconfigurations of Space, Power, and Social Networks within China's Floating Population*. Stanford, CA: Stanford University Press.

Zhao, Gang. 1994. "Looking at China's Urban History from a Macroscopic Perspective." *Social Sciences in China* 15 (3): 171–79.

Zhou, Yixing, and Laurence J. C. Ma. 2003. "China's Urbanization Levels: Reconstructing a Baseline from the Fifth Population Census." *China Quarterly* 173: 176–96.

Zhu, Yu. 2000. "In Situ Urbanization in Rural China: Case Studies from Fujian Province." *Development and Change* 31 (2): 413–34.

CHAPTER 2

Rural–Urban Inequality in China

Albert Park

Rural–urban differences in China have persistently accounted for a large share of income inequality.[1] In part, today's rural–urban gap reflects the institutional legacies of socialism. Beginning in the 1950s, Communist Party leaders clearly separated urban and rural residents through a strictly enforced residential permit (*hukou*) system (see chapter 3), establishing urban and industrial development as the main objective of economic planning. Urban workers were provided with an "iron rice bowl" of lifetime employment, as well as health care, housing, and pension benefits. Rural residents were organized into collectives, in which access to basic health care and education was substantially improved. However, in order to subsidize rapid industrialization, the planning system set prices and directed investments in a manner that discriminated against agriculture and rural areas, leading to sharp differences in the living standards of urban and rural residents.

---

1 According to recent calculations by the World Bank (unpublished), rural–urban differences accounted for 40 percent of total income inequality in 2003, a percentage similar to that in 1995. Changes in rural–urban inequality accounted for 47.4 percent of the increase in inequality between 1985 and 1995, contributing more to inequality than interprovincial, intrarural, or intraurban inequality (World Bank 1997). Sicular and others (2006) find that rural–urban differences explain 25 percent of overall inequality in 2002 for a subset of provinces.

Economic reforms begun in 1978 have yet to reverse this pattern of uneven development or fully repeal the institutions and policies that created it. Quite to the contrary, market reforms have actually increased rural–urban inequality (figures 2.1 and 2.2).

Figure 2.1 plots annual real rural and urban incomes per capita adjusted to 2003 price levels with no adjustment for cost-of-living differences, and figure 2.2 plots the ratio of real rural to urban incomes accounting for the fact that the cost of living was 29.6 percent greater in urban areas than rural areas in 2003. As is apparent from the figures, real rural incomes grew faster than real urban incomes during only two brief periods. The first was in the early 1980s, when the household responsibility system returned agricultural decision-making authority from collectives back to rural households. The improved incentives, along with substantial increases in agricultural procurement prices and other complementary investments, unleashed rapid growth in agricultural productivity, which, along with price increases, boosted rural incomes significantly. The second period was from 1994 to 1997, when the urban economy slowed following financial retrenchment while rural incomes grew with rising agricultural prices and yields. This period proved to be a brief interregnum in what has been a steadily widening gap between rural and urban incomes since 1985.

By 2005, the most recent year for which data are available, rural–urban income differences had reached their historic peak and were greater than when reforms began, with real rural income per capita being

Figure 2.1. Real Urban and Rural per Capita Income, 1978–2005

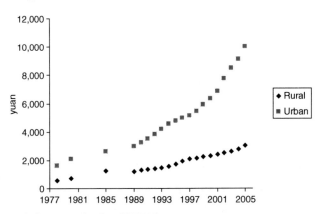

Source: Author's calculation using data from NBS (2006).
Note: Real income is in 2003 yuan, deflated by national urban and rural consumer price indices. Because of the lack of a rural CPI through 1985, the rural CPI is assumed to be equal to the urban CPI from 1977 to 1985.

Figure 2.2. Ratio of Real Rural to Real Urban per Capita Income, 1989–2005

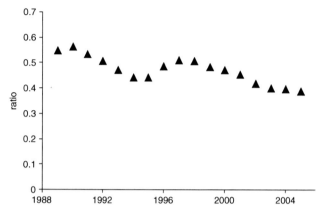

Source: Author's calculation using data from NBS (2006) and Brandt and Holz (2006).
Note: Figure plots the ratio of rural and urban incomes per capita, using urban CPI and adjusted rural CPI for 1990–2002 based on a common bundle of goods in 1990, as calculated by Brandt and Holz (2005). Use of a common bundle allows comparisons that take into account the greater cost of living in urban areas (29.6 percent greater than in rural areas in 2003). National rural and urban CPI are used to adjust incomes for 2003–05.

only 39 percent of real urban income per capita.[2] China's rural–urban gaps are much larger than those found in most other developing countries (Knight, Li, and Song 2006; Eastwood and Lipton 2004).

In addition to contributing to overall inequality, rural–urban inequality creates incentives for rural–urban migration and urbanization while at the same time being symptomatic of persistent barriers to population mobility. The size and reasons for the rural–urban gap thus carry important implications for how policy may affect urbanization and inequality and promote development through greater market integration.

The rest of this chapter is organized as follows. The next section discusses measurement issues that arise in quantifying the extent of rural and urban inequality in China. Section 3 provides an analytical framework for understanding the reasons for large rural–urban gaps in China and locates China's experience in a comparative context. Section 4 assesses the extent of rural–urban migration and urbanization in China, which are key

---

2 Chen and Ravallion (2007) report that per capita income in rural areas is 58 percent that of urban areas. Using data from the China Health and Nutrition Survey, Benjamin and others (forthcoming) find an urban–rural income ratio of 1.6. Neither of these results is reliable, however: Chen and Ravallion's result appears to arise from incorrect price deflation, and Benjamin and others' result is based on an unrepresentative sample. Brandt and Holz (2006) report a ratio of 50 percent in 2000 using their common basket spatial price deflators but using the unadjusted rural CPI; with adjustment, the ratio is 47 percent.

determinants of rural–urban differences. This is followed by a discussion of how different government policies influence rural–urban inequality. A final section concludes.

Sources of Bias in Measuring Rural–Urban Inequality

The rural–urban income gaps reported above are based on data from separate national sample surveys of urban and rural households conducted each year by the National Bureau of Statistics (NBS). These measurements are subject to a number of sources of potential bias. Although these merit scrutiny, they do not appear likely to overturn the conclusion that rural–urban income gaps in China are large.

Sampling Bias

The NBS urban household survey sample excludes urban residents living in townships as well as residents of suburban districts of province-level cities (Beijing, Chongqing, Shanghai, and Tianjin), likely leading to a slight upward bias in urban incomes (discussion with NBS staff).[3] Until 2002 the urban sample also excluded migrants living in urban areas. After they were included, they represented less than 2 percent of the sample, even though the 2000 census found that 14.6 percent of the population living in cities were migrants. Because migrants generally have lower wages than local residents, their exclusion creates upward bias in measured urban incomes.

Using rural data from 19 provinces and urban data from 11 provinces, Sicular and others (2006) find that per capita income of rural migrants living in urban areas is 60 percent that of local residents. Including migrants in calculating urban per capita income reduces the urban–rural income ratio from 2.27:1 to 2.12:1, increasing rural income from 44 percent to 47 percent of urban income. Their estimate of migrant incomes is likely to underestimate actual incomes, because it excludes urban–urban migrants and is based on a one-time survey while data for local residents are based on self-recorded diaries, which are known to produce higher income estimates.

The China Urban Labor Survey (CULS) undertaken in 2005 avoids both problems. It finds that in five large cities, the per capita income of migrants was 78 percent that of local residents; in five small cities, migrants' per capita income was higher than that of permanent residents.

---

3 Incomes of urban residents in townships are assumed to be equal to surveyed residents in county seats.

The main reason why migrants' per capita income is so close to that of urban residents is that migrants living in cities work much longer hours, have fewer dependents, and are much less likely than local residents to be unemployed or out of the labor force (Park and Wang 2007). Although migrants often send money to dependents living in rural areas, according to the CULS data, net remittances account for only 6 percent of their income (compared with 3 percent for permanent urban residents). Netting out remittances thus reduces the relative income of migrants in urban areas by just 3 percent.

Another source of sampling bias is the fact that many individuals living in collective households (including dormitories) are not sampled. In addition, the rural household survey includes as household members individuals who live away from home for more than six months a year but whose economic life remains closely tied to the household (for example, spouses and unmarried children). Many of these individuals actually reside in urban areas. Their inclusion as rural household members is likely to create upward bias in measured rural per capita income given the lack of full income pooling between migrants and their families in rural areas.

Exclusion of Some Categories of Income

NBS household surveys exclude some categories of income. According to Sicular and others (2006), including the rental value of housing as income would have raised the urban–rural income ratio by 10 percent in 1995 and 6 percent in 2002. This increase is probably overstated, because consumer price indices do not accurately reflect changes in housing prices.

Urban incomes do not include important nonwage benefits, such as housing subsidies, health care, pensions, and unemployment insurance benefits. One study that attempts to estimate the value of such benefits finds that they increase the urban–rural income ratio by about one-third (Li and Luo 2006).

Classification of Rural and Urban Areas

Reclassification of rural areas as urban areas accounts for a large share of urbanization. If more-developed rural areas are more likely to be reclassified as urban, reclassification reduces both rural and urban mean incomes, which could increase or decrease the rural–urban gap.

Benjamin and others (forthcoming) perform an exercise using data from the China Health and Nutrition Survey to argue that such reclassification increases the urban–rural income ratio. To the extent that the definition of urban is consistently applied over time, reclassification should not be a source of bias, but it certainly alters how one thinks about the contribution of rural–urban gaps to overall inequality and the causes of rural–urban inequality. Moreover, as described below, China has changed its definition of *urban* over time, leading to unknown sources of bias. Improvements in the accuracy of the definition (such as those adopted in 2000) could increase the rural–urban gap, because the most economically developed areas are more likely to be reclassified as urban.

Differences in the Cost of Living

The rural–urban income ratios plotted in figure 2.2 are adjusted to account for differences in the cost of living between urban and rural areas. If, however, the much more rapid increases in the cost of living in urban areas compared with rural areas reflect increases in the quality of goods consumed rather than increases in the prices of goods of the same quality, the comparison of real incomes in rural and urban areas will underestimate the increase in the rural–urban gap.

Understanding the Large Rural–Urban Divide

In models of free labor markets and costless labor mobility, equilibrium is achieved when wages adjust to the level at which labor supply equals labor demand. In such models, wages for workers with the same human capital converge across labor markets, regardless of differences in physical infrastructure or capital across regions. This convergence occurs because labor moves across markets until marginal productivities are equalized. If this is the case, rural–urban differences in earnings reflect differences in labor productivity. Sicular and others (2006) find that differences in the observable characteristics of rural and urban residents explain 50 percent of the rural–urban gap. According to them, 25 percent of the difference is attributable to differences in education.

Other causes of rural–urban gaps arise once the perfect-market assumption is relaxed. First, labor mobility may be hampered by the costs of moving, by search (or information) costs, or by the disutility of leaving one's home and moving to a new environment. For the poor, financing constraints may limit migration. Second, policies such as China's *hukou* system (described in chapter 3) may create policy barriers to labor mobility, effectively segmenting labor markets spatially.

Historically, rural–urban wage differentials have been observed in developing countries even when there are no obvious policy barriers to labor mobility. This is especially true during early periods of structural change. In both the United States and Japan, for example, rural–urban wage differences were large at the beginning of industrialization but converged over time, as larger shares of the labor force moved from agriculture to industry (Caselli and Coleman 2001; Hayami 2001). In the United States, rural–urban labor shifts in the South are credited with narrowing North–South wage inequality as well as rural–urban wage differences (Caselli and Coleman 2001). Although there is little direct empirical evidence on the reasons for large rural–urban gaps at low levels of development, it seems plausible that moving and search costs are substantial when the density of nonagricultural activity is low and infrastructure is underdeveloped. Highly productive early industrializers may also ration employment opportunities, leaving uneducated workers out of the industrialization game altogether. Among labor, capital, and goods markets, labor markets are typically the last to integrate (Aghion and Williamson 1999).

In China rural–urban income differences are much smaller in more-developed industrialized provinces. If labor movement out of agriculture into nonagriculture were greater in areas with larger rural–urban gaps, one would expect regional differences in these gaps and in mean income levels to converge over time. However, until the late 1990s, China's coastal provinces witnessed a more-rapid flow of labor out of agriculture, an unsustainable pattern once most of the labor in rich provinces has already left agriculture. Income and employment data suggest that since 1997 structural change in the western provinces has accelerated sharply, providing some hope that regional income differences are beginning to narrow (Du, Park, and Wang 2005). Over time, the number of migrants moving to other provinces and regions has increased. By 2004 half of all rural migrants had migrated to another province (NBS 2005).

Several lessons can be drawn from this discussion. First, large rural–urban gaps can exist absent policy barriers, especially at low levels of development. Second, rural–urban differences related to structural change are likely to be an important dimension of regional inequality. Third, China's pattern of rapid movement of labor out of agriculture with rising rural–urban income gaps is anomalous in light of the development experience of other countries. Fourth, labor market integration takes time. Increasing rural migration flows from the regions with the largest rural–urban gaps has occurred only recently.

In a world of imperfect rural–urban labor mobility, government policies that treat urban and rural areas differently can lead to gaps in rural and urban living standards. In addition to policies that directly affect labor mobility, such policies include those affecting taxation, the prices of agricultural outputs and inputs, public investment, basic social services, social insurance, and the financial sector.

Urbanization and Migration

According to official statistics, the percentage of China's population living in urban areas more than doubled during the reform period, increasing from 17.9 percent in 1978 to 42.9 percent in 2005. Possible factors that could account for the increase include more-rapid natural rate of population growth in urban areas as a result of higher birth and lower death rates; rural-to-urban migration; recategorization of rural areas as urban areas as a result of economic development; and changes in the definition of *urban*. Annual estimates of the urban population come from linear interpolations based on estimates from population censuses and mini-censuses, one of which is undertaken every five years (Chan and Hu 2003).

Because the fertility rate is much lower in urban areas than in rural areas, the first factor is unlikely to be driving urbanization. Zhang and Song (2003) estimate that three-fourths of the increase in urban population cannot be explained by the natural rate of urban population growth based on birth and death rates; they attribute this unexplained share of the increase to rural–urban migration (including both *hukou* and non–*hukou* migration). According to my calculations using the 2000 census data, only 12.2 percent of the population living in cities or towns (about 57 million people) had a *hukou* in a county or city different from their place of residence (defined as where they had lived six months or more the previous year). Thus, even if there were no migration in 1978, non-*hukou* migration could at most account for one-quarter of the increase in the urban population between 1978 and 2000. Between 1982 and 2004, 16.8–20.0 million people a year changed their *hukou* registration. Chan, Liu, and Yang (1999) report that 40 percent of *hukou* migrants come from rural areas. A simple calculation using these numbers yields an estimate of the total number of people who changed their *hukou* from rural to urban from 1982 to 2004 at 169 million, or just less than half of the total increase in the urban population over this period. Even allowing for deaths, people who change their *hukou* more than once, and *hukou* changes to rural destinations, these numbers suggest that *hukou* migration accounts for a significant share of total urbanization.

What about the importance of reclassification of rural areas as urban? Such reclassification can be the outcome of either new criteria for what is urban or evolution of rural areas into urban areas given a consistent definition for what is urban. China's official urban population statistics were revised after both the 1990 and 2000 censuses to reflect changes in definition. According to Yu (2002), however, these definitional changes did not increase the total urban population.[4] Thus, the accuracy of recategorization depends on the reasonableness of the criteria for urban classification. In 2000 the NBS shifted to a standard based primarily on population density. This standard should be less subject to influence from administrative reforms that change an area's classification in the absence of real economic or demographic changes.

Could the censuses be underestimating the true extent of urbanization by undercounting rural migrants living in cities? According to the annual rural household surveys of the NBS (2005), the number of rural migrants was 81.2 million in 2002, 89.6 million in 2003, and 93.5 million in 2004. Elsewhere, the NBS reports that in 2004 about 80 percent of rural migrants migrated for more than six months (the 2000 census also uses a six-month standard for residence) and that 95 percent migrated to cities or towns. In addition to individual migrants, the NBS estimates that rural family migration was 23.5 million in 2002, 24.3 million in 2003, and 24.7 million in 2004 (NBS 2005). If families were as likely to go to cities as individual migrants, these numbers imply that the urban population coming from rural areas was 93.5 million in 2004 (17.2 percent of the urban population). This is significantly higher than the 12.2 percent of the urban population estimated using 2000 census data. Even using official urban population data, at the current pace, more than half of China's population will be urban by 2010.

---

4 Before 1990, residents of rural towns (xiang) were defined as rural, while residents of townships (zhen) were categorized as urban. By 1990, many rural towns had been recategorized as townships, despite having large village populations. In 1990, urban areas were redefined to include urban districts (qu) or streets (jiedao) and residence committees (juweihui) in nonurban districts, such as townships, which reduced the urban population. In the 1990s, the number of urban districts increased 17 percent, often as a result of the recategorization of suburban areas that still contained rural populations. At the same time, many rural areas of townships had become quite developed. In 2000 the NBS switched to a criterion of 1,500 people per square kilometer. Using either the 1990 or the 2000 definition, the urban population in 2000 totaled 452 million. In contrast, the distribution of the urban population changed significantly as a result of the change in the definition. Chan and Hu (2003) estimate that reclassification accounted for 22 percent of urban population growth in the 1990s, but their estimate is based on the very simple assumption that the increase is equal to the population of rural towns (xiang) that became townships (zhen).

Despite rapid urbanization, it has been argued that China remains underurbanized given its level of economic development. Chinese cities are suboptimal in size (Au and Henderson 2006), and less of the population is clustered in coastal regions than would be expected with free population mobility.

Rural-to-urban migration is the critical behavior affecting both rural–urban inequality and urbanization. Such migration has increased steadily over time, and policy barriers to migration have been reduced (although the *hukou* system is unlikely to be dismantled for some time) (see chapter 3). Policy and information barriers as well as other costs continue to inhibit migration, leaving ample room for even greater migration in the future. Rising rural–urban income gaps are prima facie evidence that migration flows have not increased rapidly enough to offset rising differences in rural–urban productivity growth.

Policies Affecting the Rural–Urban Divide

If rural and urban labor markets are not fully integrated, policies that treat rural and urban areas differently affect the size of rural–urban income gaps and alter the incentives to migrate. This section examines some of the key policies contributing to rural–urban inequality in China.

Rural Industrialization

The multiplicity of collectively owned small- and medium-size rural enterprises was one of China's great reform success stories. Exploiting demand niches not met by the planning system, rural enterprises, including the self-employed, grew rapidly in the 1980s and steadily for much of the 1990s. Total rural enterprise employment increased from 28.3 million in 1978 to 92.7 million in 1990 and 135.1 million in 1996 (NBS 2006). After 1996, China experienced, for the first time, a sharp drop in rural enterprise employment, to 125.4 million in 1998. Since then there has been a gradual recovery, with employment reaching 142.7 million in 2005. The slowdown from 1996 to 1998 reflected a number of factors, including the Asian financial crisis, intensified market competition, corrections for overexpansion during 1993–94, and widespread privatization of township and village enterprises (TVEs), which frequently led to labor shedding.

TVE development in China played an important role in raising rural incomes for those able to find employment in such enterprises. In fact, given the choice, many better-educated farmers preferred local nonagricultural jobs to out-migration (Zhao 1999). The share of nonagricultural income in total rural household net income increased from 22.3 percent in 1990 to 52.4 percent in 2004. Most of the nonagricultural income (34.0 percent of net income) was from wage income. This is an impressive change in the structure of rural income.

Because such employment opportunities were highly skewed in their distribution, favoring those living in coastal areas, rural industrialization increased inequality (Rozelle 1994). This contrasts sharply with the experience of Taiwan (China), where nonfarm employment in small- and medium-size enterprises (SMEs) equalized incomes. This difference occurred because major infrastructure investments and Taiwan's small geographic size integrated the labor market across the island.

The recent widespread privatization of TVEs, along with increased market openness and intensified competition, provides opportunities for increasing rural incomes in the future. Early evidence suggests that privatized TVEs perform better than collectively owned enterprises and may therefore help make China's SMEs a more dynamic sector that will eventually increase employment opportunities for rural labor. Privatized firms are also less likely than collectively owned enterprises to privilege employment of local rural residents, which should help improve regional labor market integration. In a more open system, however, enterprises are more prone to cluster around urban or periurban areas to realize economies of scale. Therefore, future private enterprise development in China will occur mainly in urban centers. If this is the case, reducing rural–urban inequality will be particularly dependent on the ability of rural residents to migrate to urban areas.

Pricing Policies and Trade Liberalization
Under central planning, the state determined output prices for grain and other agricultural commodities at low levels to buoy urban workers' consumption and indirectly support industrial production. During the early reform period, official procurement prices were increased several times to improve farmer production incentives and increase rural incomes. In 1985, China established a dual-track pricing and procurement contracting system that required farmers to sell a fixed amount of basic grains, cotton, and vegetable oil to the state at low, state-set prices. Farmers were free to sell the rest of their output on the open market and keep the income earned. This policy acted as an effective tax when the market price was above the procurement price but became a protection price in the late 1990s, when the market price fell below the procurement

price and the government agreed to purchase quota amounts to support farmers' welfare. Procured grain was provided at subsidized prices to urban residents until 1993; termination of these subsidies contributed to the narrowing of rural–urban differences.

One reason why grain prices collapsed in the late 1990s was government administrative efforts to mandate that farmers increase planting of grain following concerns about temporary supply shortages that led to rapid grain price inflation in 1994 and 1995. These measures were motivated by concern for the welfare of urban citizens. The low grain prices hit farmers very hard and were largely responsible for slow rural income growth in the late 1990s. Many farmers responded by seeking additional off-farm employment.

After the large increases in grain prices in 1994 and 1995, real grain prices fell steadily, until increasing sharply in 2004, with lower grain sown area and lower grain output (figure 2.3). Agricultural input prices were much more stable over time, so that the profitability of grain production rose and fell with grain prices. It is not clear whether the recent increase in the grain price is a temporary or longer-term phenomenon. The government now supports higher grain prices to increase farmer incomes, is making less effort to maintain sown area in grain, and, since 2001, has provided sizable subsidies to take ecologically marginal lands out of crop cultivation.

Figure 2.3. Grain and Agricultural Input Price Indices, 1993–2005

(1993 price = 1.0)

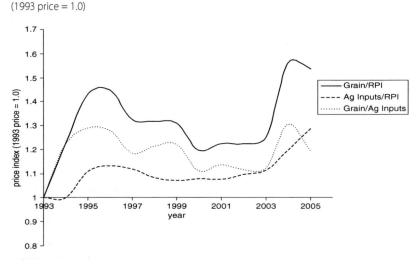

Source: Author's calculation using data from NBS (2006).

Note: Grain and agricultural inputs price indices are divided by the retail price index (RPI), using 1993 as a base.

China's World Trade Organization (WTO) commitment to increase agricultural imports for key commodities has also affected domestic agricultural prices. Before implementation of the agreement, world prices of wheat, corn, soybeans, cotton, and sugar were below domestic prices, in some cases substantially so. Lower prices as a result of trade liberalization significantly harm some specialized producers of these commodities (for example, corn producers in Jilin, soybean producers in Heilongjiang, sugar producers in Guangxi, and cotton producers in Xinjiang). Concern exists that trade liberalization will hurt northern farmers more than those in the south, because China is much more internationally competitive in rice production than in wheat and corn production, and the south is better positioned to increase livestock and horticultural goods production, in which China has a comparative advantage. However, because the increase in imports is limited for commodities with tariff-rate quotas (for example, wheat and corn), the adverse effects should be relatively modest in the intermediate term.

Supporting production adjustment (including shifts to nonagricultural activities) by farmers affected negatively by price changes through effective provision of new technologies, credit, and other necessary inputs represents a major policy challenge. If farmers can shift production in line with comparative advantage, trade liberalization can increase rather than reduce rural incomes.

The best quantitative study of the welfare impacts of China's WTO agreement is by Chen and Ravallion (2004), who solve a computable general equilibrium model calibrated using official urban and rural survey data. They find that three-fourths of rural residents lose from trade liberalization, while only one-tenth of urban residents lose. However, the magnitudes are not very large, and inequality measures are hardly affected. Overall, mean per capita farm income decreases by Y 18, mainly as a result of the drop in wholesale prices, while mean per capita urban income increases by Y 29. A more favorable outcome emerges from a study by Huang and Rozelle (2003) that points to broadly positive net outcomes of WTO accession for the average farm household and the urban consumer, although producers of exportable agricultural commodities in the eastern and southern parts of the country are among the principal beneficiaries.

Taxes and Subsidies

China's fiscal system was significantly decentralized following reforms in 1980 and 1984 (Lin and Liu 2000). Governments at all levels have encountered difficulty raising adequate revenue to fund government expenditures. The problem has led to increasing budgetary self-reliance at local levels and the reduction of fiscal subsidies from upper levels of government. County and township governments in poor areas have frequently had no alternative but to increase revenues through a variety of ad hoc fees and levies in order to meet their recurrent expenditure obligations. In some cases, the corrupt practices of village officials have also led to increased rural taxation. In many cases, such assessments are levied on a per capita or per household basis in rural villages.

For all of these reasons, taxation is regressive rather than progressive in rural China. Many farmers have seen fees increase without visible increases in public investments or services. The problem became severe in the mid- to late-1990s, leading in many cases to rural protests (Bernstein and Lu 2000).

The central government has passed laws to limit rural taxation (to 5 percent of income) and widely publicized the importance of effective enforcement of this rule. But without continuous vigilance and administrative effort, compliance is difficult to maintain. The contrast between excessive rural taxation and continued subsidies for many urban workers is quite startling in light of the large gap in welfare between rural and urban residents.

In recent years, as the government has successfully increased revenues and centralized budgetary revenue, greater redistribution has been possible. The new leadership has made significant progress in reducing rural burdens. In 2003, it eliminated educational surcharges (*jiaoyu fujiao fei*). Between 2003 and 2006, it phased out the agricultural tax, along with most other fees, eliminating farmers' tax and fee burdens in most areas.

At the same time, new spending initiatives sought to improve the welfare of rural residents. Caps on educational fees were imposed in 2002 in some areas, expanding in coverage over time. Starting in 2006, the central government provided new subsidies to eliminate the collection of most educational charges for compulsory education (primary and middle school). Since 2005, free textbooks have been provided to children from poor families. In addition to significant subsidy programs to support grain production and reduce farming on marginal lands, China also recently established a new rural cooperative health insurance system, established a new subsidy program for health expenses of the poor, and began scaling up nationally its rural minimum living standard (*Di Bao*) subsidy program.

Many of these initiatives were outlined in the 11th Five-Year Plan, adopted in March 2006, as part of an effort to "build a new socialist countryside" that increased government spending in rural areas by 15 percent over the previous year. Given these reforms, it is unlikely that differences in taxes and subsidies explain much of the current gaps between rural and urban incomes. However, fiscal imbalance and cash-starved governance in poor regions remain pervasive challenges to maintaining the quality of public services while reducing tax collection.

Agricultural Investment

During China's reform period, periods of high agricultural investments and growth have been strongly associated with reduced inequality and poverty alleviation (Rozelle 1994; Rozelle and others 1998; World Bank 2001; Chen and Ravallion 2007). But such periods have been brief and intermittent. This contrasts with the experience of Taiwan (China). From early on, Taiwan (China) emphasized the importance of raising rural incomes; it therefore invested heavily in rural infrastructure and agricultural research and extension (Park and Johnston 1995), which led to broad-based rural income growth that not only reduced income inequality but also spurred growth.

In China, industrial growth has been associated with increased inequality, mainly because until recently nonagricultural opportunities have been available to only some farmers and regions (especially those in coastal areas). The reform period has seen a steady decline in the share of government expenditures allocated to agriculture (including investments, subsidies, and research and extension), from about 14 percent in 1977 to less than 10 percent by 2004 (NBS 2006).

The disappearance of village collectives has also contributed to deterioration of rural infrastructure and investment. Collectives, for example, used to assess rural corvée labor requirements to support investments in roads, irrigation, terracing, tree planting, and other activities. The reforms have eroded their ability to mobilize labor in this way.

It is, of course, difficult to evaluate the adequacy of current public investments in rural development without carefully assessing competing public projects. A decline in agricultural investment may be appropriate given agriculture's falling overall importance in the economy. However, given the large number of people still living in rural areas, declining levels of agricultural investment have significant distributional consequences.

Some specific investments, in particular agricultural research, that have high returns receive inadequate or misplaced public investments. China invests only 0.5 percent of agricultural GDP in agricultural research, for example—a much lower percentage than other countries (developed countries such as Australia, Canada, and the United States invest 2–4 percent) (Rozelle 2003). Much research is decentralized, but revenue-scarce local governments have been unwilling to spend scarce funds on research.

Investment has also focused excessively on grain crops, ignoring technologies appropriate for poorer regions.

One example of the potential of well-targeted investments in agricultural research is China's aggressive investments in plant biotechnology, an area where China has become a world leader. The tremendous success of crops such as China's Bt cotton suggests that the returns to such investments can be spectacularly high. China should maintain its commitment to this effort, while putting in place an appropriate safety regulatory system (Rozelle 2003; Oliver and Hankins 2007).

Education and Health

Differences in basic education and health services are an important dimension of China's rural–urban divide. According to the China Health and Nutrition Survey, conducted in eight provinces, mean years of schooling were 11.0 years for urban workers and 6.6 years for rural workers (Shi, Sicular, and Zhao 2002). According to the 2000 census, urban enrollment rates are 93–95 percent and rural enrollment rates are 84–90 percent (Hannum, Wang, and Adams 2006). Enrollment rates for secondary-school-age children are 72–80 percent in urban areas and just 50–64 percent in rural areas (Hannum, Wang, and Adams 2006).

Quality differences in urban and rural schools are also significant. Many poor rural areas have yet to fully implement China's nine-year mandatory education law, mainly because poor families are unable or unwilling to pay required school fees. Fiscal decentralization has led to growing disparities in the funding of education and health services (Tsang 1994, 2002).

While gender disparities in educational attainment are not nearly as pronounced in China as in other parts of the world, they appear to increase with poverty (Hannum and Park 2002). Some minority groups also have very low levels of educational attainment. The central government has set up special funds to support schooling in poor and minority counties, but these funds remain small relative to the size of the problem.

Despite the fact that the economic returns to investment in education are likely to be extremely high, the government invested just 2.4 percent of GDP in education in 2004, a rate well below that of other developed and developing countries.[5] By way of comparison, in 1994 public spending on

---

5 If education spending from all sources, including private spending, is included, education spending rises to 4.4 percent of GDP. It is unclear how this rate compares with that of other countries.

education as a percentage of GDP was 2.2 percent in China, 2.8 percent in Pakistan, 3.6 percent in India, 3.7 percent in the Republic of Korea, 3.8 percent in Thailand, 4.7 percent in Mexico, 5.3 percent in Malaysia, and 6.6 percent in Hungary (Song 2003).

Large disparities in educational access among regions or between urban and rural areas are inefficient from the standpoint of making investments to support economic development, as Heckman (2003) notes. Recent studies have shown that the returns to a year of education in urban China are well above 10 percent. Moreover if wages are set below marginal productivities as some research suggests, or if individual educational attainment has externalities, for instance increasing the productivity of other workers, then the estimated private returns to education from microstudies may substantially underestimate the social returns to education, which could be much higher (Heckman 2003).

Rural Credit

Rural credit supports rural development by financing new and ongoing economic activities as well as household investments in education and health. Its role is especially important when there is substantial pressure on farmers to adjust their production activities in response to changing price and other incentives, because new activities usually require new investments. Credit is also necessary for farmers to achieve economies of scale through mechanization, which may be an important prerequisite for releasing additional labor for nonagricultural work.

Like much of China's financial system, China's rural financial institutions (Rural Credit Cooperatives [RCCs] and the Agricultural Bank of China) suffer from significant bad debt problems. Beginning in the mid-1990s these problems reduced the volume of new credit made available to rural borrowers, especially in poor areas, where the bad debt problem was more severe (Brandt, Park, and Wang 2004). At the same time, the lack of effective interregional financial intermediation in RCCs may have helped keep financial resources from flowing from poor areas to richer ones. To improve credit access of rural households, in the early 2000s, RCCs established a new system in which every household receives a credit limit based on an initial assessment of its creditworthiness. Some initial but scanty evidence suggests that the new system may have improved credit access of farmers, but whether this is a sustainable model remains to be seen. Since 2004, China also began experimental reforms in eight provinces to improve governance by creating larger rural cooperative banks or associations to link broader branch networks and improve incentives.

In 2006, the Peoples Bank of China began an experiment to allow private microfinance companies to operate in five provinces, and the China Bank Regulatory Commission began experimental reforms to promote village banking in poor villages of six provinces. It is too early to assess the performance of these experiments.

Overall, the record for provision of rural credit to support economic development in rural areas is mixed. In some respects, distribution of financial resources has been equitable, but rural banks are plagued by performance problems. In the more-commercial banking system that is likely to exist in the future, it will be essential to deregulate financial institutions, so that they can charge interest rates that cover transaction costs and account for risk in each region and develop financial instruments that meet the needs of local borrowers. Creating a diversified financial system, including microfinance providers, that can meet the needs of different types of borrowers in rural areas should be one goal of China's future financial reforms.

Targeted Poverty Programs

Since 1986, China has pursued an active regionally targeted investment program in a group of nationally designated poor counties. The main programs have been a subsidized loan program, a budgetary grants program, and a public works program (focused mainly on road construction and infrastructure to provide safe drinking water). Although sharp criticism has been levied at the implementation of the subsidized loan program (the largest of the three programs), there is evidence that regional targeting has increased rural incomes and achieved respectable rates of return (Jalan and Ravallion 1998; Park, Wang, and Wu 2002). However, targeting has been far from ideal, with increasing leakage over time. Many poor people residing in nondesignated counties have received no assistance. To deal with some of the targeting problems, in 2001, China switched the level of targeting to the village rather than the county and established an ambitious new community-based village investment program.

Conclusions and Policy Recommendations

A key aspect of any policy strategy for addressing rural–urban differences even as urbanization proceeds will be a vision of how patterns of labor mobility will unfold in the coming years. China's economic growth is being driven by rapid urban development in coastal areas that threaten to leave the rest of China behind. Remarkable levels of foreign direct investment and exports in these regions have created global linkages that are creating very dynamic agglomeration economies. Labor flows are responding, but the response is too slow to stop widening wage and productivity differences.

Theory suggests that when regional wage differentials become large enough, investment should begin flowing to the regions with lower wages (Hu 2002). Such movement is being encouraged in China by the government's Western development initiative, but large investment flows have yet to materialize. The situation creates some challenging policy choices, because continued freeing up of the labor market could unleash a large movement of rural labor on coastal areas. Although this may be the fastest way to share the gains of growth broadly, China appears to be relaxing *hukou* restrictions in smaller cities first, in the hope that they will attract more rural migrants and prevent congestion in large cities. The advantages of this approach need to be weighed against growth that is more focused on larger urban centers, which have greater attraction for migrants.

What are the implications of migration trends for public policy? In cities that receive increasingly large numbers of rural migrants, these pressures may create more problems than in the past, because they are adding to already large migrant populations, pushing congestion costs higher. At the same time, there may be additional scope for extending metropolitan areas in suburban or periurban areas. Large numbers of migrants are likely to affect the wages and employment of low-skilled urban workers, creating new demands on municipal governments. Government inevitably will feel pressures to influence both the volume and the spatial distribution of migration (large versus small cities, coastal versus interior cities) and to respond to pressures caused by migration. In doing so, it is important that it avoid repeating the mistakes of the past by restricting labor mobility directly, which has high economic costs and reduces the welfare of rural citizens. Instead, policies should focus on influencing the market-based incentives facing potential workers, especially through public investments, and by empowering municipal governments to mobilize necessary resources to attract migrants when the potential exists.

The initiative announced in 2004 in the State Council's Document No. 1 was designed to support more-rapid rural development through a specific set of policies and investments. It represents a good start in tackling the difficult challenge of reducing large rural–urban disparities. Clearly, no single policy change can eliminate these disparities; it will be important to push on as many fronts as possible.

This chapter emphasizes the importance of facilitating greater labor mobility as a critical part of any strategy to narrow rural–urban differences in the future. The government should plan to gradually phase out the *hukou* system and harmonize government policies to be *hukou*-blind (that is, to equalize access to education, employment opportunities, social insurance programs, and other programs; see chapter 3). Public policies aimed at influencing or responding to patterns of migration should place less emphasis on regulating labor supply decisions, instead emphasizing empowering municipal governments to realize growth potential and respond to changing demands for public expenditures.

The government can reduce rural–urban disparities and promote more-rapid economic growth by making high-return investments in rural development. Priority should be given to increasing education and health investments in rural areas. In the poorest areas, education should be made available free of charge to ensure that financial barriers prevent no children from attending school. Lack of adequate education is a barrier to labor mobility and a leading contributor to poverty. The economic and social returns to education are much greater than the private returns and therefore merit public subsidies. Investments in preventive health and other basic health services are also likely to be high-return investments. Human capital is a particularly good investment for the poor, because it stays with the individual even if he or she migrates to a new location.

Continued investments in agriculture can support rapid growth while reducing rural–urban inequality. Agricultural research has high returns and should receive strong government support. However, large investments in remote rural areas could be a questionable strategy if resources are so poor that labor out-migration is likely to be the best decision for many households. Many of China's poorest rural areas are destined to become depopulated as the process of urbanization and development continues.

The government could also consider adopting several other recommendations:

- Support employment information and credentialing systems that can help rural labor overcome information barriers.
- Promote greater labor mobility and equal treatment by supporting private sector development, by including rural workers in social insurance systems, and by enforcing established labor standards.
- Develop a diversified rural financial system made up of institutions with clearly defined ownership and the flexibility to set interest rates and design financial instruments appropriate for local demanders.

- Develop an adequate financing mechanism in the public finance system to enable redistribution that makes it possible for local governments to avoid excessive taxation of farmers and provide adequate social services and public investments in rural communities.
- Support structural adjustment (shift to new activities) in rural areas by providing appropriate training, incentives, and access to credit.
- Continue investing in targeted poverty alleviation programs, but ensure that specific investments are consistent with a coherent long-range development strategy that is appropriate given local circumstances.

References

Aghion, Philippe, and Jeffrey Williamson. 1999. *Growth, Inequality and Globalization: Theory, History, and Policy.* Cambridge: Cambridge University Press.

Au, Chun-Chung, and Vernon Henderson. 2006. "Are Chinese Cities Too Small?" *Review of Economic Studies* 73 (3): 549–76.

Benjamin, Dwayne, Loren Brandt, John Giles, and Sangui Wang. Forthcoming. "Income Inequality During China's Economic Transition." In *China's Economic Transition: Origins, Mechanisms, and Consequences,* ed. Loren Brandt and Thomas Rawski. Cambridge: Cambridge University Press.

Bernstein, Thomas, and Xiaobo Lu. 2000. "Taxation without Representation: Chinese State and Peasants in the New Reform Era." *China Quarterly* 163: 111–32.

Brandt, Loren, and Carsten Holz. 2006. "Spatial Price Difference in China: Estimates and Implications." *Economic Development and Cultural Change* 55 (1): 48–86.

Brandt, Loren, Albert Park, and Sangui Wang. 2004. "Are China's Financial Reforms Leaving the Poor Behind?" In *Financial Sector Reform in China,* ed. Yasheng Huang, Edward Steinfeld, and Anthony Saich. Cambridge: Harvard East Asian Press.

Caselli, Francesco, and Wilbur John Coleman. 2001. "The U.S. Structural Transformation and Regional Convergence: A Reinterpretation." *Journal of Political Economy* 109 (3): 584–616.

Chan, Kam Wing, and Ying Hu. 2003. "Urbanization in China in the 1990s: New Definition, Different Series, and Revised Trends." *China Review* 3 (2): 49–71.

Chan, Kam Wing, Ta Liu, and Yunyan Yang. 1999. "Hukou and Non-Hukou Migrations: Comparisons and Contrasts." *International Journal of Population Geography* 5 (6): 425–48.

Chen, Shaohua, and Martin Ravallion. 2004. "Household Welfare Impacts of China's Accession to the WTO." In *China and the WTO: Accession, Policy Reform, and Poverty Reduction Strategies*, ed. Deepak Bhattasali, Shantong Li, and Will Martin. Washington, DC: World Bank.

————. 2007. "China's (Uneven) Progress in Poverty Reduction." *Journal of Development Economics* 82 (1): 1–42.

Du, Yang, Albert Park, and Sangui Wang. 2005. "Migration and Rural Poverty in China." *Journal of Comparative Economics* 33 (4): 688–709.

Eastwood, Robert, and Michael Lipton. 2004. "Rural and Urban Income Inequality and Poverty: Does Convergence between Sectors Offset Divergence within Them?" In *Inequality, Growth, and Poverty in an Era of Liberalization and Globalization*, ed. Giaovanni Andrea Cornia. Oxford: Oxford University Press.

Hannum, Emily, and Albert Park. 2002. "Educating China's Children for the 21st Century." *Harvard China Review* 3 (2): 8–14.

Hannum, Emily, Meiyan Wang, and Jennifer Adams. 2006. "Urban-Rural Disparities in Access to Primary and Secondary Education: Recent Trends."

Hayami, Yujiro. 2001. *Development Economics: from the Poverty of Nations to the Wealth of Nations*. Oxford: Oxford University Press.

Heckman, James. 2003. "China's Investment in Human Capital." *Economic Development and Cultural Change* 51 (4): 795–804.

Hu, Dapeng. 2002. "Trade, Rural–Urban Migration, and Regional Income Disparity in Developing Countries: A Spatial General Equilibrium Model Inspired by the Case of China." *Regional Science and Urban Economics* 32 (3): 311–38.

Huang, Jikun, and Scott Rozelle. 2003. "The Impact of Trade Liberalization on China's Agriculture and Rural Economy." *SAIS Review* 23(1): 115–31.

Jalan, Jyatna, and Martin Ravallion. 1998. "Are there Dynamic Gains from a Poor-Area Development Program?" *Journal of Public Economics* 67 (1): 65–85.

Knight, John, Shi Li, and Lina Song. 2006. "The Rural–Urban Divide and the Evolution of Political Economy in China." In *Human Development in the Era of Globalization: Essays in Honor of Keith B. Griffin*, ed. James Boyce, Stephen Cullenberg, and Prasanta Pattanaik. Northampton, MA: Edward Elgar.

Li, Shi, and Chuliang Luo. 2006. *Re-Estimating the Income Gap between Urban and Rural Households in China*. Presented at Rethinking the Rural-Urban Cleavage in Contemporary China, Harvard University, Cambridge, Mass., October 6.

Lin, Justin Yifu, and Zhiqiang Liu. 2000. "Fiscal Decentralization and Economic Growth in China." *Economic Development and Cultural Change* 49 (1): 1–21.

NBS (National Bureau of Statistics). 2005. *China Rural Survey Yearbook 2005*. Beijing: China Statistics Press.

————. 2006. *China Statistical Yearbook 2006*. Beijing: China Statistics Press.

Oliver, Charles, and Jessica Hankins. 2007. "Future World Leadership in GM Crops." *China Business Review* 34(4): 36–39.

Park, Albert, and Bruce Johnston. 1995. "Rural Development and Dynamic Externalities in Taiwan's Structural Transformation." *Economic Development and Cultural Change* 44 (1): 181–208.

Park, Albert, and Dewen Wang. 2007. "Migration and Urban Poverty and Inequality in China." Unpublished manuscript.

Park, Albert, Sangui Wang, and Guobao Wu. 2002. "Regional Poverty Targeting in China." *Journal of Public Economics* 86 (1): 123–153.

Rozelle, Scott. 1994. "Rural Industrialization and Increasing Inequality: Emerging Patterns in China's Reforming Economy." *Journal of Comparative Economics* 19 (3): 362–91.

———. 2003. *Rural Development in China: New Challenges in a New Landscape*, World Bank Policy Note, Washington, DC.

Rozelle, Scott, Albert Park, Changqing Ren, and Vince Bezinger. 1998. "Targeted Poverty Investments and Economic Growth in China." *World Development* 26 (12): 2137–51.

Shi, Xinzheng, Terry Sicular, and Yaohui Zhao. 2002. *Analyzing Urban–Rural Inequality in China*. Unpublished manuscript.

Sicular, Terry, Ximing Yue, Bjorn Gustafsson, and Shi Li. 2006. "The Urban–Rural Income Gap and Inequality in China." Research Paper 2006/135, UNU–Wider, Helsinki.

Song, Shunfeng. 2003. "Policy Issues of China's Urban Unemployment." *Contemporary Economic Policy* 21 (2): 258–69.

Tsang, Mun. 1994. "The Financial Reform of Basic Education in China." *Economics of Education Review* 15 (4): 423–44.

———. 2002. "Intergovernmental Grants and the Financing of Compulsory Education in China." Teachers College, Columbia University, New York.

World Bank. 1997. *Sharing Rising Incomes: Disparities in China* Washington, DC: World Bank.

———. 2001. *China: Overcoming Rural Poverty*. Washington, DC: World Bank.

Yu, Hongwen. 2002. "Discussion of the Definition of Urban Population in China's Population Censuses." [In Chinese] Paper presented at the Eighth China Population Science Conference.

Zhang, Kevin Honglin, and Shunfeng Song. 2003. "Rural–Urban Migration and Urbanization in China: Evidence from Time Series and Cross-Section Analyses." *China Economic Review* 14 (4): 386–400.

Zhao, Yaohui. 1999. "Leaving the Countryside: Rural-to-Urban Migration Decisions in China." *American Economic Review* 89 (2): 281–86.

CHAPTER 3

Migration, *Hukou*, and the City

C. Cindy Fan

Rural–urban migration is playing an increasingly important role in shaping the economic and demographic landscape of Chinese cities.[1] Over the past two decades, China has transformed itself from a relatively immobile society to one in which more than 10 percent of the population are migrants. Although China's mobility rate is still low compared with that of advanced industrial economies, the sheer size of the migrant flows and their dramatic economic and social consequences have already profoundly affected economic growth and urban development. Looking ahead, decision makers at all levels will need to craft policies that address issues of migration and rural–urban migrants— issues that are hotly debated among scholars, Chinese policy makers, and others.

This chapter presents recent findings that describe migration patterns and changes since the 1980s. It complements and extends the discussion in chapter 2, highlighting the salient facets of migration that have direct implications for China's urbanization process.

Funding from the World Bank, the National Science Foundation (BCS-0455107 and SBR-9618500), the Luce Foundation, and the Academic Senate of the University of California at Los Angeles is gratefully acknowledged. The author also thanks Mingjie Sun and Wenfei Winnie Wang for their research assistance.

1 Rural–urban migration has been the main driver of urban growth in China since the 1980s (see Duan 2003, Lu and Wang 2006, and chapter 2 of this volume).

The chapter is divided into four sections. The first section describes the *hukou* system and its relation with population movements. The second section summarizes the magnitude, spatial patterns, and reasons for migration and describes migrant characteristics. The third section examines the effects of rural–urban migration on urban and rural areas. The final section discusses the policy implications of increased migration.

The *Hukou* System and Its Reform

China's *hukou* system became law in 1958, when the National People's Congress passed its "Regulations on Household Registration in the People's Republic of China." Under these regulations, every Chinese citizen is assigned a *hukou* location (*hukou suozaidi*) and an "agricultural" (rural) or "nonagricultural" (urban) *hukou* classification (*hukou leibie*) (Yu 2002; Fei-Ling Wang 2005). For the most part, both are inherited from one's parents. An agricultural *hukou* provides access to farmland; a nonagricultural *hukou* provides access to jobs, housing, food, and state-sponsored benefits. The *hukou* location specifies where one is entitled to receive benefits; in essence, it defines where one belongs.

Until the mid-1980s, it was extremely difficult for rural Chinese to survive in cities, because without an urban *hukou*, they did not have access to the necessities of life, such as food and housing, many of which were centrally controlled and allocated. The *hukou* system therefore kept rural–urban migration to a minimum.

During the past two decades or so, major changes in the *hukou* system have expanded options for rural Chinese to work in urban areas. These changes unleashed large waves of migration.

Temporary Migration

In October 1984, the State Council announced that peasants working in towns would be granted the "self-supplied food grain" (*zili kouliang*) *hukou*, marking the first opening in the rigid division between city and countryside.[2] In 1985, the Ministry of Public Security issued regulations for rural migrants to obtain "temporary residence permits" (*zanzhuzheng*). The same year the National Congress allowed citizens to use their identity cards as proof of identification (before 1985 only the *hukou* could be used) (Yu 2002).

---

2 This type of *hukou* had disappeared by the late 1980s (Zhong 2000).

These measures, as well as the increased marketization of food, housing, and other daily necessities, made it easier for rural Chinese to work and live in urban areas. Although some rural migrants stay in the city for extended periods of time, their lack of an urban *hukou* means that they are considered, at least in an institutional sense, temporary migrants.

"Selling" of Hukou

Beginning in the late 1980s, many city governments began charging migrants high fees—ranging from several thousand to tens of thousands of yuan—in exchange for *hukou* in towns and cities.[3] City governments justified this practice on the grounds that they should be compensated for extending urban benefits to migrants.[4] Beginning in the mid-1990s, large cities, such as Shanghai and Shenzhen, began to offer "blue-stamp" *hukou* to migrants who met high skill requirements and were able to make sizable investments (Wong and Huen 1998). Like the green card in the United States, the blue-stamp *hukou* could be converted into a permanent urban *hukou* after a specified period of time. These practices commodified *hukou* and channeled resources from a very small elite of eligible migrants to the coffers of urban governments (Cai 2001; Cao 2001).[5]

Reform in Towns and Small Cities

In 1997, the State Council approved a pilot scheme to grant urban *hukou* to rural migrants who held stable jobs and had resided in selected towns and small cities for more than two years (Yu 2002). Unlike under earlier practices, this reform did not require qualified migrants to pay a hefty sum. After testing the scheme in 450 towns and small cities, in 2001 the State Council approved plans to expand *hukou* reform (Yu 2002). Since then the principal criteria for obtaining *hukou* in small cities and towns have been a permanent and legal place of stay and a stable source of

---

3 Varieties of terms have been used to describe these fees. The most popular are *jiangshe fei* (development fee), *chengshi jiangshe fei* (urban development fee), *jiangzhen fei* (town development fee), *jiangshe peitao fei* (development and accessory fee), and *zengrong fei* (accommodation fee). The fees are often higher in large cities than in small cities and higher in the city proper of large cities than in the outskirts (Cao 2001).

4 Yu (2002) estimates that by the end of 1993, 3 million rural migrants had purchased *hukou* in a city or town, raising Y 25 billion in local government revenues.

5 Since the late 1990s, the "selling" of *hukou* has increasingly been replaced by other mechanisms (Zhang and Lin 2000; Zhong 2000; Cai 2002).

income (Cai 2003). In 1998 the State Council approved four guidelines that further relaxed the urban *hukou*.[6] In 2003, the State Council issued a directive affirming the rights of rural migrants to work in cities (Cai 2003). Adherence to these guidelines and directives is, however, up to individual city governments (Sun 2007).

Reform in Large Cities

The extent and specifics of *hukou* reform in large cities varies greatly. In general, the larger the city, the more difficult it is to obtain a local *hukou*. A number of large and medium-size cities, such as Nanjing, Xi'an, and Zhuhai, have relaxed their criteria for granting *hukou* (Cai 2002). Shijiazhuang, in Hebei Province, is among the most adventurous cities, having granted 450,000 new *hukou* between August 2001 and June 2003 (Wang 2003). In most large cities, however, *hukou* reform has been minimal; only an extremely small minority of rural migrants—who satisfy stringent criteria on educational attainment, skills, financial ability, and health—are awarded local *hukou* and given access to urban benefits (Zhang and Lin 2000; Zhong and Gu 2000; Qiu 2001; Cai 2003; Wang 2003). The legacy of blue-stamp *hukou* and the logic of creaming thus persist.

Very large cities, such as Beijing, Guangzhou, and Shanghai, where *hukou* is still a primary gatekeeper, have been especially resistant to *hukou* reform.[7] University graduates who wish to apply for government jobs in Beijing must obtain a *hukou* for Beijing city proper, for example (Beijing Chenbao 2006). Many enterprises in Beijing restrict hiring to candidates holding Beijing *hukou* (Fazhi Wanbao 2006).

City governments can also tighten the policy at their discretion. In 2002, Guangzhou reversed its *hukou* reform on the ground that migrants over-loaded the urban infrastructure; Zhengzhou followed suit in 2004 (China Daily 2004; Zhongguo Qingnianbao 2007). In May 2007, the Ministry of

---

6 These guidelines specify that (a) children can choose to inherit *hukou* from the father or the mother (previously, *hukou* was inherited from the mother); (b) rural residents who have lived in the city for more than one year and whose spouses hold urban *hukou* may be granted urban *hukou*; (c) elderly parents whose only children live in cities may be granted urban *hukou*; and (d) people who have made invest-ments, established enterprises, or purchased apartments; have stable jobs and accommodation; and who have lived more than one year in a city are eligible for local *hukou* (Yu 2002).

7 In 2001 the Beijing government began to issue three types of temporary permits, which determine the services migrants have access to and the extent of government control and monitoring (Cai 2002).

Public Security completed a report on *hukou* reform, highlighting the legal place of stay as the basic criterion for urban *hukou* but once again affirming the autonomy of city governments to establish their own criteria for granting *hukou* (Sun 2007).

Classification and Location

The distinction between nonagricultural *hukou* and agricultural *hukou* is no longer as important as it once was; some provinces (including Anhui, Gansu, Hunan, and Hubei) and some large cities (including Guangzhou and Nanjing) have eliminated it altogether (Congressional-Executive Commission on China 2005). *Hukou* location, however, continues to define a person's life chances and access to resources. The difference between a *hukou* in small cities and towns and a *hukou* in the city proper of large cities persists and is substantial.

In addition to the new measures and guidelines described above, the Chinese government established the goal that by 2005, *hukou* reform in large and medium-size cities would be completed and the dualistic registration system replaced by a unified registration system (Cai 2002). To date, neither has been fully implemented. Still, these official endorsements indicate that the central government is increasingly concerned with reforming the *hukou* system and tackling *hukou*-based barriers to migration.

At least two quantitative targets in the 11th Five-Year Plan (2006–10) suggest that the government encourages migration (Editorial Group 2006; Fan 2006). First, the level of urbanization is expected to increase, from about 43 percent in 2006 to 47 percent in 2010, indicating that a moderate pace of rural–urban migration is expected and encouraged (Guangming Ribao 2006). Second, by 2010 an additional 45 million rural workers are expected to have shifted from rural to urban sectors. Although it is too early to predict if these targets will be reached, the 11th Five-Year Plan has legitimized a development trajectory of increased urbanization and rural–urban labor transfer that will almost certainly entail further *hukou* reform.

Migration Patterns and Changes

Since the 1980s, the magnitude of migration in China has increased significantly, migration flows to the most developed regions have accelerated, and economic reasons for migrating have gained in importance. Migrant characteristics have also changed.

Magnitude and Spatial Patterns

Despite the recent proliferation of research on migration in China, much confusion remains about its magnitude. The confusion partly reflects the multitude of concepts and terms related to migration and the frequent changes of definition in census and census-type surveys in China (Duan and Sun 2006).[8] This chapter focuses on *liudong renkou* (the "floating population") and *qianyi renkou* (migrants), by far the most commonly used measures of migration in China.

The "floating population" (liudong renkou). *Liudong renkou* is a unique concept in China that is tied to the *hukou* system (Goodkind and West 2002). Individuals who are not living at their *hukou* location are considered "floating." This concept is based on the notion that the *hukou* location is where one belongs and that migration is not considered official and permanent until the migrant's *hukou* location is also changed. The floating population is a stock measure. Regardless of when actual migration occurred, a person is counted as part of the floating population as long as his or her usual place of residence is different from the *hukou* location.

In practice, a temporal criterion usually qualifies the definition of the floating population, and it varies from source to source.[9] The 1990 census specified that a person must have left the *hukou* location for at least a year before he or she is considered part of the floating population. In the 2000 census, the period was shortened to six months.

The spatial criterion was also changed: in the 1990 census, the floating population included people who had moved from one county (or county-level city or urban district) to another; in the 2000 census, the spatial criterion was changed to subcounty units (townships, towns, and streets). The 1990 census thus counted only the intercounty floating population, while the 2000 census counted both the intercounty and intracounty floating population. The intercounty floating population increased from 22.6 million (2.0 percent of the population in 1990) to 78.8 million (6.3 percent of the population) in 2000 (table 3.1).[10]

---

8 There are at least 20 different and related concepts for describing population movements and the floating population in China (Zhou 2002). China's definitions of migrants are the most complex in the world (Jiao 2002).

9 The temporal criterion can range from 24 hours to one year (Goodkind and West 2002), creating a wide range of estimates. Definitions using a short temporal criterion may include transients and travelers (Shen 2002).

10 The effect of the change of the temporal criterion—from one year to six months—is difficult to determine. However, it is reasonable to assume that the surge in the floating population was caused primarily by an increase in mobility in the 1990s rather than to definitional changes (Liang 2001).

Table 3.1. Size of "Floating" and Migrant Population, 1990 and 2000

	1990 census		2000 census	
Item	Number (million)	Percentage of population[a]	Number (million)	Percentage of population[a]
Floating population (liudong renkou)				
Intercounty	22.6	2.0	78.8	6.3
Intercounty + intracounty	—	—	144.4	11.6
Migrants (qianyi renkou)				
Intercounty	35.3	3.4	79.1	6.7
Intercounty + intracounty	—	—	121.2	10.3
Intercounty migrants				
Permanent[b]	19.1 (54.1)	1.8	20.2 (25.6)	1.7
Temporary[b]	16.2 (45.9)	1.6	58.8 (74.4)	5.0
Interprovincial[b]	11.5 (32.6)	1.1	32.3 (40.9)	2.8
Intraprovincial[b]	23.8 (67.4)	2.3	46.8 (59.1)	4.0

Source: 1990 census 1 percent sample; NBS 2002; Liang and Ma 2004.
— Not available.
a. Figures for migrants include only people over the age of five.
b. Figures in parentheses represent percentage of intercounty migrants.

Combining intercounty and intracounty migrants, the 2000 census reports a floating population of 144.4 million (11.6 percent of China's population) (NBS 2002). This number is consistent with most published sources, which estimate that the floating population was about 30 million in the early 1980s, 70–80 million in the early and mid-1990s, and 100–140 million in the late 1990s (Solinger 1999; Zhong 2000; Wan 2001; Bai and Song 2002; Jiao 2002).[11] The 2005 National One-Percent Population Sample Survey reported an increase of the floating population to 150 million in 2005 (NBS 2006). According to one estimate, the floating population is increasing by about 5 million people a year (Beijing Sheke Guihua 2000). According to this estimate, it will reach 200 million in 2015 and 250 million in 2025.

Migrants (qianyi renkou). The closest Chinese equivalents to the terms *migration* and *migrants* are *qianyi and qianyi renkou*. Unlike the floating population, *qianyi renkou* is a measure of flow. In the 1990 census, *qianyi renkou* were defined as individuals five years or older who had moved

---

11 Figures reported by the Public Security Bureau (PSB) may be considerably lower, because they include only the portion of the floating population that registers with local PSBs. For example, based on PSB data, the floating population in the mid-1990s was only 44 million (Jiao 2002). The Ministry of Public Security estimates that the floating population in 1997 was 100 million, but its data show that only about 38 million were registered (Gongan Bu 1997; Goodkind and West 2002; Shen 2002).

from one county to another within the past five years and (a) whose *hukou* had moved to the 1990 place of residence or (b) who had left their *hukou* location for more than one year. In the 2000 census, the spatial criterion was changed to subcounty-level units and the temporal criterion was changed to six months. Migrants in group (a) are usually referred to as permanent migrants; those in group (b) are usually referred to as temporary migrants (see, for example, Goldstein and Goldstein 1991; Yang 2006; and Liang and Chen 2007). A variety of other terms have also been used to describe this dichotomy. They include *hukou* and non-*hukou*, plan and nonplan (or self-initiated), formal and informal, and de jure and de facto (see, for example, Gu 1992; Yang 1994; Li 1995; Chan, Liu, and Yang 1999; Fan 1999; forthcoming).

The terms *liudong* and *qianyi* are often used interchangeably in the Chinese literature and media. Some scholars consider the terms mutually exclusive. To make it even more confusing, the terms *floating population* and *temporary migrants* are also often used interchangeably. Understanding the floating population as a stock measure and *qianyi renkou* as a flow measure is key to distinguishing between these terms.

Using the *qianyi renkou* criteria described above, the 1990 censuses documented some 35.3 million intercounty migrants, accounting for 3.4 percent of the population over the age of five; this figure had risen to 79.1 million (6.7 percent of the population) by 2000 (see table 3.1). These results support the observation that mobility increased significantly between 1985–90 and 1995–2000 (Fan 2005a; Liang 2001). By 2002, the sum of intercounty and intracounty migrants had reached 121.2 million, accounting for 10.3 percent of the population over the age of five.

Among intercounty migrants, 45.9 percent were temporary migrants in 1990 and 74.4 percent were temporary migrants in 2000. The number of permanent migrants hovered near 20 million, but the number of temporary migrants increased from 16.2 million to 58.8 million. The dramatic surge in temporary migrants reflects not only *hukou* reform but also the increased prominence of market forces in determining population movements in China. The increase also suggests that rural migrants, who constitute the bulk of temporary migrants, are playing an increasingly important role in shaping Chinese cities.

Interprovincial migration, which is typically over longer distances, accounted for 32.6 percent of all intercounty migration in 1990 and 40.9 percent in 2000. These figures indicate that the friction of distance has declined over time for Chinese migrants (Du and Gao 2004; Fan 2005b).

Between the 1990 and 2000 censuses, intraregional flows declined in relative importance, while interregional proportions increased, rising from 57.3 to 71.8 percent of all flows (table 3.2). This trend is consistent with the observation that more migrants traveled long distances in the 1990s than in the 1980s. Of the six off-diagonal cells in table 3.2, only two—central-to-eastern and western-to-eastern—increased between the two censuses, indicating an acceleration and concentration of migration flows from the two noncoastal regions to the eastern region. The flow from the central region to the eastern region is especially noteworthy, increasing from 21.0 to 41.8 percent between the two censuses. These trends indicate that interprovincial migration is overwhelmingly from inland to coastal areas and that the concentration of migrants in the eastern region (the most urbanized of the three regions) is high and increasing (the province of Guangdong alone received 36.2 percent of all interprovincial migrants between 1995 and 2000). Provincial net migration volumes and rates also increased between 1990 and 2000, with sending provinces losing more migrants and receiving provinces gaining more migrants in the 1990s than in the 1980s (Fan 2005a).

Reasons for Migration

Both the 1990 and 2000 censuses asked migrants to select one of nine options as their primary reason for migrating. These census data reveal not only the motives for migrating but also the means of doing so, the circumstances under which migration takes place, what migrants plan to

Table 3.2. Interprovincial Migration within and between Regions, 1990 and 2000
(percentage of total migration flows)

Destination	Origin			
	Eastern	*Central*	*Western*	*Total*
1990				
Eastern	24.4	21.0	11.5	57.0
Central	10.7	9.2	6.3	26.1
Western	3.7	4.1	9.1	16.9
Total	38.8	34.3	26.9	100.0
2000				
Eastern	18.4	41.8	18.2	78.4
Central	3.8	4.0	2.4	10.2
Western	2.4	3.2	5.8	11.4
Total	24.5	49.0	26.5	100.0

Source: State Statistical Bureau 1992; NBS 2002.
Note: Because of data limitations, Tibet is excluded from the computation. Chongqing is combined with Sichuan, because it did not become a separate provincial-level unit until 1996.

do at the destination, and above all the degree of state involvement (Fan 1999; forthcoming). (table 3.3).

The reasons for migration can be represented by two intersecting dichotomous sets. The first set distinguishes economic reasons from social (including family and life-cycle) reasons (Rowland 1994). "Job transfer" (the transfer of workers by the state to specific jobs and regions); "job assignment" (the assignment of jobs by the state to recent graduates); and "industry/business" (defined as self-initiated moves for engaging in industrial, commercial, or trade sectors) are economic reasons for migrating. Research shows that most migrants who cite "industry/business" as their reason for migrating are of rural origin and do not have urban *hukou* (Fan 1999). Social reasons include "friends/relatives" (migration to seek the help of friends and relatives); "joining family"; and "marriage." "Retirement" and "study/training" are not readily categorized as economic or social reasons.

The second set involves "state-sponsored," "planned," or "official" migration versus migration that is "self-initiated," "unofficial," or driven by the "market." The first type of migration is usually associated with permanent migration (with *hukou* change); the second type is usually associated with temporary migration (without *hukou* change). Generally, "job transfer" and "job assignment" are part of state planning and are thus usually accompanied by *hukou* change. Because admission to universities is highly competitive, "study/training" migrants who enter universities are awarded urban *hukou* in the city where their university is located. "Industry/business" and

Table 3.3. Self-Declared Reasons for Intercounty Migration, 1990 and 2000
(percent)

Reason	1990 census			2000 census		
	All	Permanent migrants	Temporary migrants	All	Permanent migrants	Temporary migrants
Job transfer	12.0	18.1	4.8	3.1	5.1	2.4
Job assignment	6.8	10.2	2.7	2.6	7.8	0.8
Industry/business	23.6	1.8	49.3	46.4	3.9	65.0
Study/training	12.9	21.4	2.7	13.7	39.9	4.7
Friends/relatives	9.7	6.6	13.4	5.0	3.4	5.6
Retirement	1.6	2.1	1.0	n.a.	n.a.	n.a.
Joining family	11.0	13.7	7.8	10.0	7.9	10.7
Marriage	13.8	15.6	11.6	7.3	17.2	3.9
Housing change	n.a.	n.a.	n.a.	4.5	10.4	2.5
Other	8.7	10.4	6.7	4.4	4.2	4.4

Source: 1990 census 1 percent sample; Liang and Ma 2004.
n.a. = Not applicable.
Note: The options in the two censuses were the same, except that the 2000 census omitted "retirement" and included a new option ("housing change").

"friends/relatives" constitute self-initiated migration and are usually not accompanied by *hukou* change. "Retirement," "joining family," and "marriage" may or may not involve *hukou* change. Generally, marriage migrants moving from one rural area to another can obtain *hukou* (and have access to farmland) at their new location; it is much more difficult for rural–urban marriage migrants to obtain urban *hukou*. Because the vast majority of marriage migrants are rural–rural migrants, marriage as a migration reason tends to describe permanent migrants whose moves are accompanied by *hukou* change (Fan and Huang 1998; Fan forthcoming).

A new category, "housing change," was included in the 2000 census, in part because of rapid increase in housing construction in many cities since the 1990s. It primarily describes intracounty moves and migration of short distance.

As expected, according to the 1990 census, "study/training," "job transfer," and "job assignment" were prominent reasons for permanent migrants. The proportions of "job transfer" and "job assignment" migrants dropped sharply between the two censuses, however, supporting the observation that market mechanisms are increasingly overtaking state-sponsored channels in job-related moves. Marriage continued to be a prominent reason for permanent migration in the 2000 census. "Industry/business" was an important and leading reason for temporary migration in the 1990 census, but its dominance increased further, so that in the 2000 census it accounted for 65.0 percent of all temporary migrants. The overwhelming objective of rural migrants is to increase income and diversify their sources of household income (Croll and Huang 1997; Fan 2002); these migrants have little access to state-sponsored channels of migration (Solinger 1999). The 2000 census results show that economic motivations are becoming increasingly prominent (Yang 2004). At the same time, the larger proportion of temporary migrants in the "joining family" category suggests that more rural–urban migrants are bringing their families to cities (Zhou 2004).

Migrants' Characteristics
Migrants in China tend to be young, single, and male (Cao 1995; Chan, Liu, and Yang 1999; Cai 2003). Since the 1980s, female migration has increased more rapidly than male migration.[12] Rural–urban migrants have a mean age in the mid-20s (Wang and others 2002). They are more likely to be male than female, but the gender ratio varies considerably

---

12 The proportion of women among interprovincial migrants increased from 41.3 percent in the 1990 census to 47.7 percent in the 2000 census (Fan forthcoming).

from place to place (Wang and others 2002). Female migrants are younger than male migrants, and they are more likely to be single (Fan 2004b; Wang and others 2002). Rural–urban migrants' modal educational attainment is junior secondary; they have more formal education than rural nonmigrants but less than urban residents (Cai 2003; de Brauw and others 2003; Du, Park, and Wang 2005). The effect of education is likely nonlinear: the most- and least-educated people are less likely to migrate than those in the middle, because those in the middle have the desire to economically better themselves as well as the means to pursue migrant work (Li and Zahniser 2002; Du, Park and Wang 2005).

Recent studies have highlighted a new generation of rural–urban migrants who have more education than earlier migrants and little farming experience (Qiu, Xie, and Zhou 2004). These recent migrants may be less concerned with augmenting family income than with the prospect of obtaining urban *hukou* and staying in urban areas. They are also likely to be selective about the type of urban work they perform (Jian and Zhang 2005).

Studies have shown that permanent migrants tend to be associated with high education, urban origins, and urban destinations, while temporary migrants are associated with low education and rural origins (Fan 2002). The state is selectively awarding skilled and urban migrants permanent residence in the city while relegating less-qualified and rural migrants to unofficial and temporary statuses. The *hukou* system has played an important stratification role by engineering a two-track migration system under which a superior track (permanent migration) is set aside for qualified workers and urban residents and an inferior track (temporary migration) is designated for less-skilled migrants and migrants from rural areas (Gu 1992; Chan, Liu, and Yang 1999; Fan 1999).

Impacts of Rural–Urban Migration

The notion that rural–urban migration has been a key component of China's economic development is widely accepted (Cai 2001). The impacts of migration on urban and rural areas are deep and multifaceted, and evaluations of these impacts are mixed.

Impacts on Urban Areas

The impact of rural migrants on urban areas is hotly debated (Jiao 2002). Migrant labor is seen as important for stimulating the urban economy and boosting the expansion of urban industries and services (Cao 1995; Zhong and Gu 2000). Because most rural–urban migrants engage in low-paid, manual and services types of work, they fill jobs that are shunned by most urbanites, who can specialize in more prestigious jobs. Migrants in cities also increase consumption, which creates employment for others (Zhong and Gu 2000).[13]

By augmenting labor in urban areas, rural migrants indirectly suppress wage increases in cities (Qiu, Xie, and Zhou 2004). It is well documented that rural migrants' labor cost is substantially lower than that of local urban labor (Cai 2002).[14] Moreover, the large agricultural labor surplus supports a continuous supply of new, young, and cheap migrants for cities (Yang and Ding 2005). Rural migrants are, therefore, a source of "perpetually young" labor for urban development; they are especially relevant for cities experiencing or expecting to experience population aging (Wang and others 2002). Recent labor shortages in the Pearl River delta and other areas specialized in labor-intensive manufacturing, however, suggest that rural migrants are becoming more selective in urban work; they are more mobile than they once were and more willing to follow better paid jobs to new and different locations (Jian and Zhang 2005).

Despite migrants' contributions to the urban economy, public and official evaluations of rural–urban migration are mixed. Rural migrants are criticized for overloading urban infrastructure such as transportation and housing, engaging in criminal activities, violating the birth-control policy, and spreading sexually transmitted diseases (Cao 1995; Solinger 1999; Zhong and Gu 2000; Yang 2006; Yang, Derlega, and Luo 2007; Messner, Liu, and Karstedt forthcoming). Migrants are also blamed for exacerbating urban unemployment, especially given the increase in laid-off urban employees from state-owned enterprises (Jiao 2002; Yang and Ding 2005). This criticism prompted many cities to tighten migration control in the mid-1990s (Cai 2002), although research has shown that migrant labor and urban local labor are complementary rather than competitive (Zhong 2000; Wang and others 2002). Workers laid off from state-owned enterprises are more experienced and skilled than the average rural–urban migrant.[15] Some studies nevertheless warn that the

---

13 Based on a survey conducted in the mid-1990s, Zhong and Gu (2000) report that migrants' consumption accounts for more than half of total retail consumption in Wuhan.

14 Cai (2002) cites reports that estimate that the cost ratio between local labor and migrant labor is 5:1 in Shanghai and 1.8:1 in Nanjing.

15 A study by Jiao (2002) concludes that the replacement ratio between the two types of labor is only 0.1.

competition between migrants and laid-off workers in cities may have increased (Cai 2002). In general, the consensus among researchers is that the positive impacts of rural–urban migrants on urban areas outweigh their negative impacts (Jiao 2002).

In China's large cities, the social and economic segregation of rural migrants, the status hierarchy based on geographic origin, and the segmentation the urban labor market persist (Gu 1992; Cao 1995; Chan, Liu, and Yang 1999; Solinger 1999; Cai 2002; Fan 2002; Yu 2002). In these cities, most rural migrants occupy the lowest social and occupational rungs and are treated as outsiders rather than being assimilated (Solinger 1995; Fan 2002). Under the dualistic *hukou* structure, rural Chinese are still excluded from the system of entitlements designed only for urbanites. Rural migrants lack access to retirement, health and unemployment benefits, government-sponsored housing schemes, jobs that prioritize urban residents, and the urban education system (Lu 2005). The education of migrant children, who numbered more than 14 million in 2000 and nearly 20 million in 2005, is rapidly becoming a burning question in Chinese cities (Fang Wang 2005).

Impacts on Rural Areas and Rural–Urban Inequality
It is widely acknowledged that labor migration helps raise income and diversify income sources for rural households and alleviates poverty in rural areas (Cai 2001; CASS/NBS 2003). Estimates of remittances vary, but most studies find that they account for at least 20 percent of the total income of migrant households (Du and Bai 1997; Li 1999; Wang and Fan 2006). Overwhelmingly, rural households use remittances to fund household projects (such as building or renovating a house); support household members (by financing education, for example); maintain regular household activities (such as living expenses and agricultural input), and lift households out of financial difficulties (by repaying debts) rather than to engage in new investment activities (Murphy 2002; Fan 2004a; Wang and Fan 2006).

When rural Chinese migrate to the city, their direct economic contribution to the countryside is lost, except when they return during planting and harvesting seasons. Even after factoring in this opportunity cost, labor migration is still desirable. Li (1999) shows that the marginal contribution of migrant workers to household income is higher than that of nonmigrant workers. He argues that migration raises the productivity of nonmigrants, because the departure of migrants results in reallocation of resources within the household and increased efficiency of the remaining labor. Hare and Zhao (2000) find that marginal returns to labor from migration are higher than returns from agriculture.

The rural–urban income gap in China is large and increasing, as Albert Park indicates in chapter 2 and other researchers, including Knight and Song (1999) and Sicular and others (2007), have noted. Li (2003) shows that if urban nonmonetary income is taken into account, the ratio of urban income to rural income in China was 3.62:1 in 2000—the largest gap in the world. The Chinese government reports that urban income is five to six times as high as rural income (Guomin Jingji 2005). At the 16th National Congress of the Chinese Communist Party in November 2002, former President Jiang Zemin stated that a widening rural–urban gap impedes progress toward a *xiaokang* society and that this trend should be reversed (CCP 2002).[16] This point is also emphasized in the 11th Five-Year Plan (2006–10) (Guomin Jingji 2005). In this light, the economic benefits of rural–urban migration to the countryside have national importance, as they are expected to reduce, if not eliminate, rural–urban inequality.

Skeptics question the equilibrating effect of migration. Croll and Huang (1997) note that remittances are an unstable source of income. Migration is also seen as accelerating brain drain from already deprived rural areas (Cao 1995). Labor migration may also discourage profitable sectors from moving inland and accelerate industrial agglomeration in coastal areas, thus increasing the coastal-inland gap (Hu 2002).

These arguments notwithstanding, most researchers conclude that rural–urban migration has positive effects on rural areas and that its negative effects are small. Moreover, many studies have shown that migrants bring back not only remittances but also new skills, information, and ideas that are beneficial to economic development in the place of origin (Zhong 2000; Fan 2004a).

A small body of work since the late 1990s has focused on urban–rural return migration. While systematic data on return migration are sparse, research based on surveys suggests that significant proportions of rural–urban migrants have returned to their places of origin (Bai and Song 2002; Murphy 2002). Other studies note that the desire for peasant migrants to settle in cities is not as strong as expected and that the

---

16 A *xiaokang* society is a society in which most of the population is of modest means or middle class. Although the term has its roots in classical literature, the concept has been widely used by China's national leaders as a goal to reach in the next two decades. Its newfound popularity is probably a response to increased criticisms of widening gaps in Chinese society (see Yusuf and Nabeshima 2006).

majority wish to return (Solinger 1995; Cai 2000; Wang 2003; Zhu 2007). Most studies on return migrants highlight their positive contributions, including their skills, capital, experience, demonstration effect, information transfer, and entrepreneurial activities (Ma 2002; Murphy 2002; Qiu, Xie, and Zhou 2004). Wang and Fan (2006) argue, however, that return migrants are negatively selected, and they question the extent of the returnees' economic contributions to their communities of origin. In short, the literature's main findings indicate that rural–urban migration has positive impacts on the countryside but that its impacts on overall rural–urban inequality are mixed.

Policy Implications

Chinese society is increasingly mobile. Both the magnitude and geographic extent of migration have expanded since the 1980s, and both trends are expected to continue (Zhang and Lin 2000).

The roles of economic and market forces in shaping migration have increased (Fan forthcoming; Poncet 2006). Migration is considered the engine of urbanization and economic development in China, and it is generally acknowledged that the overall impacts of migration on both rural and urban areas are positive. At the same time, the *hukou* system is increasingly criticized for impeding labor flows, the efficient allocation of human resources, and the establishment of a nationally integrated labor market (Cao 1995; Zhong 2000; Zhang and Lin 2000; Cai 2001; Qiu 2001; Yu 2002). It is also seen as a major, albeit diminishing, source of the inequality between rural and urban Chinese, a gap that threatens social stability and undermines the government's new goal of "getting rich together" (*gongtong fuyu*), as embodied in the 11th Five-Year Plan (Du, Park, and Wang 2005; Fan 2006; Guomin Jingji 2005). Problems in accurately documenting urban statistics are also attributable to the *hukou* system (Wan 2001; Chan 2003).

Despite criticisms of the *hukou* system, most researchers favor an "orderly" reform rather than wholesale abolition of the system.[17] This in part reflects the resistance of urban residents, who want to protect their interests and entitlements (Cai 2001), but it also reflects concern over

---

17 These views are consistent with the gradualist approach that has characterized China's economic reforms since the late 1970s. This approach is sometimes described as "crossing the river by feeling the stones."

explosive growth of cities and the spread of slums, with the associated social problems and poverty traps. Moreover, abolition of the *hukou* system cannot be achieved without reforming housing, health insurance, social security, labor, and employment policies (Qiu 2001).

Most scholars favor a two-pronged approach that gradually reduces the prominence of the *hukou* system. They suggest that urban entitlements be reduced so that urban residents are encouraged to compete in the labor market rather than relying on state protection (Cai 2001; Zhong 2000). They also argue that certain conditions—including freer capital flows, higher educational attainment of migrants, and a smaller rural–urban income gap—must be met before *hukou* reform can be thoroughly implemented, in order to ensure that migrants will not flood cities and cripple the urban infrastructure (Zhang and Lin 2000; Cai 2001).

Given the likelihood that the *hukou* system will not be dismantled in the foreseeable future, researchers have highlighted several issues that require policy makers' attention. The first has to do with the criteria for awarding urban *hukou* to rural migrants. Most scholars favor merit-based criteria, which are viewed as useful for monitoring the number, quality, and composition of migrants (Zhang and Lin 2000). This "elite" migrants approach has characterized migration policies in Beijing, Shanghai, Shenzhen, and other large cities. Related to this is the view that the urban *hukou* should be more accessible in small towns and more strictly controlled in large and mega cities (Wan 2001; Cai 2003).

Another issue concerns the functions of *hukou*. An increasingly popular view is that *hukou* should serve the purpose of population registration rather than migration control (Zhong 2000). Some scholars suggest that the *hukou* should be replaced by a single identity card that is individual rather than household and location based. Such a card could replace the multiplicity of permits required of rural migrants and enable better and more standardized data collection (Qiu 2001).

Many researchers, including Jiao (2002), have urged policy makers to pay more attention to the rights and well-being of rural–urban migrants, whose voices often go unheard and who have few resources for collective activities, such as bargaining. Many scholars have pointed to the need to educate migrants' children, with some researchers recommending legalizing selected *liudong ertong xuexiao* ("migrant children's schools") and integrating them into the urban education system

(Zhong and Gu 2000; Zhou and Chen 2004; Fang Wang 2005).[18] Cai (2003) warns that without a systematic plan to educate migrants' children, these children will repeat their parents' marginality, creating a vicious intergenerational cycle.

Policies that serve migrants on a long-term basis can help foster their sense of belonging and contributing to the cities in which they live. Such policies can also address concerns over equity. The desire to prevent further polarization between rural and urban people is at the heart of the debate on migration policy and will be the basis for further *hukou* reform.

The debate, however has tended to focus on the city rather than the countryside. This approach is inappropriate, because rural migrants in China straddle the city and the countryside, with most remaining heavily involved in the economic and social infrastructure of their home villages (Fan forthcoming). Failure to recognize this will result in piecemeal policies that ignore the needs of those who still depend on the countryside and plan eventually to return to it. Agricultural productivity, nonagricultural economic opportunities, the cost and quality of education and other services, and the left-behind children and elderly are just some of the concerns that should be addressed if a migration policy is to be comprehensive and effective.

References

Bai, Nansheng, and Hongyun Song, eds. 2002. *Huixiang, Hai Shi Jincheng: Zhongguo Nongcun Waichu Laodongli Huiliu Yanjiu (Return to the Village or Enter the City: Research on the Return Migration of Rural Migrant Labor in China)*. Beijing: Zhongguo Caizheng Jingji Chubanshe (China Financial and Economic Publishing House).

Bejing Chenbao (Beijing Morning News). 2006. *"Beijing Gongwuyuan Kaoshi 15 Ri Qi Wangshang Baoming Xuyao Beijing Hukou. (Online Application for the Examination for Beijing Government Positions Begins on the 15th; Beijing Hukou Is Required)."* May 8.

---

18 Many migrants' children in cities are enrolled in schools organized by migrants. These schools receive minimal or no support from city governments (Kwong 2004). It is estimated that in 2004 there were 280 such schools in Beijing alone, enrolling about 50,000 migrant children (about one-fifth of all school-age migrant children in Beijing) (Li 2004). Migrants can also send their children to local schools by paying an extra fee *(jiedufei)* (Zhang and Lin 2000; Cai 2003). Although some cities have eliminated or reduced the extra fee, many migrants may still prefer to send their children to migrant children's schools, which are less expensive (Zhou and Chen 2004; Zhongguo Renmin Daxue 2005; Liang and Chen 2007).

Beijing Sheke Guihu (Beijing Social Science Planning). 2000. "*Zhongguo Liudong Renkou Meinian Jiang Zengjia Wubaiwan.*" ("China's Floating Population Increases by Five Million Every Year)." October 20.

Cai, Fang. 2000. *Zhongguo Liudong Renkou Wenti (China's Floating Population).* Zhengzhou: Henan Renmin Chubanshe (Henen People's Publishing House).

————, ed. 2001. *Zhongguo Renkou Liudong Fangshi Yu Tujing (1990–1999 Nian) (The Means and Paths of Population Migration in China* (1990–1999)). Beijing: Shehui Kexue Wenxian Chubanshe (Social Science Documentation Publishing House).

————, ed. 2002. *Zhongguo Renkou Yu Laodong Wenti Baogao: Chengxiang Jiuye Wenti Yu Duice (Report on China's Population and Labor: Employment Issues and Strategies in Urban and Rural Areas).* Beijing: Shehui Kexue Wenxian Chubanshe (Social Sciences Documentation Publishing House).

————, ed. 2003. *Zhongguo Renkou Yu Laodong Wenti Baogao: Zhuangui Zhong Di Chengshi Pinkun Wenti (Report on China's Population and Labor: Urban Poverty in Transitional China).* Beijing: Shehui Kexue Wenxian Chubanshe (Social Sciences Documentation Publishing House).

Cao, Jing-Chun. 2001. "*Guanyu Lanyin Hukou Wenti Di Sikao* (Some Thoughts on the Blue Stamp *Hukou*)." *Population and Economics* 6: 15–21, 66.

Cao, Xiangjun. 1995. "*Zhongguo Nongcun Laodongli Liudong Yu Renkou Qianyi Yanjiu Zongshu* (Summary of Research on Rural Labor Flows and Population Migration in China)." *Nongcun Jingji Yanjiu Cankao (Rural Agricultural Research)* 2: 23–33.

CASS (Chinese Academy of Social Sciences), and NBS (National Bureau of Statistics). 2003. *2002–2003 Nian Zhongguo Nongcui Jingji Xingshi Fenxi Yu Yuce (Analysis and Forecast on China's Rural Economy 2002–2003).* Beijing: Shehui Kexue Wenxian Chubanshe (Social Sciences Documentation Publishing House).

CCP (Chinese Communist Party). 2002. *Zhongguo Gongchandang Di Shiliu Ci Quanguo Daibiao Dahui Wenjian Huibian (Collection of Documents from the 16th National Congress of the Chinese Communist Party).* Beijing: Renmin Chubanshe (People's Publishing House).

Chan, Kam Wing. 2003. "Chinese Census 2000: New Opportunities and Challenges." *China Review* 3 (2): 1–12.

Chan, Kam Wing, Ta Liu, and Yunyan Yang. 1999. "*Hukou* and Non-*Hukou* Migrations in China: Comparisons and Contrasts." *International Journal of Population Geography* 5 (6): 425–48.

China Daily. 2004. "*Hukou* System Must Reform Step by Step." September 16. Beijing. http://en-1.ce.cn/Business/Macro-economic/200409/16/t20040916_1772934.shtml/

Congressional-Executive Commission on China. 2005. "Recent Chinese *Hukou* Reforms." http://www.cecc.gov/pages/virtualAcad/Residency/hreform.php

Croll, Elisabeth J., and Ping Huang. 1997. "Migration for and against Agriculture in Eight Chinese Villages." *China Quarterly* 149: 128–46.

de Brauw, Alan, Jikun Huang, Scott Rozelle, Linxiu Zhang, and Yigang Zhang. 2002. "The Evolution of China's Rural Labor Markets during the Reforms." *Journal of Comparative Economics* 30 (2): 329–53.

Du, Fenglian, and Wenshu Gao. 2004. "Zhongguo Chengshi Liudong Renkou: Tezheng Jiqi Jianyan (Migrants in the Cities of China: Characteristics and Its Testing)." *Shichang Yu Renkou Fenxi (Market & Demographic Analysis)* 10 (4): 16–21.

Du, Yang, Albert Park, and Sangui Wang. 2005. "Migration and Rural Poverty in China." *Journal of Comparative Economics* 33 (4): 688–709.

Du, Ying, and Nansheng Bai, eds. 1997. *Zouchu Xiangcun (Leaving the Village).* Beijing: Jingji *Kexue* Chubanshe (Economic Science Press).

Duan, Chengrong. 2003. *"Lun Liudong Renkou De Shehui Shiying: Jiantan Beijingshi Liudong Renkou Wenti (On the Social Adaptability of the Floating Population)."* *Yunnan Daxue Xuebao (Shehui Kexueban) (Journal of Yunnan University (Social Science))* 2 (3): 54–60.

Duan, Chengrong, and Yujing Sun. 2006. "Woguo Liudong Renkou Tongji Koujing Di Lishi Biandong (Changes in the Scope and Definition of the Floating Population in China's Censuses and Surveys)." *Renkou Yanjiu (Population Research)* 30 (4): 70–76.

Editorial Group for Guomin Jingi He Shehui Fazhan Di Shiyi Ge Wunian Guihua Gangyao Xuexi Fudao. 2006. *Guomin Jingi He Shehui Fazhan Di Shiyi Ge Wunian Guihua Gangyao Xuexi Fudao (Summary of the 11th Five-Year Plan for National Economic and Social Development: Study Guide).* Chinese Communist Party School, Beijing.

Fan, C. Cindy. 1999. "Migration in a Socialist Transitional Economy: Heterogeneity, Socioeconomic, and Spatial Characteristics of Migrants in China and Guangdong Province." *International Migration Review* 33 (4): 950–83.

———. 2002. "The Elite, the Natives, and the Outsiders: Migration and Labor Market Segmentation in Urban China." *Annals of the Association of American Geographers* 92 (1): 103–24.

———. 2004a. "Out to the City and Back to the Village: The Experiences and Contributions of Rural Women Migrating from Sichuan and Anhui." In *On the Move: Women and Rural-to-Urban Migration in Contemporary China,* ed. Arianne M. Gaetao, and Tamara Jacka, 177–206. New York: Columbia University Press.

———. 2004b. "The State, the Migrant Labor Regime, and Maiden Workers in China." *Political Geography* 23 (3): 283–305.

———. 2005a. "Interprovincial Migration, Population Redistribution, and Regional Development in China: 1990 and 2000 Census." *Professional Geographer* 57 (2): 295–311.

———. 2005b. "Modeling Interprovincial Migration in China,1985–2000." *Eurasian Geography and Economics* 46 (3): 165–84.

———. 2006. "China's Eleventh Five-Year Plan (2006–2010): From 'Getting Rich First' to 'Common Prosperity.'" *Eurasian Geography and Economics* 47 (6): 708–23.

———. Forthcoming. *China on the Move: Migration, the State, and the Household.* London: Routledge.

Fan, C. Cindy, and Youqin Huang. 1998. "Waves of Rural Brides: Female Marriage Migration in China." *Annals of the Association of American Geographers* 88 (2): 227–51.

Fazhi Wanbao (Legal System Evening News). 2006. "Zhaopinhui Zhi Ren Beijing Hukou, Yi Zhanwei Ban Xiaoshi Ju 10 Ren (Job Fair Recognizes Only Beijing *Hukou*; 10 People Rejected from One Booth)." July 19.

Goldstein, Sidney, and Alice Goldstein. 1991. *Permanent and Temporary Migration Differentials in China.* Papers of the East–West Population Institute 117, Honolulu.

Guangming Ribao. 2006. "Zhou Yixing: Chengzhenhua Bushi Yuekua Yuehao (Zhou Yixing: Rapid Urbanization Is Not Necessarily Good)." March 27.

Gongan Bu Huzheng Guanli Ju (Ministry of Public Security Household Registration Division). 1997. 1997 *Nian Quanguo Zhanzhu Renkou Tongji Ziliao Huibian (Collection of Data on Temporary Population in China in 1997).* Beijing: Zhongguo Renmin Gongan Daxue Chubanshe (Chinese People's Public Security University Press).

Goodkind, Daniel, and Loraine A. West. 2002. "China's Floating Population: Definitions, Data and Recent Findings." *Urban Studies* 39 (12): 2237–50.

Gu, Shengzu. 1992. "Zhongguo Lianglei Renkou Qianyi Bijiao Yanjiu (Comparison of Two Types of Migration in China)." *Zhongguo Renkou Kexue* (Chinese Journal of Population Science) 4 (1): 75–84.

Guomin Jingji He Shehui Fazhan "Shiyiwu" Guihua Ruogan Wenti Xuexi Wenda Bianxie Zu. 2005. *Guomin Jingji He Shehui Fazhan "Shiyiwu" Guihua Ruogan Wenti Xuexi Wenda (People's Economic and Social Development "11th Five-Year Plan" Study Questions and Answers).* Beijing: Xinhua Chubanshe (Xinhua Publishing House).

Hare, Denise, and Shukai Zhao. 2000. "Labor Migration as a Rural Development Strategy: A View from the Migration Origin." In *Rural Labor Flows in China,* ed. Lorainne A. West and Yaohui Zhao, 148–78. Berkeley, CA: Institute of East Asian Studies.

Hu, Dapeng. 2002. "Trade, Rural-Urban Migration, and Regional Income Disparity in Developing Countries: A Spatial General Equilibrium Model Inspired by the Case of China." *Regional Science and Urban Economics* 32 (3): 311–38.

Jian, Xinhua, and Jianwei Zhang. 2005. "*Cong 'Mingong Chao' Dao 'Mingong Huang': Nongcun Shengyu Laodongli Youxiaozhuanyi De Zhidu Fenxi* (From 'The Wave of Migrants' to 'The Shortage of Migrants': The Institutional Analysis of the Effective Transfer of Rural Surplus Labor"). *Renkou Yanjiu (Population Research)* 29 (2): 49–55.

Jiao, Jianquan. 2002. "A Study on Floating Population from Rights Point of View." *Renkou Yu Jingji (Population and Economics)* 3: 73–75.

Knight, John, and Lina Song. 1999. *The Rural–Urban Divide: Economic Disparities and Interactions in China.* Oxford: Oxford University Press.

Kwong, Julia. 2004. "Educating Migrant Children: Negotiations between the State and Civil Society." *China Quarterly* 180: 1073–88.

Li, Haizheng, and Steven Zahniser. 2002. "The Determinants of Temporary Rural-to-Urban Migration in China." *Urban Studies* 39 (12): 2219–35.

Li, Shi. 1999. "Effects of Labor Out-Migration on Income Growth and Inequality in Rural China." *Development and Society* 28 (1): 93–114.

———. 2003. "A Review of Income Inequality in China." *Jijixue Jikan (China Economic Quarterly)* 2 (2): 309–404.

Li, Si-Ming. 1995. "Population Mobility and Urban and Rural Development in Mainland China." *Issues and Studies* 31 (9): 37–54.

Li, Xiao. 2004. "Finding Balance: Meeting the Needs of Migrant Kids." June 23. http://www.chinagate.com.en/english/10249.htm

Liang, Zai. 2001. "The Age of Migration in China." *Population and Development Review* 27 (3): 499–528.

Liang, Zai, and Yiu Por Chen. 2007. "The Educational Consequences of Migration for Children in China." *Social Science Research* 36 (1): 285–47.

Liang, Zai, and Zhongdong Ma. 2004. "China's Floating Population: New Evidence from the 2000 Census." *Population and Development Review* 33 (3): 467–88.

Lu, Xianghu. 2005. "*Zhidu Shi Ruhe Zu'ai Woguo Nongcun Renkou Xiang Chengshi Qianyi De? Lun Zhidu Dui Chengxiang Renkou Qianyi De Zuoyong Jili* (How Does Institution Prevent Rural Population from Migrating to Cities? An Analysis of the Effects of Institutions of Rural-Urban Migration)." *Diaoyan Shijie (Research World)* 6: 30–32.

Lu, Xianghu, and Yonggang Wang. 2006. "*Zhonguo Xiang-Cheng Renkou Qianyi Guimo De Cesuan Yu Fenxi (1979–2003) (Estimation and Analysis of Chinese Rural–Urban Migration Size)." *Xibei Renkou (Northwest Population)* (1): 14–16.

Ma, Zhongdong. 2002. "Social Capital Mobilization and Income Returns to Entrepreneurship: The Case of Return Migration in Rural China." *Environment and Planning A* 34 (10): 1763–84.

Messner, Steven F., Jianhong Liu, and Susanne Karstedt. Forthcoming. "Economic Reform and Crime in Contemporary China: Paradoxes of a Planned Transition." In *Urban China in Transition*, ed. John Logan. London: Blackwell.

Murphy, Rachel. 2002. *How Migrant Labor Is Changing Rural China*. Cambridge: Cambridge University Press.

NBS (National Bureau of Statistics). 2002. *Zhongguo 2000 Nian Renkou Pucha Ziliao (Tabulation of the 2000 Population Census of the People's Republic of China)*, vols. I and III. Beijing: Zhongguo Tongji Chubanshe (China Statistics Press).

———. 2006. "2005 Nian Quanguo 1% Renkou Chouyang Diaocha Zhuyao Shuju Gongbao (Announcement of Major Statistics from the 2005 National 1% Population Sample Survey)." http://www.cpirc.org.cn/tjsj/tjsj_cy_detail.asp?id=6628

Poncet, Sandra. 2006. "Provincial Migration Dynamics in China: Borders, Costs and Economic Motivations." *Regional Science and Urban Economics* 36 (3): 385–98.

Qiu, Haiying. 2001. "*Nongcun Laodongli Huiliu Yu Laodongli Miji Xing Chanye Di Kaifa (Return Labor Migration and the Development of Labor-Intensive Industry)*." *Renkou Xuekan (Population Journal)* 3: 52–55.

Qiu, Ziyi, Ping Xie, and Fanglian Zhou. 2004. "*Renkou Liudong Dui Jingji Shehui Fazhan Di Yingxiang* (Impacts of Migration on Socioeconomic Development)." *Renkou Xuekan (Population Journal)* 1: 47–52.

Rowland, Donald T. 1994. "Family Characteristics of the Migrants." In *Migration and Urbanization in China*, ed. Lincoln H. Day and Xia Ma, 129–54. Armonk, NY: M.E. Sharpe.

Shen, Jianfa. 2002. "A Study of the Temporary Population in Chinese Cities." *Habitat International* 26 (3): 363–77.

Sicular, T., X. Yue, B. Gustafsson, and S. Li. 2007. "The Urban–Rural Income Gap and Inequality in China." *Review of Income and Wealth* 53 (1): 93–126.

Solinger, Dorothy J. 1995. "The Floating Population in the Cities: Chances for Assimilation?" In *Urban Spaces in Contemporary China*, ed. Deborah Davis, Richard Kraus, Barry Naughton, and Elizabeth J. Perry, 113–39. Cambridge: Cambridge University Press.

———. 1999. *Contesting Citizenship in Urban China: Peasant Migrants, the State, and the Logic of the Market*. Berkeley: University of California Press.

Sun, Rongfei. 2007. "*Huji Gaige Wenjian Bao Guowuyuan* (Hukou *Reform Document Submitted to the State Council*)." May 23. http://news.cqnews.net/system/2007-05/23/000804562.shtml State Statistical Bureau. 1992. *Zhongguo Renkou Tongji Nianjian (China Population Statistical Yearbook)* 1992. Beijing: Zhongguo Tongji Chubanshe (China Statistical Publishing House).

Wan, Chuan. 2001. "A Commentary on Professor Zhang Qing-Wu's Academic Viewpoints of Household Register Administration." *Renkou Yu Jingji (Population and Economics)* 4: 75–79.

Wang, Fang. 2005. "*Zhongguo Chengzhenhua Jingcheng Zhong De Liudong Renkou Zinu Shou Jiaoyu Wenti* (Issues on the Education of Migrant Children during the Process of Urbanization in China)." *Fazhan Zhanlue (Development Strategy)* 9: 27–31.

Wang, Fei-Ling. 2005. *Organizing through Division and Exclusion: China's* Hukou *System.* Stanford, CA: Stanford University Press.

Wang, Guixin, Hui Gao, Wei Xu, and Guoxiang Chen. 2002. "*Xiao Chengzhen Wailai Laodongli Jiben Zhuangkuang Ji Dui Xiao Chengzhen Fazhan Yingxiang Fenxi* (Analyses of the Situation of Labor Force and Its Influences on the Development of Little Towns)." *Renkou Xuekan (Population Journal)* 3: 3–7.

Wang, Wenfei Winnie, and C. Cindy Fan. 2006. "Success or Failure: Selectivity and Reasons of Return Migration in Sichuan and Anhui, China." *Environment and Planning A* 38 (5): 939–58.

Wang, Wenlu. 2003. "Changes in Household Registering System against the Urbanization Background: Shijiazhuang City as a Case." *Renkou Yanjiu (Population Research)* 27 (6): 8–13.

Wong, Linda, and Wai-Po Huen. 1998. "Reforming the Household Registration System: A Preliminary Glimpse of the Blue Chop Household Registration System in Shanghai and Shenzhen." *International Migration Review* 32 (4): 974–94.

Yang, Shangguang, and Jinhong Ding. 2005. "*Liudong Renkou De Chengshi Jiuye Xiaoying* (The Employment Migration and the Differential Effect of Manpower Capital in the Yangtze Metropolitan Delta)." *Huadong Shifan Daxue Xuebao (Zhexue Shehui Kexue Ban) (Journal of East China Normal University (Philosophy and Social Sciences))* 37 (3): 82–88.

Yang, Xiushi. 2006. "Temporary Migration and HIV Risk Behaviors in China." *Environment and Planning A* 38 (8): 1527–43.

Yang, Xiushi, V. J. Derlega, and H. Luo. 2007. "Migration, Behaviour Change, and HIV/STD Risks in China." *AIDS Care: Psychological and Socio-Medical Aspects of AIDS/HIV* 19 (2): 282–88.

Yang, Yunyan. 1994. *Zhongguo Renkou Qianyi Yu Fanzhan Di Changqi Zhanlue (Long-Term Strategies of Population Migration and Development in China).* Wuhan: Wuhan Chubanshe (Wuhan Publishing House).

———. 2004. "*Jiushi Niandai Yilai Woguo Renkou Qianyi De Ruogan Xin Tedian* (The New Characteristics of China's Migration since 1990s)." *Nanfang Renkou (South China Population)* 19 (3): 13–20.

Yu, Depeng. 2002. *Chengxiang Shehui: Cong Geli Zouxiang Kaifang: Zhongguo Huji Zhidu Yu Hujifa Yanjiu (City and Countryside Societies: from Segregation to Opening: Research on China's Household Registration System and Laws)*. Jinan: Shandong Renmin Chubanshe (Shandong People's Press).

Yusuf, Shahid, and Kaoru Nabeshima. 2006. *China's Development Priorities*. Washington, DC: World Bank.

Zhang, Ping, and Zi Lin. 2000. "Market Economic Development and Reform of Household Registration System in China." *Renkou Yu Jingji (Population and Economics)* 6: 35–41.

Zhong, Shuiyang. 2000. *Renkou Liudong Yu Shehui Jingji Fazhan (Migration and Social Economic Development)*. Wuhan: Wuhan University Press.

Zhong, Shuiyang, and Shengzu Gu. 2000. "Development of Urban Service Sector and Employment of Floating Population." *Renkou Yu Jingji (Population and Economics)* 2000 (5): 35–38.

Zhongguo Qingnianbao (China Youth News). 2007. "Diaocha: Jiucheng Yishang Minzhong Renwei Youbiyao Jinxing Huji Gaige (Survey: More Than 90 Percent of People Think That Hukou Reform Is Necessary)." February 26.

Zhongguo Renmin Daxue Renkou Yu Fazhan Yanjiu Zhongxin (Renmin University of China Population and Development Research Center). 2005. "*Zhongguo Renkou Qianyi Liudong Yu Renkou Fenbu Yanjiu* (Research on Migration and Population Distribution in China)." In *2000 Nian Renkou Pucha Guojia Zhongdian Keti Yanjiu Baogao (National Level Key Research Reports on the 2000 Census)*, ed. National Bureau of Statistics, 912–1035. Beijing: Zhongguo Tongji Chubanshe (China Statistics Press).

Zhou, Hao. 2002. "A Review, Summary and Discussion of Population Migration Study in China." *Renkou Yu Jingji (Population and Economics)* 1: 56–59.

Zhou, Hao. 2004. "*Zhongguo Renkou Qianyi De Jia Ting Hua Qushi Ji Yingxiang Yinsu Fenxi* (The Analysis on the Trend and Factors of Family Migration)." *Renkou Yanjiu (Population Research)* 28 (6): 60–67.

Zhou, Hao, and Ling Chen. 2004. "*Dui Liaodong Ertong Xuexiao Zhi Helixing Di Sikao Yu Jianyi* (Consideration and Policy Suggestion on the Rationality of School for Temporary Migrant Children)." *Renkou Yu Jingji (Population and Economics)* 1: 47, 69–73.

Zhu, Yu. 2007. "China's Floating Population and their Settlement Intention in the Cities: Beyond the *Hukou* Reform." *Habitat International* 31 (1): 65–76.

CHAPTER 4

Poverty and Vulnerability

John G. Taylor

Economic reforms and urbanization have substantially reduced poverty in China. Between 1981 and 2004, the number of people living on US$1 a day declined from 634 million to 128 million (Chen and Ravallion 2007).[1] China has also made progress in the nonincome areas of poverty, reducing hunger, child mortality, and maternal mortality; improving maternal health and education, particularly at the primary level; and promoting women's participation in political decision making.

Although the decline in poverty slowed in the mid- and late-1990s, when the focus of antipoverty efforts shifted to hard-core poverty in isolated remote areas, the number of poor people continued to fall. In 2002 the number of poor was estimated officially at 28.2 million, about 3 percent of the rural population.[2] In 2003, however, for the first time

---

1 Chen and Ravallion (2007) define poverty as living on US$1 a day at 1985 purchasing power parity (Y 879 per capita). Based on the Chinese government's definition, which defines the poor as people with average per capita incomes of less than Y 625 a year, the number of people living in poverty fell from 250 million in 1978 to 32 million in 2000. This figure represents the average per capita net income for all nationally defined poor counties. Since 2001, researchers at the Leading Group for Poverty Alleviation and Development have referred both to the "absolute poor" (people with net incomes below Y 629 in 2001 prices) and to "low-income people" (people with incomes below Y 869 in 2001 prices). The "low-income" definition is very close to the World Bank level of Y 879.

2 This figure is based on the official poverty line of annual per capita net income of Y 627 at 2002 prices.

since 1978, there was a slight reversal in this trend, with poverty levels rising by 800,000 to 29 million.

Within this overall picture, there remain wide variations, both between and within provinces with respect to levels of per capita and household income and consumption and human development, particularly in health, education, and social safety net provision. These variations are accompanied by continuing specific vulnerabilities, affecting in particular women, ethnic groups (national minorities), and people with disabilities.

Faced with these issues, and the possibility of their affecting the ongoing development process, the Chinese government has adopted an approach calling for the building of a *xiaokang* (harmonious) society, in which everyone will benefit from a life that is both moderately affluent (materially and socially) and sustainable. Equity in the process of development has become a major issue, with the government placing a high priority on reducing inequalities (Murphy 2004; Prime Minister's Report 2004). The government's current "five integrations" strategy aims to create policies that are more coordinated and balanced at the urban–rural, regional, social, and economic levels. In particular, urban poverty is to be addressed more systematically. The extent of the problem and how to tackle it are the focus of this chapter.

Who Are the Urban Poor?

Despite increasing awareness of urban poverty, defining the urban poor in China is beset with difficulties, because China does not have an official urban poverty line for the country as a whole. The poverty line varies from city to city, with benefits lines determined by costed basic items of expenditure. Official definitions of the urban poor exclude most migrants.

Since 2000 the government has defined the urban poor as people covered under the Minimum Living Security Standard scheme (MLSS), or *Di Bao*. According to official figures, 21 million urban residents received *Di Bao* in 2003 (Hussain 2003; Ravallion and Chen 2003).[3] In one of the most thorough research exercises undertaken on urban poverty (Wang 2002), Chinese researchers from the National Bureau of Statistics (NBS)

---

3 The methods and cutoffs used to determine urban households' eligibility for *Di Bao* vary widely across cities, with the maximum per capita net income ranging from Y 1,211 to Y 2,310 a year. Some cities compile detailed lists of basic goods and services to establish poverty lines; others rely on informed guesses. In Beijing, *Di Bao* provides Y 280 per capita a month, plus a "food and fuel" card worth Y 40 a month. Migrant workers, university students, city farmers, and released prisoners do not qualify for *Di Bao* (see Guan 2005).

defined the urban poor as people with annual expenditure of less than Y 2,310 per capita (in 1998 prices). The NBS assessment is based on an averaging of city poverty lines. Based on these various definitions, about 4.7–6.5 percent of the urban population is estimated to be poor.

One of the most important groups among the urban poor are the elderly, a group that includes many laid-off workers. During the past decade, levels of urban poverty have been pushed upward primarily by workers made redundant from the closure of state-owned enterprises and the dismantling of the "iron rice-bowl" welfare systems once provided by these enterprises. If elderly urban inhabitants are childless, their situation is particularly difficult. In the absence of family support, they are totally dependent on pension contributions from their former employers, which are not always forthcoming.

Alongside the elderly are the disabled, who officially represent 40 percent of the urban poor. Other groups of poor include migrants from rural areas and farmers displaced as a result of changing land use in urban and periurban areas. Data from a 2003 survey by the Ministry of Land Resources (DFID 2004) indicate that there are 20 million farmers with urban residence (*hukou*) who have lost their rights to land. They tend to receive low levels of compensation and have few skills with which to obtain nonagricultural work.

The urban poor tend to have the following characteristics (Zhou 2000):[4]

- *Lower than average incomes.* On average, the incomes of the urban nonpoor are 2.3 times higher than those of the poor.
- *Lower than average levels of expenditure.* On average, nonpoor households' expenditures are 2.9 times higher than those of poor households.
- *Unemployed or jobless.* The proportion of the poor seeking work is about three times that of the nonpoor.
- *Female.* More women are living in poverty than men (12.1 percent of women and 11.7 percent of men).
- *Lower than average levels of educational attainment.*
- *Poor health.*[5]

---

4 The information in this section is based on the NBS survey of poor urban households and on participatory poverty assessments conducted by researchers at the Centre for Integrated Agricultural Development at the Chinese Agricultural University, notably Zhuo Xuejun (2000).

5 Data on health and education conditions for poor urban workers are presented later in the chapter.

Support for and Problems Faced by the Urban Poor

At first sight, the *Di Bao* program appears to be effective in meeting the needs of the urban poor. Basic items of expenditure are met, with some local governments also providing nonmonetary benefits (health care, schooling entitlements, and discounts on the use of utilities) to *Di Bao* participants. Local authorities and neighborhood committees try to ensure that recipients are genuinely eligible, taking into account factors such as financial assets and housing conditions. Recent research indicates that the program does a good job of targeting those most in need: larger households living in small dwellings, nonowner occupiers, people caring for disabled or ill family members, retirees, laid-off workers, and the unemployed (Chen, Ravallion, and Wang 2006). It would thus appear that the needs of the chronically poor are being met.

Research indicates, however, that there is a large gap between *Di Bao* payment levels and poor urban families' estimates of what they need to meet their subsistence needs. Using data from the 2004 Urban Short-Form Survey conducted by the NBS, Park (2005) estimates that based on subjective perceptions, 6.7 percent of the urban population considers itself poor but only 1.6 percent receives *Di Bao*. This finding is reinforced by Chen, Ravallion, and Wang (2006), who conclude that the program is more successful at reaching the chronically poor than the poor. Data from their household surveys, conducted in 35 cities, show that about three-quarters of households eligible for *Di Bao* do not receive it. Moreover, 81 percent of *Di Bao* recipients consider their incomes inadequate to meet their needs.

Coverage is also uneven. The 2004 NBS survey concluded that 85 percent of the poor live in China's smaller (prefecture-level) cities, which have more limited fiscal resources. According to the survey, 18.5 million urban residents received *Di Bao* payments, although 27.8 million were eligible. In addition, safety net benefits do not accrue to most migrants, the vast majority of whom lack urban *hukou*.

The Predicament of Rural–Urban Migrants

Officially, the urban poor represent less than one percent of the poor in China. If, however, some recent estimates of the migrant population living below the poverty line are included in this figure, both the incidence and the share of urban poverty rises. Migrant workers constitute a larger proportion of the urban poor, and the share of the urban poor increases to 10–12 percent of the poor nationwide.

Despite their contributions to the economy, migrants are disadvantaged. Most perform work that residents do not want to do, for which they are paid less than residents. Migrants are also ineligible for social benefits. Where they lack sustaining social networks, their vulnerability is particularly acute.

It is difficult to estimate the extent of poverty among migrants, because they do not hold urban *hukou* and are therefore not eligible for most welfare services. A survey conducted in 1999 by the NBS provides some information; recent research by the Asian Development Bank adds data through 2001 (ADB 2001).

The surveys find that the poverty rate is 50 percent higher among urban migrants than among permanent residents. The NBS estimates that 3 million migrants are living in poverty, but this figure appears to have been based on income available to migrants after remittances had been sent back to their village families.

Female migrants are particularly at risk. According to a survey of migrant women and children undertaken by the Ministry of Health (2003b) in Beijing 93 percent of resident women but only 10 percent of migrant women gave birth in hospitals, and 71 percent of women dying during or as a result of child birth were migrants.[6] The vast majority of migrant women cannot afford to purchase most medicines or medical care, a situation that is exacerbated by widespread irregularities in payment by their employers.

Children of migrants face systematic barriers in access to education. These children are permitted to attend public schools, but without urban *hukou*, they have to pay higher tuition fees, which makes it difficult for them to do so. Unable to afford these fees, many migrant families leave children in their villages of origin.

Urban housing for rural migrants often lacks basic amenities and is of lower quality than the average for urban residents in the same income category (Wang 2004). A study of migrant housing in two Chinese cities finds that 80 percent of migrants rent, 7 percent share a room with another family, 50 percent live in only one room, 29 percent occupy two rooms, 4 percent have exclusive use of a shower or bath, 8 percent have use of a toilet, and 28 percent have no access to a kitchen (Wang 2004). Migrants also spend a higher proportion of their income on housing than do residents holding urban *hukou*.

---

6 The figures for female migrants dying during or as a result of childbirth in other cities in 2000 were 79 percent in Guangdong in 2001 and 72 percent in Shanghai.

Migrants face less-healthy living conditions than other city dwellers. Many cities have begun moving heavily polluting industries to periurban areas, where large numbers of poor migrants live. The polluted water and air in these areas affects their health.

Unemployment

Official data indicate that national unemployment in China stood at 3.6 percent in 2001 and 4.2 percent in 2005. A survey conducted by the Chinese Academy of Social Sciences, in collaboration with the University of Michigan, ("No Right to Work" 2004) finds that total unemployment rose from 7.2 in 1996 to 12.2 percent in 2001 (it has since declined). The Ministry of Labour and Social Security projects that the national unemployment rate will average about 5 percent by 2010 ("Unemployed Urbanites" 2006).

Since the mid-1990s, the ranks of the urban poor have increasingly included workers made redundant by the restructuring (closure or downsizing) of state-owned enterprises. For older laid-off workers, alternative employment or sources of income are limited. In 2000, two-thirds of laid-off workers received neither unemployment insurance nor *Di Bao* payments.

Health and Education

Many of the clinics serving low-income households in urban areas provide limited services, at a cost poor households can sometimes ill afford.[7] Data from the 2003 National Health Services Survey indicate that the average visit to a health clinic costs a patient Y 97.7 in rural areas and Y 163.5 in urban areas, these figures are 75 percent and 38 percent higher than in 1998 (Ministry of Health 2003a). The average costs of hospitalization stood at Y 3,227 in 2003, with urban costs at Y 5,518.

About 55 percent of urban residents are not covered by public health insurance programs (Liu, Nolan, and Wen 2004). This represents a 20 percent decline since 1993. Rising medical costs are accompanied by increases in the number of patients relying on self-care and the number of patients buying directly from pharmacies.[8] The cost of medicine is relatively high.[9] According to the Ministry of Health's 2003 survey,

---

7 Health care costs are rising rapidly and account for 12 percent of household consumption.

8 In 2003, 36 percent of patients in the National Health Services Survey sample self-medicated, a 7 percentage point increase since the previous survey, in 1998.

9 The average cost of medicine purchased in pharmacies is Y 72 (Y 112.4 in urban and Y 50.4 in rural areas).

35.5 percent of urban people who needed to do so did not seek medical assistance because it was unaffordable.[10] Data from the Beijing University School of Public Health and the Ministry of Health Maternal and Child Surveillance Network Reports indicate that 80.9 percent of urban children under the age of seven received health care in 2002. The infant mortality rate was 15.4 deaths per 1,000 live births nationally and 11.1 in urban areas. The under-five mortality rate was 19.3 deaths per 1,000 live births nationally and 13.8 in urban areas. The maternal mortality rate has decreased gradually in urban areas, from 43.1 deaths per 100,000 live births in 1996 to 28.7 in 2002, with the largest percentage decrease (12.5 percent) occurring between 2000 and 2002. Over the same period, the rural maternal mortality rate fell from 62.4 to 47.8 deaths per 100,000 live births.

Fees and other costs of education constitute a substantial percentage of the income of low-income households. Girls have less access to education than boys at the secondary and even the primary level (UNDP 2004). Faced with difficulties in meeting school costs, parents tend to withdraw their daughters before their sons (Beynon and Zheng 2001).[11] About 9 percent of children age 7–15 from poor households are not enrolled in school—almost twice the rate for children from nonpoor families. A key problem is the lack of state policies to assist poor households in meeting the costs of schooling.

Substantial intersectoral and regional inequities exist in both education and health. Average infant mortality rates were three to five times higher in western provinces than in coastal provinces. School enrollment rates ranged from 60–70 percent in western and central China to 99 percent in the most-developed eastern provinces (UNDP 2004).

Improving Service Delivery

The Chinese government, particularly the Ministry of Civil Affairs and local civil affairs departments, is concerned about urban poverty, particularly in the context of growing conflicts between urban communities and planning agencies. The government is calling for improvements in consultation with urban communities to address weaknesses in urban planning and devise means of addressing the types of poverty experienced by

---

10 The ministry's report concludes that "medical impoverishment is one of the most important reasons for poverty" (Ministry of Health: 2003a, 7).

11 In the participatory poverty assessment undertaken in Yunnan in 2001, villages in poor counties stated that they prioritize school attendance by boys.

groups of urban residents. Studies of urban poverty (Zhou 2000; Wang 2002; ADB 2004) conclude that cities have both underestimated and understated the needs of the urban poor. They also reveal a lack of support for women and the most vulnerable poor urban groups, particularly children and the disabled.

To push the urban poverty agenda forward and work more efficiently with nongovernmental and community-based organizations in urban areas, the Ministry of Civil Affairs has begun to explore ways of assessing types and levels of urban poverty in order to develop appropriate poverty reduction measures that target and monitor poor urban households.[12] It has focused on the use of participatory approaches, particularly the possible uses of participatory monitoring and evaluation.[13]

For the central government, bearing more of the costs of primary education and basic health care must be a priority. In 2004, public spending on education as a share of GNP was 2.4 percent and it remained well short of the 4 percent of GNP target. The target of spending 4 percent of gross national product (GNP) on education has yet to be met. To do so, both the central government and local governments must ensure that resources are earmarked for education and that, as required by government policy, basic education is universally provided for a minimum of nine years.

Government expenditure on health as a percentage of total government expenditure fell from 25.0 percent in 1990 to 14.2 percent in 1997 and to 10.2 percent in 2001 (WHO 2006). In 2003 it represented just 2.0 percent of GDP (UNDP 2005). As a percentage of total health expenditure, government spending fell from 46.6 percent in 1996 to 39.1 percent in 2005 (WHO 2006), while private expenditure rose from 53.4 percent to 60.9 percent. The current level of health funding is inadequate to meet required low-cost interventions in critical areas such as immunization and maternal and child health services.

Essential interventions for health care should receive adequate funding. Health insurance schemes should be extended to cover poor households, with subsidies granted to meet a substantial proportion of the annual

---

12 Recent reports also note a lack of coordination among organizations attempting to meet the needs of the urban poor—particularly between the Ministry and Departments of Civil Affairs, the Ministry of Education, local governments, associations for people with disabilities, the All-China Women's Federation, the All-China Communist Youth League, and the China Social Work Association.

13 For example, the ministry has been interested in research recently undertaken by the Jiangxi Poverty Alleviation and Development Office (PADO) examining the extent to which participatory assessment tools used in rural areas can be developed for use in poor urban communities.

fees required by the scheme. In urban areas, in particular, moves to subsidize health care (especially hospital costs) for households need to be strengthened.

Basic programs need to focus more on delivering essential, low-cost interventions. Better immunization and greater use of mineral and vitamin supplements need to be promoted, and more detailed information should be provided on nutrition, basic health, and maternal and child services. Given the relation between tuberculosis and HIV/AIDS, free diagnosis and treatment of tuberculosis would be advantageous. Overall, health services need to be adequately maintained and upgraded, and health management and supervision strengthened with the help of resource planning at the local level. Prices for health services need to be aligned more closely with service costs and guidelines established for the roles played by nongovernmental organizations in service delivery within the context of poverty reduction initiatives.

In improving service delivery for poor and vulnerable households in areas such as basic health, maternal and child care services, tuberculosis programs, improved immunization, and greater use of mineral and vitamin supplements, one of the most important constraints is the inability of township governments to meet the matching requirements of counterpart funding. A second constraining factor is that expenditure on infrastructure improvements for the provision of health care and education at the local level is not always followed by improvements in service provision. New health clinics often remain underutilized, with patients preferring the services of their local doctors, in less well-equipped facilities. Inadequate information has been disseminated on new services, and insufficient funds have been provided to train staff for new clinics. Moreover, new clinics often charge more for medicines than local doctors do.

Commitment by local government agencies and health bureaus to meet the needs of poor households is essential to overcome these problems. This commitment has at times been inadequate. Success in tackling HIV/AIDS, for example, relies heavily on information campaigns organized at the county level and below. Yet local politicians continue to fear that their areas will be stigmatized if they acknowledge the existence of HIV/AIDS, causing investment, business, or tourism to suffer. Communicable diseases and poor health need to be addressed by improved organization of basic immunization and nutritional information, primary responsibility for which lies at the local level.

Improving the capacity of county and township governments to deliver health and education services also requires enhancing management skills for resource planning. More attention needs to be paid to reducing financial barriers and extending coverage of preventive programs, by consulting with stakeholders, improving monitoring procedures, and establishing information bases to enable different approaches to be tested. Failure to implement and sustain institutional improvements will adversely affect service delivery.

In education, addressing school dropout rates, particularly for girls, is crucial. The roles and commitment of local agencies will be critical in developing and implementing recently proposed national tracking systems. Locally based campaigns to convince poor households of the benefits of school attendance for their daughters will also be an important part of educational strategies, although based on experience, commitment to such campaigns will require considerable strengthening.[14] Greater commitment to educate the children of migrant families is also needed. Improving the educational and skill levels of migrants will contribute to the development of the labor market. Doing so will require tackling the highly variable levels of municipal support for the implementation of policies to improve educational conditions for the children of migrant families, particularly in cities outside the southern and eastern seaboards.

Despite the central government's commitment to improving the targeting of programs to poor and migrant households, little has been done in this area. A notable exception is in Jiangxi, where the Poverty Alleviation and Development Office (PADO) has begun to work on proposals for ways in which participatory assessment tools used in rural areas can be developed for use in assessing the needs of poor urban communities. This work could be extended. Priority could be given to the development of manuals for use in participatory assessments of urban poverty and capacity-building programs for officials, relating the findings of participatory assessments to suggestions for the development of integrated social protection schemes.

Enhancing the Safety Net

By extending the recent reforms made in urban social security schemes (exemplified in the recent social security reform pilot program in Liaoning[15]) and by its intentions to expand the unemployment insurance

---

14 Educating girls will also contribute to better health of children, because better-educated mothers tend to pay closer attention to the health of their children and are better equipped to take advantage of modern medical advances (Yusuf, Nabeshima, and Ha 2006).

15 In 1999 the central government made the decision to integrate the subsectors of social security (pensions, death, disability, health, and unemployment) at the municipal, provincial, and national level and to integrate the information systems linking the three government levels in these subsectors. This effort has been piloted in Liaoning Province.

and *Di Bao* programs, the government is creating the basis for widening the provision of social security.[16] In continuing this work, it is desirable that social security be extended to migrants, with priority given to covering, at the very least, all long-term migrants, who should be given the same coverage as urban residents. An additional problem area is that of municipal compliance rates, which are low and for most of areas of social security (pensions, disability, health, and unemployment), variable because of the inability of many cities to provide sufficient pooling to ensure sustainability.

Noncontributory safety net provision currently includes support for workers laid-off from state-owned enterprises. This program provides a very basic living allowance and limited subsidized medical care.[17]

With regard to pensions, the government has made progress in setting up a new social security trust fund. Lack of public confidence will make it difficult to develop contributory schemes, however. To pay retirees from the old system, local governments often use funds that should be going into personal accounts. Private enterprises have little incentive to join a system whose contributions go mainly to pay off the liabilities of an earlier system.

Solving pension problems will require radical solutions. To ensure that coverage under the new pension system is affordable, the central government will have to assume more of the old system's liabilities. To secure adequate funding in the longer term, the government may decide that accounts will eventually have to be transferred to asset managers, that contributions will have to be rerouted from workers and employers to fund managers, and that a central supervisory board will need to be created. Such developments may also require the involvement of foreign financial services firms, given the lack of experience of Chinese firms in managing pension assets.

In developing insurance schemes, the issue of mobility needs to be addressed squarely, recognizing that people need to be able to access support when and where they need it. The problem is that, in order to make benefits transferable, social security contributions and expenditures need to be pooled, and it is not year clear how this ought to be done. The best level for pooling may be the province, with basic schemes for catastrophic illness and unemployment set up as a starting point. Employees in larger enterprises could be an initial pilot group in rural areas.

---

16 A World Bank (2003) report addresses the costs and sustainability of expanding social security provision. It stresses the importance of centralizing the financing and provision of social security and protection to the provincial level.

17 The basic living allowance provided is set at 70–80 percent of the local minimum wage.

An effective pensions policy is essential for enhancing social welfare by meeting the needs of the aging population and broadening and deepening capital markets. Developments remain at an early stage, however. Various alternatives have been proposed. The World Bank and others have suggested a three-pillar system, combining social pooling with funded individual accounts. Such a system would provide a basic pension for retired workers, keeping them above the poverty line; it would be combined with mandatory, fully funded individual accounts paid for by workers and enterprises. A third pillar would consist of a supplementary pension, which employers could choose to provide and workers could choose to contribute to (World Bank 1997). Whichever option is chosen, an appropriate system needs to be given priority, taking advantage of current high growth and savings rates. Pension reform would help sustain the momentum of state-owned enterprise reform.

The risks to this process are clear. Developing a basic pensions system requires contribution levels that enterprises may not be able to meet. Many employees are rightly suspicious of pension schemes and will require considerable reassurance and detailed information before they are willing to contribute. Moreover, arrangements are not yet in place to handle the huge sums involved in managing pension funds. Alongside the development of the basic scheme, the government will need to finance pensions already being paid as well as the accumulated pension rights of workers under the old state system. This debt will have to be funded through the sale of state-owned enterprise assets, government bonds, and additional contributions from employees, none of which is currently very appealing.

Similar arrangements could be made for poor urban families. Individual accounts could pay for low-cost health care, with insurance— pooled across enterprises—covering serious medical problems.[18] Issues of confidence, appropriate use of funds, limited local funding, and a switching of central government funding will all have to be addressed.

In dealing with these issues, it will be important to keep in mind the overwhelming evidence of recent surveys that indicates that households, particularly poor households, prioritize concerns about health and mounting health care costs above concerns about unemployment and

---

18 The piloting and development of community-based health insurance schemes in urban areas since the mid-1990s—based on individual savings accounts contributed by employers and employees—has not included poor urban households. The scheme had 109 million beneficiaries at the end of 2003 (see Liu, Nolan, and Wen 2004).

insecurity in old age.[19] Poor people believe that health is the most important area in which governments need to assist in the maintenance of their livelihoods.

References

ADB (Asian Development Bank) 2001. *Urban Poverty in the PRC 2001*. Manila: Asian Development Bank.

————. 2004. "Understanding Urban Poverty." In *Poverty Profile of the Peoples Republic of China*, 5–106. Manila: Asian Development Bank.

Beynon, Louise, and Zheng Baohua. 2001. *Listening to the Voices of the Poor: Lessons and Recommendations from the PPA Study in Nanhua County, Yunnan*, in *Addressing the Poverty Constraints and Project Needs of Poor Rural Communities*. Department for International Development, Beijing.

Chen, Shaohua, and Martin Ravallion. 2007. "Absolute Poverty Measures for the Developing World, 1981–2004." Policy Research Working Paper No. 4211. World Bank, Washington, DC.

Chen, Shaohua, Martin Ravallion, and Youjuan Wang. 2006. *Dibao: A Guaranteed Minimum Income in China's Cities?* World Bank Policy Research Working Paper 3805, Washington, DC.

DFID (Department for International Development). 2004. *Urban Poverty in China*. Beijing.

Guan, Xinping. 2005. *Poverty Problems and the MLSS in Urban China*. Social Policy Research Center, Chinese Academy of Social Sciences, Beijing.

Hussain, Athar. 2003. *Urban Poverty in China: Measurement, Patterns and Policies*. Geneva: International Labour Office.

Liu, Gordon, Brian Nolan, and Chen Wen. 2004. "Urban Health Insurance and Financing in China." Department of Health Economics and Management, Beijing University.

---

19 For example, a recent participatory assessment undertaken by researchers supervised by the Sociology Institute of the Chinese Academy of Social Sciences, based on fieldwork with household members and migrants from 12 villages in six provinces, concludes that education and health are the primary concerns of rural household members and their migrant members in urban areas. (Respondents also indicated that these were the main concerns of nonmigrant urban residents.) The results of this assessment will be included in a forthcoming World Bank report, *China's Evolving Poverty Reduction Agenda*. In a recent willingness-to-pay survey supervised by the author to assess the impact of proposed increases in water prices by a water supply company in Beipiao City (Liaoning), members of most of the 600 households surveyed cited health and education as their major concerns. The results of this survey are being drafted in a report for the Department for International Development and Ministry of Water Resources entitled *Water Resources Demand Management Project*.

Ministry of Health, People's Republic of China. 2003a. *Characteristics and Trend of Need, Demand, and Utilization of Health Services in Chinese Residents: Major Findings from the Third National Health Services Survey.* Beijing.

———. 2003b. *Current Situation Analysis on Women and Children's Healthcare for the Migrant Population, Need Assessment for their Healthcare, and Study on the Mode of Service Provision.* Beijing.

Murphy, David. 2004. "The Dangers of Too Much Success." *Far Eastern Economic Review* 10 (June): 28–31.

"No Right to Work." 2004. *Economist*, September 9.

Park, Albert. 2005. "Vulnerability and Relative Poverty in Urban China." Paper presented to the First Workshop on "Broadening China's Poverty Reduction Agenda: Establishing the Factual Basis for a Scientific Approach to Policy," Beijing, March 11.

Ravallion, Martin, and Shaohua Chen. 2007. "China's (Uneven) Progress against Poverty." *Journal of Development Economics* 82 (1): 1–42.

"Prime Minister's Report to the PRC 10th National People's Congress." 2004. May 3. http://www.gov.cn.

UNDP (United Nations Development Programme). 2004. "Human Development and Equity." Draft concept note for the *China Human Development Report.* Beijing.

———. 2005. *China Human Development Report: Development with Equity.* Beijing.

"Unemployed Urbanites to Number 10 million by 2010." 2006. *China Daily.* July 11.

Wang, Ya Ping. 2003. "Living Conditions of Migrants in Inland Chinese Cities." *Journal of Comparative Asian Development* 2 (1): 47–69.

———. 2005. "Low-Income Communities and Urban Poverty in China."*Urban Geography* 26 (3): 222–42.

Wang, Youjun. 2002. *Analysis of PRC's Urban Policy.* Asian Development Bank, Manila.

World Bank. 1997. *China 2020: Development Challenges in the New Century.* Washington, DC: World Bank.

———. 2003. *China: Promoting Growth with Equity.* World Bank, East Asia and Pacific Region, Poverty Reduction and Economic Management Unit, Beijing.

WHO (World Health Organization). 2006. *Basic Indicators for Member States: China.* Geneva: WHO.

Yusuf, Shahid, Kaoru Nabeshima, and Wei Ha. 2006. "What Makes Cities Healthy?" World Bank, Policy Research Working Paper, WPS 4107, Washington, DC.

Zhou, Xuejun. 2000. *Voice of the Poor: Report on a Participatory Urban Analysis in Beijing.* Center for Integrated Agricultural Development, Chinese Agricultural University, Beijing.

CHAPTER 5

Finance for Urban Centers

Patrick Honohan

A major characteristic of China's economic transformation is urbanization
on an unprecedented scale. The construction and real estate sectors now
account for nearly 20 percent of GDP; investment in housing, the bulk of
it in urban areas, grew almost 19 percent a year between 2000 and 2004.
Gross investment in urban infrastructure by Shanghai alone amounted to
almost $300 billion between 1990 and 2004 (Yusuf, Nabeshima, and
Perkins 2006). Financing the infrastructure, housing, and working and
fixed capital needs of an increasingly diverse set of enterprises—industrial
and service—presents a huge challenge, in terms of both the volume and
efficient allocation of resources.

Thanks to China's deep banking system and high level of household
and corporate savings, funds are available in the aggregate, but the
financial sector has succeeded only partially in guiding these funds to
where they are needed for greatest economic efficiency. This problem is
becoming a matter of greater concern as urbanization increases the flow
of resources into very long-lived assets.

By far the largest component of China's financial system is banking,
a sector whose structure has been evolving rapidly over the past few
years. Four enormous state-controlled commercial banks represent the

The author is indebted to extensive contributions and suggestions by Genevieve Boyreau-
Debray, Loic Chiquier, Bob Cull, Mansoor Dailami, Yongbeom Kim, Kaoru Nabeshima,
David Scott, and Shahid Yusuf. Research assistance was provided by Hanqing Shi.

core of the system; together they control assets equivalent to about 100 percent of GDP. While in practice each bank still retains a degree of the sectoral specialization implied by its names (agriculture, construction, industry and commerce, and foreign trade), all four now offer commercial banking services on a nationwide basis. In the past, these banks were tasked with supporting state-owned enterprises (SOEs). They paid little attention to the ability of those enterprises to repay. As a result of the proliferation of the resulting nonperforming assets, public funds on the order of $400 billion have been applied to recapitalizing the banks ahead of their partial privatization to strategic foreign investors and the investing public on the Hong Kong and Shanghai exchanges ("China to Open" 2006).[1]

While the four banks still account for some 60 percent of deposits (and a somewhat smaller percentage of loans, following the sale of a sizable chunk of their nonperforming loans), other banks are making steady inroads into the urban financial market. Some have national licenses, although they concentrate on the largest cities; 113 cities also have city commercial banks.[2] The China Development Bank, funded largely by bonds sold to other intermediaries, is the most important player in credit and investment banking at the longer-term end of the market.

At first glance, China's banks, stock exchanges, and large insurance companies and the impressive physical presence of financial firms in Shanghai, Beijing, and other centers might suggest that the country's cities have the main elements of a financial system that can provide credit and risk capital. But a closer look reveals important shortcomings in the functioning of these institutions—shortcomings that can be traced to continued ambiguity over the role of the government in finance.

Not enough bank credit seems to be going to the cities and provinces where it is most needed, in part, no doubt, because locally owned private banking has faced significant regulatory obstacles and has hardly begun to be established. As for the securities markets, more than 1,430 equities are listed on the Shanghai and Shenzhen markets, most of them representing subsidiaries carved out of the more-saleable assets owned by a larger state- or collectively owned group. Typically, only about a third of the subsidiary's shares were sold on the market. In effect, the

---

1 At the time of writing, only the Agricultural Bank had not yet been partially privatized.
2 Thirteen banks have national licenses. All but one is majority controlled by the government or government-owned enterprises, though several also have foreign equity stakeholders. Foreign banks also operate in China, although they remain small, especially in the local currency market, where they accounted for less than one percent of loans in yuan in 2006 ("Not Too Big" 2007).

stock exchange is still dominated by government-controlled enterprises; it does not primarily provide a channel through which entrepreneurs can tap China's ample savings. This will change in the future, because firms that account for 93 percent of market capitalization have abolished the nontradable share categories and the government has lifted the ban on new listings ("China: Stock Market" 2006).

The growing housing finance market is also subject to constraints, in part because of the persistence of efforts to plan and manage the functioning of the market. Meanwhile, though urban infrastructure is being built, it is being done so without the full benefit of modern techniques of infrastructure finance that could harness a spectrum of maturities and instruments and reassign costs and risks so that they are transparently borne by those who can best absorb them.

Allocating Financing Efficiently across Provinces

Ample though its savings are, China cannot afford to misallocate them. Despite the enormous investment needs of the urban explosion, banks have not been performing their classic function—familiar from numerous historic episodes of urbanization around the world—of channeling investable funds from mature surplus regions to dynamic urban economies. Indeed, it is far from clear that credit is flowing smoothly to the right borrowers in the right cities. Recent research reveals the limited interprovincial capital mobility in China and the fact that the net banking flows that do occur do not flow to the provinces—and presumably by extension to the cities—with the most-rapid growth prospects.

Conditions in China would seem to be ideal for an integrated financial market. Not only are the main banks in each city and province the same, but the two organized securities markets seem open to enterprises from all provinces. The legal and regulatory system is common across provinces, and language problems are of relatively minor importance. Given these favorable conditions, why are funds not flowing to the places where they are needed to promote the development of China's most promising cities?

One reason relates to the governance of the state-owned commercial banks. Although each is apparently a single legal entity, these banks have operated in a highly decentralized way, and their regional management has been strongly influenced by provincial and local governments (Yi 2003). Recent steps to centralize management control, notably through the appointment process for managers, have reportedly not yet fully eliminated the divided loyalties of regional management. And by all accounts, it would be a mistake to assume that the arrival of technical support and board representation from foreign strategic shareholders will have solved all of these problems.

One apparent consequence of this governance structure can be detected from the pattern of financial flows. The evidence suggests that a part of the savings of Chinese households has been wasted by being invested in the wrong geographical areas. If the allocation of loanable funds across provinces is wasteful, it would not be surprising if the pattern of allocation within provinces (between urban and rural areas, between different cities and different borrowers) is also prone to waste. While this conjecture must be qualified by the finding of Cull and Xu (2003) that access of enterprises to bank lending is correlated on a firm-by-firm basis with the enterprise's profitability, productivity, and employment growth, Cull and Xu (2000) also find that this relation has weakened over time.

One indication of the inefficiency of the banking sector comes from banking statistics and the allocation of bank loans across provinces. In international comparisons, deeper national financial systems are systematically associated with more rapid growth.[3] In China, however, provincial banking depth and provincial output growth are inversely related (Boyreau-Debray 2003), and provincial enterprise profitability is negatively associated with lending growth (Podpiera 2006). A perverse relation is also apparent in the market valuation of tradable shares in companies listed on the Shanghai or Shenzhen stock exchanges compared with estimates of provincial capital productivity. These anomalous patterns strongly suggest that the flow of investable funds from China's formal financial system[4] is not governed solely by the logic of the market.[5]

---

3   For a summary of this literature, see Honohan (2004). Most of the cross-country studies do not include China, apparently because of difficulty in matching the authors' preferred concepts of financial depth. China's exceptionally deep financial system and rapid economic growth at first sight suggest that its experience is fully consistent with the global correlation. However, more complex econometric models that take account of additional dimensions of financial sector development reduce China's ranking in this regard.

4   This is not necessarily true of investment funds from nonbanking sources, which are becoming increasingly important in China. Boyreau-Debray and Wei (2004) show that, in contrast to bank- or government-financed funds, self-financed corporate investment is higher in areas in which the marginal productivity of capital is higher. For a perspective on the institutional background that could ensure that nonstate and nonbank finance in China is more effectively channeled, see Allen, Qian, and Qian (2002).

5   The interprovincial pattern of some alternative indicators of financial development, such as greater diversity in sources of finance, is correlated with growth, as predicted by conventional theory (Boyreau-Debray 2003). These points are foreshadowed by Lardy (1998). The idea of a dividing line between coastal and noncoastal provinces should not be taken too simplistically, however, given the findings of Cull, Shen, and Xu (2003) on Sichuan Province.

One possible explanation for the peculiar pattern of investment is that the allocation of financial resources across provinces reflects the desire to ensure that adequate credit is available in poorer regions. However, the data do not support this view. Indeed, regression analysis fails to detect any significant correlation between mean provincial output per capita and bank credit.[6] Credit is thus not being systematically channeled to poor regions.[7]

The concentration of SOEs, rather than income, appears to be the most important determinant of net banking inflows. Lending is not going to where it achieves the best pay off in terms of economic growth but instead to where the state-owned banks' traditional clients are found. Presumably, the progressive commercialization of the state-owned commercial banks will eventually weaken this link, but while it persists, a price is being paid in terms of provincial growth. Poor provinces with good growth potential but relatively few state enterprises are receiving a suboptimal supply of funds. It is likely that even in provinces that are net recipients of funds, many enterprises with promising growth prospects are also being starved of funds. The empirical evidence points not only to problems in the geographic distribution of the volume of funds but to deeper contrasts between how financial intermediation has been functioning in China and how market finance is supposed to function. The most obvious structural difference that might explain this contrast is the continuing predominance of state ownership in banking in China, especially in noncoastal provinces.

It has been argued that foreign direct investment (FDI) partially offsets the distortion of banking flows, by favoring some of China's more dynamic cities.[8] This offset is only partial, however.

Analysis of interprovincial patterns of finance suggests unexploited potential for better credit allocation. One of the main barriers to exploitation of this potential has been the de facto local government control or

---

6 Dayal-Gulati and Husain (2002) make a similar finding, showing that more bank credit actually slowed the speed of interprovincial income convergence. The credit data they use refer only to state-owned commercial banks, however, not to the system as a whole.

7 Such a policy goal would be difficult to rationalize. Less-prosperous provinces might need support or subsidy from the rest of the country because of their poverty and hence their inability to generate the necessary tax revenues to cover the cost of essential public services, including income support of needy households. But such resource transfers should be on a grant basis, through mostly fiscal channels, if they are to redress the poverty imbalance.

8 See Huang and Di (2004) for an argument that FDI differentially substitutes for financial market deficiencies in different Chinese provinces.

influence over the allocation of credit. This control does not come solely through exercise of ownership rights. Instead, it derives from the influence of regional governments and elites on the behavior and decisions of regional bank managers, especially managers of state-owned banks but also managers of other banks, many if not most of which are largely controlled by regional governments or owned by SOEs. By capturing the allocation of credit in this way, these government and quasi-government bodies may have thought that they were advancing the public interest. In fact, they are retarding the long-term growth and full convergence of Chinese productivity and per capita output with levels of advanced economies.

The authorities have wisely acted to alter the lines of responsibility in the banks, centralizing decisions and appointment processes with a view to weakening the influence of local governments on banking policy (Yi 2003; Zhou 2004). They have sold strategic stakes in three of the large banks to foreign investors and launched initial public offerings. Other joint stock banks, including city commercial banks, have also been partially privatized. These measures need to be supplemented by a more open approach to the establishment of private banks not linked with government or SOEs. Expansion of existing banks into a wider geographic area could also be encouraged.[9]

It might be argued that China is growing so rapidly that improvements in the allocation of credit cannot credibly enhance its growth trajectory. There are several reasons why such an argument has less weight than appears. First, much of China's growth has been achieved by a shift of labor resources away from subsistence agriculture into the modern sector, supported by capital accumulation on a vast scale, as reflected in a national saving ratio sustained at more than 35 percent for two decades (Young 2000). The huge sacrifice in current consumption (and the willingness of households to place their savings in low-yielding bank deposits) has masked the considerable inefficiencies that have been involved in the process. Second, economic depreciation of the capital thus formed may be a good deal higher than it would have been with better investment decisions; if so, net national product is growing less rapidly than appears. Third, an efficient financial sector would reduce the vulnerability of the growth process to a financial crisis.

---

9 To date, only two of the city commercial banks have been allowed to venture outside their own city—Bank of Shanghai into Ningbo and Bank of Beijing into Tianjin.

Several types of policy action could help. Political appointment of top managers of state-owned banks could be terminated; these positions should be filled on the basis of relevant skills, not as part of a rotation of senior government officials. Removing the automatic revolving door between banking and policy would greatly reduce the risk of confusion of roles. While the partial privatization of state-owned commercial banks will help improve governance, control of these banks still lies in the political sphere. More needs to be done to establish and maintain a sharp distinction between the government's role as owner of these banks, aimed at maximizing their value as commercial concerns, and its role in developing and enforcing prudential, competition, and monetary policies. The long-established political links to bank management at the city level will be hard to dissolve entirely, but efforts to do so are highly desirable.

Ensuring that Urban Enterprises Are Well Run

Although governments provide the major economic base and rationale for a few great world cities, the dynamism of most cities comes from trade, commerce, finance, and production. Wholesale financial services agglomerate in urban centers. Partly because of the high skill levels and corresponding remuneration and the costly ancillary services that high finance can command, cities that excel in this field typically act as magnets for other leading enterprises, support cultural activities, and attract tourism in a virtuous circle. Hong Kong (China) is a classic example, now joined by Shanghai and other Chinese cities.

In general, the engines of urban dynamism are enterprises. Most urban economies can flourish only if enterprises have access to finance, and—even more important—existing enterprises make the most of their position and potential by being well managed.[10] One way of ensuring that enterprises are well managed is to allow corporate control to be contested. For medium-size and large enterprises, the equity market provides an important potential tool for enabling corporate control to pass into more-effective hands.

---

10 Following the approval of bill issuance by the People's Bank of China in May 2005, $27 billion worth of bills were traded in the first three-quarters of 2006. Other types of short-term debt instruments are also coming into widespread use. These include drafts (which must be settled within 90 days) and entrustment loans (loans between firms mediated by banks) ("Out of the Shadows" 2006).

China's equity markets made a brave start; the number of equities listed on the two mainland exchanges, Shanghai and Shenzhen, is impressive. Primary and rights issues of equities have raised an annual average of about 1 percent of GDP in recent years and close to 2 percent of GDP in 2007—a sizable sum, albeit dwarfed by the annual average net increase of about 17 percent of GDP in nongovernment lending by the banking system ("China: Stock Market Surge" 2007). Indeed, compared with other aspects of China's growth record, the contribution of the equity market to China's growth is modest.

One reason for this is the nature of ownership rights in listed enterprises and the related barriers to change of control of underperforming enterprises. The way in which nontraded shares are traded—an issue the authorities have only recently tackled—illustrates the ambiguous and gradual manner in which the state has been disengaging its control over enterprises.

In mid-2006, before the dramatic surge in stock prices, total equity market capitalization was about 25 percent of GDP. The boom in the stock market raised total equity market capitalization to about 100 percent of GDP by August 2007. Whatever the level of capitalization at a particular date, it overstates actual capitalization, for two reasons.[11] The first is the standard adjustment that needs to be made in any stock exchange to identify the free float of shares—that is, those not tied up in strategic stakes held by controlling shareholders and others considered unlikely to offer their holdings for sale on the market. Despite an increase during 2005–06, the proportion of freely tradable shares in China was still less than 40 percent of the total, equivalent to a relatively modest 10 percent of GDP.

The second reason why China's equity market is smaller than appears is the nonstandard nature of nontradable shares. The so-called legal person (LP) and state-share categories refer to separate classes of shares, which are conceptually distinct from those listed on the Shanghai or Shenzhen markets. (LP shares are generally held by SOEs.) While these shares convey equal voting rights and claims on dividends (when paid), until mid-2005 they could not be transferred between different classes of owners,[12] and transfers of LP shares between enterprises took place at prices that seemed very far from market exchange prices.[13]

---

11 Throughout, the discussion relates to A shares.
12 Until 2005 neither state shares nor LP shares could be sold to the general public.
13 For the historical evolution of these distinct classes of shares, see Walter and Howie (2003).

The unusual characteristics of the LP and state shares created considerable uncertainty about the value of the company as a whole. In particular, the fear that the LP and state shares might at some point be unloaded onto the market is believed to have depressed the price of A shares. The high elasticity with which share prices have moved in response to the issue of new tradable shares suggests that the market viewed the value of the enterprise as being divided between tradable and other shares on a fixed basis, independent of the number of shares issued.[14] That is to say, when new tradable shares were issued, the market assumed that the issuance would dilute the ownership share of existing holders but not affect the value of the state and LP shares.[15] Thus, tradable shares have not appeared to convey the same kind of entitlement that equity shares have in most advanced securities markets—even in cases where there are multiple categories of shareholding, as is the case in several European exchanges.

In April 2005, the authorities finally grasped the nettle created by the multiple share categories and began a process of converting state and LP shares into tradable shares. Each listed enterprise made the conversion independently; most compensated existing holders with an additional tranche of tradable shares, ostensibly to make provision for the fact that there would now be no legal obstacle to disposing of the remaining shares on the market.

Not long after the announcement of this conversion policy (and the accompanying one-year moratorium on new share issues), the four-year decline in A-share values went into reverse, and the index rose rapidly for the following few years, almost quadrupling by mid-2007. The process of conversion was rapid, with 93 percent of market capitalization and more than 85 percent of the number of listed enterprises having converted by September 2006.

The conversion program can be seen as a significant step toward reducing the ambiguity of the government's claim on listed enterprises. But the apparent arbitrariness of the conversion process and the compensation paid to holders of already tradable shares (in the form of

---

14 Walter and Howie (2003) interpret the relation as implying paradoxically that the market attached almost no value to the LP and state shares; however, the relation is equally consistent with the more-plausible interpretation given here.

15 There have been transactions in LP shares, at heavy discounts relative to A shares (Green 2003). The discount could be interpreted as implying that these transfers are at administered prices rather than fair-market value.

shares) also shows the pervasiveness of unwritten reserve powers in this area. Who is to say that the compensation is appropriate, especially if, as argued earlier, the market previously assumed that the claims of state and LP shareholders on the company were de facto independent of the relative number of tradable and other shares outstanding? Who is to say whether shareholders really have the final say over the management and wider governance of listed enterprises (especially for listings that represent only the attractive assets of wider state enterprise groupings)? Does ultimate control of the corporate finances of listed companies still lie in the political realm? It may take more than this rationalization of share categories to clarify and build market confidence that the various levels of government really are transferring genuine ownership and control of these enterprises into private hands, as they say they are.

It is not only minority shareholders' behavior that is affected by the ambiguous dividing line between government and enterprise management in so many Chinese enterprises. Indeed, arguably much more important is the barrier this ambiguity erects to takeovers of enterprises by more effective management teams, often through merger or acquisition by a better-placed or more-skilled incumbent.[16]

Lack of a market for enterprise control is problematic not only for the listed enterprises—which after all, include the elite of Chinese industry—but also particularly for small underperforming enterprises whose control lies partly in the hands of city governments. It is not surprising that, in order to ensure no disruption to the employment or flow of tax revenues from locally controlled enterprises, governments act to block takeovers or mergers, especially if the purchasing enterprise is not from the same city (Yi 2003). The opportunity for raising productivity through rationalization and more efficient management is lost by the failure to pursue the logic of market-driven control of the deployment of enterprises' productive resources.

Even where city and provincial governments are not interfering directly, they may be influencing the efficiency and productivity of enterprises by failing to create the conditions for productivity-enhancing

---

16 Many advanced economies have witnessed episodes of excessive merger and acquisition activity; a number of studies claim to show that value destruction has been at least as frequent a consequence as value creation. Like other transition economies, however, China is still at the point where allocation of enterprise ownership and control is far from what can deliver the most-efficient outcome.

investment. In particular, although private property rights are protected (since the 1999 constitutional amendment, albeit not to the same extent as state property), the perception is that these rights differ across cities and enterprises. Cull and Xu (2004) examine survey responses by 2,400 enterprises in 18 cities during 2003. They find a systematic relation between the enterprises' self-assessment of the degree to which their property rights were likely to be protected and their willingness to reinvest profits. Assuring enterprises throughout China that their property rights will be protected will likely require that the central authorities play a stronger role in ensuring local compliance with national policy on property rights protection.[17]

The conversion of shareholdings by state and legal persons into standard tradable shares has been successfully accomplished. The conversion represents an essential step toward achieving transparency in the role of government agencies in corporate governance. But this process will not be fully accomplished without a coherent privatization program for moving most enterprises from state to private hands. Privatization itself will not be very effective if the security of property rights in every Chinese city is not strengthened. Strengthening these rights will require action at political, legislative, and judicial levels (Yusuf, Nabeshima, and Perkins 2006).

It is somewhat ironic that one of the ways reformers are advocating to reduce overinvestment by cash-rich enterprises is to force the payment of dividends to the state or to a state holding company (Naughton 2006). Higher wholesale deposit interest rates, and an active market for corporate control, would represent an alternative and potentially more dynamic solution to this problem.

The wider message is clear. Governments, at the municipal and higher levels, have the important tasks of building and maintaining the soft infrastructures (including legal and information infrastructures) that support productivity-enhancing enterprises. If these tasks are to lead to an expansion of financial and producer services and the associated growth of urban economies, authorities at various levels must refrain from creating ambiguity over who controls and who can control the destiny of enterprises.

---

17 Qian (2003) suggests that the early success of township and village enterprises (TVEs), despite the lack of formal property rights, may reflect the political protection implicitly given to them by their links to local governments. The subsequent performance of TVEs shows the limitations of such an approach.

Financing Physical Infrastructure

Two key dimensions of urban physical infrastructure are housing and large public works. Each calls for a different financing solution.

Housing Finance

Although China's population growth and household formation rates are not high, the combination of rapid economic growth and urbanization has generated a huge demand for urban residential units and their financing. China is currently in the most-rapid phase of its urbanization. The proportion of the population in urban areas rose from 21 percent to 36 percent in the last 18 years of the 20th century. The following five years saw this percentage jump to 43 percent, still a relatively low rate, which can be expected to continue growing to beyond 60 percent before 2020. If it does, some 200 million more people will become city dwellers by 2020.

Rising living standards generally translate into higher expected quality of accommodation. Many of the apartment blocks built in the big cities in the boom years of the 1970s and 1980s are being razed to make way for larger and better units. The scope for quality improvements is considerable. By 2005, 82 percent of urban households owned their own homes, but by one estimate, 38 percent lived in housing of poor quality.

Financing the construction and purchase of these dwellings is already transforming the business model of China's banks. Negligible a decade ago, by 2006 mortgage lending accounted for about a tenth of the banks' local currency loan portfolio, and other real estate finance accounted for almost half as much again.[18] All types of banks have been active, although the Big Four have shifted into mortgages more than others, and they accounted for more than two-thirds of new bank mortgage lending in 2005.

The vigor of the banking response could conceal some problems in the future. Credit underwriting standards vary widely, and there is little relation between loan pricing and perceived credit risk. Many banks seem to be more eager to build market share than to ensure that the business is profitable. In the competition for market share, banks have been offering mortgages at the lowest long-term rate permitted by the People's Bank of China, without distinguishing borrowers by risk category. Indeed, as fixed-term mortgages have become established, they, too, have been

---

18 The mortgage market in China started in 1988. During 2005 the value of total outstanding mortgages exceeded 10 per cent of GDP for the first time. It still has some way to go to reach the levels attained in the Republic of Korea (27 percent), Hong Kong (China) (44 percent), or Singapore (61 percent) ("Mortgage Industry" 2006).

offered at the lowest permitted rate, without regard to the additional risks involved (Chiquier 2006). To be sure, loan delinquency rates have so far proved manageable, but this may change if mortgage portfolio growth rates and the increase in housing prices slows.

Banking systems that are more market-oriented have not been free of the problems associated with the underwriting and pricing of mortgages and mortgage-related products. But banks controlled by government-owned entities and still not fully committed to the goal of profitability are particularly prone to errors of this type.

Another segment of the Chinese mortgage market is even more ambiguously positioned in regard to viability. The Housing Provident Funds (HPFs) were established for public sector employees in the early 1990s in an attempt to move away from employer-provided housing toward an individual responsibility scheme. The funds are financed partly by mandatory employee contributions and partly by employer contributions. Ostensibly designed mainly to help low-paid workers obtain affordable housing (while also accumulating resources for eventual use in pension outlays), the funds' 10 million or so subsidized mortgages appear to have gone to the more prosperous of their 63 million savers. The local governments that control the funds have also diverted some of the resources to other uses. This kind of scheme is another half-way step between plan and market that fails to deliver the intended social goal, is susceptible to corrupt practices and subversion, and interferes with the development of a robust and sustainable mortgage system. Although HPFs account for just 12 percent the value of the mortgage market ("Mortgage Industry" 2006), the rapid emergence of banks as mortgage providers has removed most of the initial rationale for the pro-vision of housing finance through special channels. As the HPFs are still increasing their share of mortgage finance nationwide, it is worth reforming their structure in order to remove or redirect the misaligned subsidy and to centralize underwriting and other investment decisions.[19]

The mortgage insurance industry that has emerged in China displays features of fragmentation and the lack of a coherent business model. Indeed, although they have now diversified into insuring bank mortgages, many of the one hundred or so Housing Guarantee Funds (HGFs) started as a way of insuring the loans of HPFs. As such, they too inhabit an

---

19 In 2005, the People's Bank of China revised the rules to allow securitization of mort-gage loans and trading of such securities on the interbank market ("Mortgage Industry" 2006).

uncomfortable halfway house between government-controlled business and the market. Mortgage insurance works best when a strongly capitalized and specialized insurer pools the risks of numerous lenders, offering scale and diversification economies and pricing risks on the basis of loss experience accumulated on a nationwide basis. Charging arbitrary but seemingly low premia, the HGFs (many of them controlled by local governments or government-owned companies) inhibit the emergence of stronger and more viable mortgage insurers.

Infrastructure Finance

Considerable uncertainty exists regarding the financing costs of the vast program of infrastructure investment now under way. Much of the infrastructure investment is being financed through conventional bank loans, some of them made to contractors with an explicit or, more likely, implicit guarantee from the city and other local authorities that wish to see the projects completed.[20] It is not clear just how much of current infrastructural spending has been financed in such inefficient ways.

Although it may very well have to pay for the infrastructure in the end, the local government is unlikely to have had the opportunity to control the design, prioritization, or contract cost of the project or to monitor the progress of spending. Where a contractor has borrowed the funds and begins to foresee that the project will be financially unsuccessful, he will have an incentive to loot the project, diverting all possible resources to his personal benefit, thus deepening and accelerating insolvency and increasing the cost of the project to the local government.

Here again the problem is one of ambiguity over the dividing line between public and private. A poorly conceived and executed semi-privatization of the financing of public infrastructure is the least attractive form of financing.[21]

---

20 This is not the only issue in infrastructure financing. Indeed, international experience with respect to approaches to infrastructure financing varies widely even in countries, such as Germany, Japan, and the Republic of Korea, that have relied on bank finance (see Robaschik and Yoshino 2000, who note that German policy banks have generally lent through private banks, whereas Japanese policy banks take the credit risk directly themselves).

21 It is true that the rapid infrastructural development of Germany and Japan, in the 19th century and after World War II, was accomplished without the benefit of such sophisticated financial instruments. But it is not only that the sophistication of modern finance offers new opportunities for improved allocation of risk, it is also the case that the greater potential in current conditions for risk transfer to the state, especially in China, makes the use of such opportunities essential. These points are linked to much wider issues of defining the best role for public ownership and regulation in infrastructure (see Kessides 2003).

Some of the risks of infrastructure investment can by transferred to investors who have the capacity to bear such risks through structured bond financing (Dailami and Hauswald 2003). Bonds whose returns are sensitive to cost overruns or revenue shortfalls could be attractive to insurance companies and other collective investment vehicles (including foreign investors). Because a diversified portfolio of such bonds need not be especially risky, they could be attractive even at a modest premium yield over government bonds.

China's bond market is still immature. Until 1988, no trading in treasury bonds was allowed; hence no secondary market existed (Zhou 2005). Several reforms were introduced after 1988 to make the bond market more like bond markets elsewhere. Before 1991, treasury bonds were issued through administrative assignment. Since 1995, they have been issued through syndications and auctions. To establish a benchmark, long-term bonds were introduced starting in 2001.[22] Since 2003, the Ministry of Finance has announced the schedule of new issuances in advance (Zhou 2005).

Since 2004, several initiatives have been introduced to stimulate the growth of bond markets. These initiatives include issuing subordinated bonds by commercial banks;[23] promoting the securitization of credit assets;[24] authorizing the Agricultural Development Bank of China to issue policy-related financial bonds; allowing railway bonds and corporate bonds to be circulated in the interbank market; introducing forward transactions in the interbank bond market;[25] and authorizing the Asian Development Bank and the International Finance Corporation to issue bonds denominated in yuan in China (Mu 2005).[26] To facilitate the infrastructure construction, the People's Bank of China issued "The Administrative Rules for Fund Management Firms by Commercial Banks" on February 20, 2005 to allow commercial banks to set up fund management firms (Mu 2005).

---

22 In 2001, 15- and 20-year bonds were introduced; 30-year bonds were introduced in 2002 (Zhou 2005).

23 The People's Bank of China issued "The Administrative Rules on Financial Bonds in the Interbank Bond Market" on May 12, 2005 (Mu 2005).

24 The government issued the "Administrative Rules for Credit Asset Securitization Pilot Operations" on April 20, 2005 (Mu 2005).

25 Forward transactions in the interbank bond market were introduced in "The Administrative Rules for the Forward Bond Transactions in the National Interbank Bond Market" on May 11, 2005 (Mu 2005).

26 "The Provisional Administrative Rules for International Development Institutions RMB Bonds" was issued February 18, 2005.

Currently, the full range of financial derivatives that can be used to structure bonds is not available in China, not least because of regulatory impediments, some of them introduced to stem abuses in the past. The credibility of such instruments depends on achieving an adequate level of accounting and auditing for the relevant bodies. Now is the time to move progressively and carefully toward removing the legal and regulatory barriers that hamper the introduction of such bonds, though the need to build the technical skills and regulatory infrastructure required to ensure that they work well should not be underestimated.

The recent introduction of mortgage-backed securities is a useful step along this road. Removal of unduly restrictive regulation on the investment portfolio of insurance firms will also help ensure that the natural purchasers of such instruments are permitted to do so.

City governments should move away from the use of special-purpose vehicles and other rough-and-ready attempts to shift infrastructure financing off their balance sheets when the likelihood is that they will pay for them in the end, toward a more sophisticated approach, such as that described above. Well-designed infrastructure bonds can help provide what is needed: a clear dividing line between the risks to be absorbed by government and those to be absorbed by the market.

Concluding Remarks

China's cities will continue to absorb vast financial resources as they grow and consolidate in the years and decades ahead. For this flow to be ensured, several deficiencies in China's financial sector need to be corrected. The flow of investable banking funds must chase productive and well-managed firms rather than be diverted into less productive uses in the less dynamic regions and firms. Takeovers and market discipline on listed enterprises need to be more effective to ensure that these enterprises become engines of urban dynamism. If China's cities are to be well built, arrangements for mortgage and infrastructure finance need to embrace modern financial techniques more effectively.

A common theme underlies several of these shortcomings. Along several dimensions, ambiguity in the role of some level of government or its agencies is resulting in suboptimal credit and investment decisions affecting cities. This phenomenon is not unique to China, but it is arguably much more acute in China than in most countries—a legacy of both the transition process and the shifting balance of power between regional authorities and the central authority. Resolution of these issues will be part of ongoing administrative and policy reform on a wide front, at both the city and national levels.

References

Allen, Franklin, Jun Qian, and Meijum Qian. 2002. "Law, Finance, and Economic Growth in China." *Journal of Financial Economics* 77 (1): 57–116.

Boyreau-Debray, Genevieve. 2003. "Financial Intermediation and Growth: Chinese Style." World Bank Policy Research Working Paper 3027, Washington, DC: World Bank.

Boyreau-Debray, Genevieve, and Shang-Jin Wei. 2004. "Can China Grow Faster? A Diagnosis of the Fragmentation of the Domestic Capital Market." IMF Working Paper 04/76, International Monetary Fund, Washington, DC

"China: Stock Market Strengthens but Outlook Is Cloudy." 2006. *Oxford Analytica.* October 10.

"China: Stock Market Surge Set to Continue." 2007. *Oxford Analytica.* October 9.

"China to Open Renminbi Business to Foreign Banks." 2006. *China Daily.* November 16.

Chiquier, Loic. 2006. "Housing Finance in East Asia." World Bank, Financial and Private Sector Development Vice Presidency, Washington, DC.

Cull, Robert, and Lixin Colin Xu. 2000. "Bureaucrats, State Banks, and the Efficiency of Credit Allocation: the Experience of Chinese State-Owned Enterprises." *Journal of Comparative Economics* 28 (1): 1–31.

———. 2003. "Who Gets Credit? The Behavior of Bureaucrats and State Banks in Allocating Credit to Chinese State-Owned Enterprises." *Journal of Development Economics* 71 (2): 533–59.

———. 2004. "Institutions, Ownership, and Finance: The Determinants of Profit Reinvestment among Chinese Firms." *Journal of Financial Economics* 77 (1): 117–46.

Cull, Robert, Minggao Shen, and Lixin Colin Xu. 2003. "Comparing Financing Patterns: Coastal vs. Inland Provinces in China." World Bank, Development Research Group, Washington, DC.

Dailami, Mansoor, and Robert Hauswald. 2003. "The Emerging Project Bond Market: Covenant Provisions and Credit Spreads." World Bank Policy Research Working Paper 3095, Washington, DC.

Dayal-Gulati, A., and A. M. Husain. 2002. "Centripetal Forces in China's Economic Takeoff." *IMF Staff Papers* 42 (3): 364–94.

Green, Stephen. 2003. *China's Stock Market*. London: Economist Books.

Honohan, Patrick. 2004. "Financial Development, Growth and Poverty: How Close Are the Links?" In *Financial Development and Economic Growth: Explaining the Links*, ed. Charles Goodhart, 1–37. London: Palgrave.

Huang, Yasheng, and Wenhua Di. 2004. "A Tale of Two Provinces: The Institutional Environment and Foreign Ownership in China." William Davidson Institute Working Paper 667, Ann Arbor, MI. http://ssrn.com/abstract=529142

Kessides, Ioannis. 2003. *Infrastructure Regulation: Promises, Perils and Principles*. Washington, DC: AEI-Brookings Joint Center for Regulatory Studies.

Lardy, Nicholas R. 1998. *China's Unfinished Revolution*. Washington, DC: Brookings Institution Press.

"Mortgage Industry Untapped, Says BIS." 2006. *Shanghai Daily*. December 11.

Mu, Huaipeng. 2005. "China's Bond Market: Innovation and Development." Paper presented at the Second Annual Asia Pacific Bond Congress, Hong Kong (China), June 16.

Naughton, Barry. 2006. "Claiming Profit for the State: SASAC and the Capital Management Budget." *China Leadership Monitor* 18: 1–9.

"Not Too Big a Bang." 2007. *Business China*. January 1.

"Out of the Shadows." 2006. *Economist*. December 16.

Podpiera, Richard. 2006. "Progress in China's Banking Sector Reform: Has Bank Behavior Changed?" IMF Working Paper 06/71, International Monetary Fund, Washington, DC.

Qian, Yingyi. 2003. "How Reform Worked in China?" In *In Search of Prosperity: Analytic Narratives of Economic Growth*, ed. Dani Rodrik. Princeton, NJ: Princeton University Press.

Robaschik, Frank, and Naoyuki Yoshino. 2000. "Public Banking in Germany and Japan's Fiscal Investment and Loan Program: A Comparison." University of Duisburg Working Paper 54, Germany.

Walter, Carl E., and Fraser J. T. Howie. 2003. *Privatizing China*. Singapore: John Wiley.

Yi, Gang. 2003. "Changes in China Capital Market." Paper presented at the World Bank/DRC Workshop on National Market Integration, September. Beijing.

Young, Alwyn. 2000. "Gold into Base Metals: Productivity Growth in the People's Republic of China during the Reform Period." NBER Working Paper 7856, National Bureau of Economic Research, Cambridge, MA.

Yusuf, Shahid, Kaoru Nabeshima, and Dwight Perkins. 2006. *Under New Ownership: Privatizing China's State-Owned Enterprises*. Stanford, CA: Stanford University Press.

Zhou, Chengyue. 2005. "China's Treasury Bonds Market: Opening Up and Development." Paper presented at the conference "Developing Bond Markets in APEC: Toward Greater Public-Private Sector Regional Partnership," Tokyo, June 21.

Zhou, Xiaochuan. 2004. "Some Issues Concerning the Reform of the State-Owned Commercial Banks." Speech delivered to the International Institute of Finance Spring Membership Conference, Shanghai, April 16.

CHAPTER 6

Energy Policy

Edward S. Steinfeld

Having negotiated a tortuous path through sweeping reform and rapid economic development for 25 years, Chinese society finds itself coping with the relatively new phenomena of rapid urbanization and soaring demands for energy. As with so many other challenges in recent Chinese history, these new challenges have emerged as by-products of earlier societal achievements—the inevitable offshoots of phenomenal economic growth—accelerating at previously unimagined speed. This chapter explores the nature of an urbanizing China's rapidly accelerating demand for energy, the complexities involved in meeting that demand, and the even broader policy and institutional challenges surrounding long-term resource and environmental sustainability.

The Nature of the Challenge

In 1980, China's urbanization rate hovered just below 20 percent, a rate lower than Pakistan (28.1 percent), India (23.1 percent), and Indonesia (22.1 percent) (see table 1.1). By 2005 China's levels had surged to 42.9 percent, outstripping Pakistan (34.9 percent) and India (28.7 percent) and almost reaching the level of Indonesia (48.1 percent).

During this period, Chinese energy consumption soared. In 1973 China consumed 7.9 percent of the world's energy; by 2005 the figure had risen to 14.2 percent, making China the world's second-largest consumer, trailing only the United States (IEA 2007a). Since 1993 China has been a net importer of oil, and it continues to be the world's largest consumer (and producer) of coal, which accounted for more than 76.4 percent of China's primary energy supply in 2004 (IEA 2007b).

Certainly since 2002, China's electric power sector has been growing at a torrid pace. Total generating capacity increased by nearly a third between 2003 and 2006 (MIT 2007). In 2005, the system added about 70 gigawatts (GW) of generating capacity, an amount on par with the scale of the entire British power grid (MIT 2007). Many observers doubted that China could increase its capacity by another 70 GW. Nonetheless, the following year witnessed an additional 102 GW of capacity expansion (McGregor 2007). Concomitantly, and far more quickly than previously predicted, in 2006 China became the world's largest global emitter of carbon dioxide (Landsberg 2007).

In theory, the connection between urbanization and rising energy consumption appears obvious. As people shift from rural lifestyles to high-density, multistory urban dwellings, demand for energy-intensive climate control and extensive lighting should surge. So, too, should demand for energy-intensive appliances, automobiles, and the extensive long-distance transportation networks needed to channel goods into urban markets. Urban lifestyles presumably also generate demands for entirely new, and decidedly energy-intensive, production systems, such as the refrigerated food supply chain, from upstream industrial-scale preparation to supermarket retailing.

China's soaring energy consumption have not yet reflected these new drivers of energy demand (Rosen and Houser 2007; Zheng 2007); that is, the long-term consumption ramifications of urbanized lifestyles have not yet begun to kick in. Chinese per capita energy consumption remains well below levels found in advanced industrial societies: in 2005, annual per capita energy consumption stood at 1.56 tons of oil equivalent (toe) (Zheng 2007), a fraction of levels in Europe (3.46 toe), Japan (4.12 toe), and the United States (7.88 toe) (Rosen and Houser 2007). Within China, however, the per capita energy consumption of urban citizens is 3.5 times that of rural citizens. Given the country's accelerating pace of urbanization, it would be foolish to assume that over the long run, residential energy consumption in China will not rise, in all likelihood substantially. There is every reason to believe that the China of tomorrow will exhibit an energy-demand pattern similar to that of urbanized societies throughout the world.

For the time being, industrial consumption drives Chinese energy demand—to a greater extent than virtually anywhere else in the world. In 2005, the industrial sector accounted for 71 percent of China's energy demand, with the remainder split between transport (10 percent) and residential, commercial, and agriculture use (19 percent). In India the industrial sector accounts for 49 percent, transport accounts for 21 percent, and residential, commercial, and agriculture use accounts for 30 percent. Far at the other end of the spectrum, in the United States industry accounts for only 25 percent of energy demand, while transport accounts for 33 percent and residential, commercial, and agricultural uses for 43 percent (Rosen and Houser 2007).

The fact that the effects of urbanization on energy consumption have yet to be felt has sweeping implications. At the very least, it means that China's accelerating demand for energy—with all the pressures it is exerting on global resources and the global environmental commons—is unlikely to be anywhere close to peaking. Chinese energy demand rose steeply through the 1990s and will likely continue to do so in the coming decades, even if reductions in energy intensity are achieved (tables 6.1–6.3).

Although residential energy consumption can be expected to rise, little reason exists to believe that industrial consumption will fall substantially, either in the aggregate or as a portion of total consumption. The expansion of energy-intensive heavy industry in China, a phenomenon that began in the 1990s, is related to the build-out of urban infrastructure on a national scale. Chinese firms are churning out the steel, aluminum, concrete, and other basic building materials going into the nation's new roads, mass-transit systems, and vast urban residential and commercial real estate development projects. Conceivably, this phenomenon could peter out over time once basic infrastructure is established, but the time frame for this will likely extend across decades.

Moreover, beyond just supplying domestic infrastructural needs, Chinese industry is increasingly producing for global markets. Indeed, urbanization has moved hand in hand with the development of technology and energy-intensive manufacturing for the global market. It is not just that the world's electronics, automotive parts, and consumer goods are being assembled in China. The most energy-intensive components for these products—everything from steel and aluminum to semiconductors—are being produced in China. The globalized supply chain now permits the most energy-intensive (and often lowest value added) production aspects of global products to be delinked from the less energy-intensive but often highest-value production aspects (design, research and development, marketing, and so forth) of those products. It is precisely these energy-intensive but often low-value production activities that are now concentrating so heavily in China. These activities make China a critical link in global supply chains but also a repository

Table 6.1. Energy Production and Consumption, 1991–2005

Item	1991	1995	1996	1997	1998	1999	2000	2001	2002	2003	2004	2005
Primary energy production												
Raw coal (tens of thousands of metric tons)	108,741	136,073	139,670	137,282	125,000	104,500	99,800	116,078	138,000	166,700	199,232	220,473
Crude oil (millions of barrels)	14,099	15,004	15,733	16,074	16,100	16,000	16,300	16,396	16,700	16,960	17,587	18,135
Natural gas (10^8 cubic meters)	161	179	201	227	233	252	272	303	327	350	415	493
Hydro (10^8 kilowatts)	1,251	1,906	1,880	1,960	2,080	2,038	2,224	2,774	2,880	2,837	3,535	3,970
Nuclear (10^8 kilowatts)	n.a.	128	143	144	141	149	167	175	251	433	505	531
Total energy consumption												
Raw coal (tens of thousands of metric tons)	110,432	137,677	144,734	139,248	129,492	126,365	124,537	126,211	136,605	163,732	193,596	216,723
Crude oil (millions of barrels)	12,384	16,065	17,436	19,692	19,818	21,073	22,439	22,838	24,780	27,126	31,700	32,535
Natural gas (10^8 cubic meters)	159	177	185	195	203	215	245	274	292	339	397	479
Hydro (10^8 kilowatts)	1,251	1,906	1,880	1,960	2,080	2,038	2,224	2,774	2,880	2,837	3,535	3,970
Nuclear (10^8 kilowatts)	n.a.	128	143	143	144	149	167	175	251	433	505	531

Source: NBS various years.
n.a. Not available.

Table 6.2. Projected Demand for Primary Energy and Oil in Selected Countries in 2025
(millions of barrels of oil equivalent a day)

Country	Primary energy		Oil	
	2001	*2025*	*2001*	*2025*
United States	96.3	132.4	19.6	27.3
China	40.9	109.2	4.9	14.2
Japan	21.9	24.7	5.4	5.3
India	13.8	29.3	2.2	4.9
World	403.9	644.6	78	119.2

Source: U.S. Department of Energy 2007.

for the indirect energy demands of global consumers. To the extent that global demand for consumer products remains robust, so, too, will China's demand for energy.

That China's energy demands for the foreseeable future are linked to the dual phenomena of urbanization and globalization is important in two respects. On the urbanization front, it means that nonproduction-related energy consumption will likely increase significantly only in the future, particularly once the growing numbers of urban residents begin consuming at levels comparable to global norms. On the globalization front, it means that China's appetite for energy is in many ways a reflection of the global appetite—particularly in advanced industrial markets—for consumer goods, production of which is increasingly concentrating in China. In this sense, the problem of Chinese energy demand, both in its origins and its potential solutions, must be understood as global in nature. In essence, Chinese and global sustainability have become one in the same.

Energy Intensity and per Capita Consumption

Energy intensity (consumption per unit of GDP) in China is one of the highest in the world: in 2002, it was more than 7.0 times that of Japan, 3.5 times that of the United States, and 1.7 times that of Indonesia (Sun 2003). Historically, as economies shift from agriculture to industry, energy intensity rises steadily; peaks with the deepening of heavy industry; begins dropping as technological transformation occurs; and then continues to descend with the shift into the more service-oriented, less manufacturing-intensive activities typical of postindustrial economies. Energy intensity peaked in the United States in 1920 and globally in 1955 (Sun 2003).

Table 6.3. Alternative Projections of Growth in Final Energy Demand in China, by Sector

End-use sector	Asia Pacific Energy Research Centre			International Energy Agency			Tsinghua University		
	Projected demand in 2020 (Mtoe)	Annual growth 1999–2020 (percent)	Share of total demand (percent)	Projected demand in 2030 (Mtoe) (percent)	Annual growth 2000–30 (percent)	Share of total demand in 2030	Projected demand in 2030 (Mtoe)	Annual growth 1999–2030 (percent)	Share of total demand in 2030 (percent)
Industry	605	2.7	46	553	1.9	43	696	1.6	41
Transport	205	5.3	16	236	4.1	23	339	4.0	20
Residential	397	1.5	30	217	3.1	17	464	1.8	27
Commercial	73	4.7	5	111	4.8	9	97	2.8	6
Other	43	3.2	3	97	1.6	8	101	4.1	6
Total	1,322	2.7	100	1,264	2.6	100	1,697	2.2	100

Source: APERC 2004.

Whether China has reached peak levels is debatable; the trends are ambiguous. In the first two decades of reform, particularly in the late 1990s, energy intensity declined, partly as a result of technological upgrading in heavy industry and power generation and partly as a result of the shutting down of obsolete firms (table 6.4). The decline may also have been an artifact of statistical anomalies surrounding underreported coal production and consumption. Whatever the cause, energy intensity appeared to be on the rise by 2002, the point, not coincidentally, at which the growing gap between the supply of and demand for electric power generation began resulting in more frequent service interruptions in booming manufacturing centers.

The globalization of production and the fragmentation of industrial supply chains—phenomena intimately linked to China's economic development—may have substantially changed the traditional relation between development and energy intensity. Because energy-intensive production activities can be geographically delinked from production-related services and management that are not energy intensive, countries like China may end up with disproportionately high levels of

Table 6.4. Energy Intensity, 1991–2005
(tons coal equivalent / GDP)

Year	Energy intensity
1991	5.12
1992	5.12
1993	4.42
1994	4.18
1995	4.01
1996	3.88
1997	3.53
1998	3.15
1999	2.90
2000	1.40
2001	1.33
2002	1.30
2003	1.36
2004	1.43
2005	1.22

Source: NBS various years.
Note: GDP for 1991–99 calculated at 1990 prices; GDP for 2000–04 calculated at 2000 prices; 2005 GDP calculated at 2005 prices.

energy-intensive production, while advanced industrial societies continue to produce higher-value services that are not energy intensive. Whole industries need not move globally, only particular segments of those industries. For prolonged periods, economies such as China's are therefore not likely to attract a full-package of industrial activities (services and production) but a package heavily tilted toward energy-intensive activities. This is true both regionally and globally: more advanced economies, particularly in northeast Asia, have moved both manufacturing assembly operations and their industrial-driven energy needs and energy externalities to China (Gaulier, Lemoine, and Unal-Kesenci 2006). Although China is more energy intensive than advanced industrial economies, its per capita energy consumption is nevertheless relatively modest. Low per capita consumption figures, however, do not suggest that China, even if it were to achieve its efficiency targets, could simply do with its energy crunch what it has in so many other areas of economic and institutional reform—that is, grow its way out of the problem. To the contrary, low per capita consumption suggests that energy demand in China is likely to rise substantially. Although high U.S. consumption patterns might not presage China's future, the more modest patterns associated with Japan, the Republic of Korea, or the European Union—already several times China's current consumption levels—probably serve as indicators of the direction in which China is heading.

Moreover, because of several factors—some specific to China, others related to broader changes in the global organization of production—energy intensity is unlikely to decline as quickly as that of previous modernizers. Because it enjoys the mixed blessing of vast domestic coal reserves, for the foreseeable future China will probably continue to rely on coal as the main source of energy. With its high carbon content, coal burns less efficiently than other hydrocarbons (such as oil or natural gas). The more carbon in a hydrocarbon fuel, the less energy it has (lower hydrogen to carbon ratios entail lower efficiency of combustion). To the extent that China remains dependent on coal, it will have to forgo the efficiency gains associated with the switch even to alternative fossil fuels. In addition, higher quality coal is concentrated in the north and northwest, thus necessitating energy-consuming (often oil-consuming) transport to industrial centers along the eastern and southeastern coast (60 percent of railroad transport is powered by coal). China's problem, therefore, is not just that fuel has to be transported over great distances but that the material being transported is not energy dense.

China's Unique Energy Security Challenge

The nature of China's "energy security" challenge goes beyond the fact that growth and modernization alone are not solutions to the supply-demand gap. In the broadest sense, energy security involves the accommodation of difficult-to-reconcile objectives: adequate energy for long-term economic growth, energy that can be secured without exposure to undue geopolitical risk, energy supply and utilization consistent with long-term public health, and energy supply flexible enough to meet rising popular expectations for public and private goods.

Under normal circumstances, these demands would be difficult to meet. China's circumstances are not "normal," however, for several reasons. First, on the domestic front, the variables feeding into the energy security calculus are shifting with extreme rapidity. China is simultaneously experiencing an industrial revolution, an economic boom, a rapid phase of urbanization, and, in many respects, an information revolution, particularly at the level of the individual citizen. Citizens have increasingly come to expect not only macroeconomic growth and the energy necessary to fuel that growth but also a wide array of goods associated with advanced economies (consumer goods, ranging from refrigerators to automobiles, and public goods, ranging from clean air to comprehensive health care). This expectation means that energy provision—in terms of both quantity and quality—has become central to the issue of good governance. Put simply, good governance in China today entails fueling an industrial revolution as dramatic as anything experienced by 19th century England but doing so in a manner acceptable to a public whose living standard expectations are decidedly 21st century and cosmopolitan.

Second, these challenges must be resolved at a time when at least one key global energy resource, petroleum, appears to be approaching depletion in the medium term. Optimistic forecasts suggest that peak global oil production (Hubbert's Peak, or the point at which expansion of production ceases and a depletion curve ensues) will occur around 2035; more pessimistic views assert that this point has already been reached (Deffeyes 2005). The amount of oil recorded each year as known reserves peaked in 1961. Since then, technological advances have permitted commercially sustainable drilling in the North Sea, Africa, and the Arctic. Much of the "easy oil" appears to have been extracted, however, and new finds are becoming smaller and smaller. The "easy oil" that does exist remains primarily in the Persian Gulf and more broadly in member nations of the Organization of the Petroleum Exporting Countries (OPEC).

In 2006 Gulf countries accounted for 31.1 percent of global crude oil production. Saudi Arabia alone accounted for 12.9 percent of global production (IEA 2007a). Given political instability in the region, the security and reliability of these flows are uncertain. Precisely as China moves toward becoming a modern economy, the future availability of petroleum is in serious doubt.

Whether and when peak global oil production will be reached is uncertain. What is clear, however, is that China is viewed by many of the world's largest energy producers and consumers alike as putting a major new strain on global energy resources and markets. China's consumption patterns, and the choices China makes to secure the resources needed to meet those consumption needs, have become matters of concern for a number of countries. Geostrategically, "business as usual" on the energy front for China may entail increased competition and conflict with other major consuming nations, particularly the United States. China has little choice, then, but to seek to redefine traditional developmental paths and chart an alternative energy course into the future.

Internalizing Externalities

Charting a path to the future involves complex decisions, ultimately about price. In the case of energy, however, calculation of price entails the internalization of extensive and highly ambiguous externalities. Coal, for example, appears inexpensive in the near term for China. But if coal is burned without environmental cleanup mechanisms, flue gas desulfurization systems, and related technologies, it imposes a costly public health toll. To the extent that the public deems urban environmental conditions unacceptable, such sentiments also have political ramifications.

Factoring these costs in raises the cost of domestic coal. But replacing coal with alternative energy sources, such as imported petroleum or natural gas, also creates negative externalities, such as the need to invest in military assets to protect sea lanes or in diplomatic relationships with suppliers. Taking these considerations into account, coal—albeit coal produced using sophisticated decarbonization, gasification, or liquefaction processes—may be the least costly fuel after all.

Some "clean-coal" technologies, while promising, are unproven technologically and commercially. Development costs may be high, but they may permit the realization of positive externalities in industrial innovation and global competitiveness. Even in the relatively near term—the 5- to 10-year horizon—externalities make the calculation of cost in the energy sector exceedingly complex, enough so to force policy makers to consider all options.

Given the scope of its energy needs, and its centrality in global production networks, China appears likely to be the place where "new to the world" energy-related innovations—in civilian nuclear power, clean-coal technologies, efficiency-related upgrades on the consumption side, and a variety of other areas—will be implemented for the first time. Whether it is foreign or domestic players who design and implement these innovations is open to question; that China will be the venue is almost beyond doubt. How this emerging reality will then feed back into Chinese economic development and affect China's position globally on the industrial innovation front represents an important issue for policy makers and commercial actors alike.

Trends in Energy Consumption

China accounted for 14.2 percent of the world's total energy consumption in 2005 (IEA 2007a). Virtually across the board in the energy sector, China represents the fastest-growing market in the world. Electric power generation, 70–80 percent of which is consumed by industry (a range that has remained relatively stable in the reform era) faces tremendous expansion pressures to meet the relatively conservative projections for industrial demand growth. The industrial sector is the driver of outcomes today; demand in the transport, urban residential, and commercial sectors remains relatively small but will grow significantly in the future (table 6.5).

Transport and Automobiles

For decades, primary energy consumption in China has been dominated by the electric power sector. This trend continues today at steady growth levels, predictably driving demand for domestic coal.

A newer, more dynamic, and less predictable phenomenon is the rising demand from the transport sector, demand that involves liquid hydrocarbons—petroleum today, but possibly liquefied natural gas and coal-based liquids in the future. As the government ramps up infrastructure investment and continues to promote the automobile industry, transportation-related energy demand is projected to rise 4.0–5.5 percent a year in the medium term. Noteworthy is both the pace of growth and the fact that the required fuels are domestically scarce.

The increase in demand for petroleum is already evident. By the start of 2004, China was just overtaking Japan as the world's second-largest

Table 6.5. Total Energy Consumption, by Sector, 1997–2005
(ten thousand tons coal equivalent)

Sector	1997	1998	1999	2000	2001	2002	2003	2004	2005
Industry	92,375.3	88,521.9	87,151.2	95,442.8	98,273.3	104,088.1	121,731.9	143,244.0	159,491.6
Total residential consumption	16,368.0	14,392.7	15,213.9	15,964.6	16,567.5	17,527.4	19,827.2	21,281.0	23,449.5
Transport, storage, and post	7,286.3	7,957.0	9,011.8	10,067.1	10,363.0	11,171.0	12,818.8	15,104.0	16,629.2
Farming, forestry, animal husbandry, fishery, and water conservancy	5,905.4	5,790.3	5,993.4	6,045.3	6,400.3	6,612.5	6,716.0	7,679.9	7,918.4
Wholesale and retail trade and catering	2,394.4	2,552.1	2,901.5	3,038.8	3,265.0	3,520.3	4,179.6	4,820.3	5,031.1
Construction	1,179.0	1,612.1	1,979.4	2,142.5	2,234.0	2,543.7	2,859.6	3,258.6	3,411.1
Other	4,702.8	5,212.6	5,562.5	5,851.5	6,096.4	6,334.1	6,818.7	7,838.8	8,691.2
Total	137,799.0	132,213.9	133,831.0	138,552.6	143,199.2	151,797.3	174,951.6	203,227.0	224,682.0

Source: NBS various years.
Note: Totals may not sum correctly because of rounding errors.

consumer of petroleum products. Almost a decade earlier in 1993, China had become a net importer of oil (U.S. Department of Energy 2006). China's oil demand is projected to reach 14.2 million barrels a day by 2025 (see table 6.2).

Chinese demand for oil imports rose steadily throughout the 1990s, at 4 percent a year; by 2005, domestically produced crude oil accounted for only 55 percent of total Chinese oil consumption. Strong demand for oil has made China a significant enough oil importer to move markets. The spring 2004 spike in oil prices was at least partly related to China's surging demand for imports, particularly in the context of an increasingly uncertain geopolitical situation in the Persian Gulf. Economic development naturally increases demand for transportation- and transport-related fuels. Rapid industrialization drives demand for electric power, which drives demand for coal, which must be transported through an increasingly extensive rail and road system. Similarly, expansion and integration of markets for intermediate industrial and final consumer goods means that increasing amounts of material must be transported by air, rail, and road. Throughout the 20th century, modernization has entailed the expansion of transport economies. And unlike electric power generation, transport depends almost exclusively on oil: transport accounted for 60.3 percent of world oil consumption in 2005, the single-largest sector by far (IEA 2007a).

In China, this natural shift is being accelerated and encouraged by governmental policy. The automobile sector has been promoted as a key "pillar" industry, on the basis of a series of presumed spillover effects. Its extensive network of supporting and related industries is expected to provide employment, and its technology intensity is expected to promote innovation and global competitiveness. Its final product simultaneously drives the deepening of financial markets (through auto financing), stimulates growth (through personal consumption), and meets demands for mobility and modernity on the part of an increasingly sophisticated emerging middle class.

China is hoping that the automobile industry will do for it in the 21st century what the industry did for the United States and Japan in the 20th century. The danger is that China is pursuing this industrial strategy at a time when petroleum resources globally are becoming stretched and popular awareness of the potential impact on already strained domestic environmental and infrastructure conditions is growing. In this sense, China is on a trajectory comparable to other developing nations, such as Thailand, where rapid growth in personal transportation led to severe traffic congestion and severe environmental problems in urban areas.

China's automobile sector has boomed since 2001. In 2002, China produced and sold 1 million cars, up 50 percent from the previous year. In 2006, China surpassed Japan as the world's second-largest auto market (behind the United States), with total sales of 7.2 million units ("China 2007 Auto Output"). By 2030 the total number of vehicles, estimated at 37 million vehicles in 2006, is expected to grow to 370 million (Rosen and Houser 2007). Between 2002 and 2012, Chinese purchases are expected to account for one-fifth of all new car sales in the world (Rosen and Houser 2007).

Automobiles create a variety of negative externalities. Although use of newer vehicles tends to increase fuel efficiency on a vehicle-mile basis, the trend globally in recent years has been toward decreases in fuel efficiency on a passenger-mile basis, as rising levels of automobile ownership have increased the use of single-occupant vehicles, increasing traffic congestion. Such conditions are already apparent in most major Chinese cities. Particularly when promoted officially as the anchor of a consumer economy and socially as a key indicator of sophistication and modernity, automobiles encourage extremely inefficient utilization of energy, with substantial environmental costs. Advances in internal combustion engine technology, infrastructure, and "smart" traffic management systems will lead to efficiency gains in the future, but they are likely to be offset by the inefficiencies of declining mass-transit use and the rising costs of pollution. China's macroeconomic growth requires the expansion of the transport economy, but automobiles need not be a primary mode of transportation. That they have become one is a reflection of choice rather than necessity.

This choice induces energy-related externalities in urban planning. Promotion of automobiles necessitates massive road and infrastructure construction. Severe constraints on land in Chinese cities and limited public funds mean that construction of this infrastructure comes at the expense of mass-transit systems. At the individual consumer level, automobile ownership has enabled movement, particularly by the wealthy, to suburbs, where parking is available, larger homes (associated with more energy-intensive heating and cooling, more appliances, and so forth) are possible, and commuting in a single-occupant vehicle is common.

The substantial investments being made in the extensive supporting energy infrastructure for automobiles—petroleum distribution facilities, filling stations, and so forth—raise the costs of switching to alternative transportation fuels in the future. This extensive supporting infrastructure creates a variety of vested interests that also make it difficult to switch to alternative fuels and alternative modes of transportation.

The decision to promote automobiles will have tremendous ramifications for China's ability to adapt to changing energy circumstances in the future. Significant vulnerabilities (urban pollution and congestion, dependence on external and uncertain sources of oil, and so forth) and substantial opportunity costs (investment in a public transport infrastructure, investment in alternative fuels, and so forth) are being incurred as a result.

Urban Residential and Retail Energy Demand

The second major shift in energy demand is coming from rising urban residential and commercial utilization. Urbanization and rising incomes are usually accompanied by steep increases in household electricity consumption. Acquisition of energy-consuming durable goods (washing machines, televisions, refrigerators, and PCs) becomes the norm, and demand for energy-intensive heating and cooling rises. In 1990, there were about 42 refrigerators and 59 color televisions and 0.34 air conditioners for every 100 urban households in China. By 2005, those figures had grown to 91, 135, and 81, respectively (NBS 2006).

Globally, increasing urban demand for electricity has moved forward in tardem with global information technology (IT) revolution. On the one hand, the proliferation of computers, routers, and related IT infrastructure has permitted the realization of certain energy efficiencies. Lean production has led to efficiencies in transport and transport-related fuels; digital transmission of information has reduced the need for face-to-face interaction and related travel; and IT–related smart traffic management systems ease energy-wasting congestion. On the other hand, increases in efficiency have been outmatched by the even greater increases in aggregate energy demand as residential and commercial consumers around the world are surrounding themselves with IT-related products and equipment. The net result has been that in the context of the IT revolution, countries as diverse as the United States and China have experienced increased demand for electricity in the urban household and retail sectors.

Urban populations are more directly exposed to the pollution effects of power generation. Thus, clean power generation becomes a primary concern, as does the desire to move heavy industry outside cities, increasing the need for energy-consuming transportation development. Pressure for clean power encourages the promotion of noncoal-fired power plants, increasing demand for fuels such as natural gas or liquefied natural gas, which, particularly in the east and southeast, increasingly come from overseas. Urban consumer electricity demand entails more-complex power management than traditional industrial utilization. Consumer demand fluctuates on a seasonal and daily basis; it not infrequently exhibits significant surges. Variability and intermittency create pressures for movement toward more flexible fuels and generating facilities and more-distributed modular power systems. Traditional large-scale coal-fired plants become far less attractive, whereas smaller-scale systems, often utilizing natural gas or other more energy-dense fuels, which can be brought on and off line, gain in appeal. As distributed power systems (based on fossil fuels or renewable alternatives) proliferate, pressures increase to find an effective currency for energy, a storage fuel (liquefied hydrogen, liquefied coal, coal-based syngas, or a variety of other options) that can be transported easily across complex networks of smaller power-generation facilities and multiple utilizations.

Rising urban demand creates pressures for substantial change in urban energy infrastructure, energy management, and technological development. Concerns about energy consumption should force thoughtful consideration of public choices about urbanization strategy. Even with an effective push toward efficient distributed power systems, China will still likely suffer stiff energy penalties if policies of dispersed urbanization are pursued. This is particularly true in transport, because smaller-scale, more-dispersed locales are less suited than large compact settings to extensive intraurban public transportation development. At the same time, dispersed urbanization creates pressures for more-extensive, energy-intensive interurban transport, whether by road, rail, ship, or air.

Trends in Energy Production and Supply

Domestic production and supply of all fuels have increased since 2001. Despite those efforts, supply has been outstripped by demand.

Coal

In 2005, 76.4 percent of China's primary energy production came from coal, 12.6 percent from petroleum, 3.3 percent from natural gas, and less than 7.7 percent from nuclear, hydropower, and wind (NBS 2006). In terms of the narrow definition of cost, coal is the cheapest fuel for large power plants. The power industry in China is by far the largest consumer of primary energy. Moreover, heavy industry—which is likely to remain a substantial component of the Chinese economy, regardless of gradual shifts toward services and more information-intensive sectors—is a massive consumer of crude coal.

While over the long run, coal's share in overall national energy consumption will gradually fall, absolute demand for coal will continue to rise, and for the foreseeable future, coal will remain the mainstay of China's energy supply (MIT 2007).

Efficiency gains can be realized at various stages, including in the processing and conversion, transportation, storage, and final consumption of coal. Several projects exist for the colocation of large coal-fired power plants near large, high-quality, low-sulfur content mines. One advantage of locating coal near these mines is that crude coal no longer need be transported across great distances. Options for utilizing the power that is generated include transmitting coal by wire across power lines, with some loss resulting in the process; creating coal-based liquid fuels, which could be transported relatively cheaply and could substitute for petroleum in the transport sector; producing coal slurry, which could be transported by pipeline; and, potentially in the future, producing liquefied hydrogen.

A number of experimental projects are under way, including the Shenhua Group's coal liquefaction facility in Inner Mongolia and a variety of other efforts involving coal gasification and coalbed methane production (UNESCO 2007). China has also expressed interest in experimental de-carbonization and carbon dioxide sequestration technologies for coal-based power generation.

Petroleum

Use of petroleum and natural gas, while still a small portion of China's total energy supply, has accelerated in recent years. This trend is consistent with pressures associated with modernization and other policy-induced factors (particularly the emphasis on automobile production and ownership). Rising use of petroleum and natural gas increases dependence on overseas energy resources (table 6.6).

In response to this growing dependence on imported oil, Chinese firms have been acquiring interests in overseas upstream exploration and production. Concessions have been acquired in Azerbaijan, República Bolivariana de Venezuela, Indonesia, Islamic Republic of Iran, Iraq, Kazakhstan, Peru, and Sudan (U.S. Department of Energy 2006). The potential geopolitical risks are obvious, as is the challenge of competing with other import-dependent oil consumers in East Asia, namely, Japan and the Republic of Korea.

Natural Gas

Natural gas, which has never been an important fuel in China, began to receive substantial attention in the mid- to late-1990s. Accounting for 3 percent of total energy consumption in 2005 (NBS 2006), natural gas

Table 6.6. Imports and Exports of Energy, by Type, 1991–2005

(ten thousand metric tonnes, unless otherwise noted)

Item	1991	1995	1996	1997	1998	1999	2000	2001	2002	2003	2004	2005
Imports												
Coal	136.8	163.5	321.7	201.3	158.6	167.3	212.0	249.0	1081.0	1109.8	1861.4	2,617.1
Crude oil	597.3	3400.6	2261.7	3546.6	2732.0	3661.4	7027.0	6026.0	6941.0	9102.0	12272.0	12,681.7
Gasoline	11.2	15.9	7.9	8.4	1.5	0.0	n.a.	n.a.	n.a.	n.a.	n.a.	n.a.
Diesel	319.6	612.3	465.1	742.8	310.8	30.9	25.9	27.5	47.7	84.9	274.9	53.2
Kerosene	2.6	76.1	65.9	138.1	129.1	211.2	255.5	201.9	214.5	210.3	282.0	328.3
Fuel oil	124.6	659.1	942.6	1,371.1	1,627.2	1,757.0	1,480.0	1,823.6	1,659.7	2,395.5	3,059.2	2,608.6
Liquefied petroleum gas	n.a.	232.6	355.0	358.2	476.6	322.3	481.7	488.9	626.2	636.7	641.0	617.0
Other petroleum products	11.5	95.7	106.5	176.1	190.6	208.1	161.5	201.3	384.3	432.1	384.2	443.4
Natural gas (10^8 cubic meters)	n.a.	n.a.	n.a.	n.a.	n.a.	n.a.	n.a.	n.a.	n.a.	n.a.	n.a.	n.a.
Electricity (10^8 kWh)	31.1	6.4	1.2	0.9	0.2	3.7	15.5	18.0	23.0	29.8	34.0	50.1
Exports												
Coal	2,000.1	2,861.7	3,648.4	3,073.0	3,229.7	3,743.9	5,505.0	9,012.0	8,384.0	9,402.9	8,666.4	7,172.4
Crude oil	2,259.8	1,822.7	2,040.3	1,982.9	1,560.0	716.7	1,031.0	755.0	766.0	813.3	549.2	806.7
Gasoline	250.2	185.5	131.4	178.2	182.0	413.8	455.2	572.5	612.0	754.2	540.7	560.0
Diesel	121.0	130.6	157.4	232.1	98.5	60.5	55.5	25.6	124.0	224.0	63.7	147.6
Kerosene	32.1	37.4	74.4	72.3	91.6	125.0	198.8	182.2	170.0	201.7	205.0	268.7

(continued)

Table 6.6. Imports and Exports of Energy, by Type, 1991–2005 *(continued)*
(ten thousand metric tonnes, unless otherwise noted)

Item	1991	1995	1996	1997	1998	1999	2000	2001	2002	2003	2004	2005
Fuel oil	69.5	27.8	36.6	51.7	57.5	25.5	33.4	44.1	64.0	76.1	181.7	230.0
Liquefied petroleum gas	1.1	7.1	33.3	39.2	50.2	7.5	1.6	2.1	5.6	2.4	3.2	2.7
Other petroleum products	148.8	131.1	117.3	155.7	202.5	221.0	280.5	325.5	246.0	261.8	360.7	473.0
Natural gas (10^8 cubic meters)	n.a.	n.a.	n.a.	n.a.	n.a.	n.a.	n.a.	n.a.	n.a.	n.a.	24.4	29.7
Electricity (10^8 kilowatts)	2.6	60.3	37.1	72.0	71.7	91.5	98.8	101.9	97.0	103.4	94.8	111.9
Coke	108.3	886.1	768.6	1,058.1	1,146.4	997.4	1,520.0	1,385.0	1,357.0	1,472.1	1,501.2	1,276.4

Source: NBS various years.
n.a. Not available.

is expected to become an increasingly important fuel in the future as Chinese cities seek cleaner sources of energy (author interviews). Construction of the extensive infrastructure needed to support this fuel—pipelines to distribute gas; shipping trains, port terminals, and gasification facilities needed to handle imported liquefied natural gas—is well under way (Watts 2006).

Nuclear Power

Nuclear power has been developing rapidly, albeit from a low base, particularly with respect to the electricity sector. Generally speaking, nuclear power is a more expensive means of generating electricity than coal or natural gas.

In 2005, the government declared its goal of adding 40 GW of civilian nuclear power capacity by 2020. China's nine civilian nuclear reactors had a total generating capacity of roughly 7 GW in 2006 ("China's Goal" 2006). Nuclear power accounted for 2.3 percent of Chinese electricity generation and 0.85 percent of total Chinese energy production in 2004 (IEA 2007b). Even with the most ambitious growth program, nuclear power will likely account for little more than 5 percent of total energy supply in the coming decades.

Hydropower

Hydropower represents an important component of Chinese electric power generation, although it accounts for a relatively small component of total energy production. In 2004 hydropower accounted for 2 percent of total Chinese energy production and 16 percent of electric power generation (IEA 2007b).

Increasing hydropower's contribution to China's overall energy mix is difficult, because the sources of hydropower tend to be in the center and west of the country, far from the main areas of regional demand along the coast. The costs and energy inefficiencies associated with large-scale national transmission and distribution systems are immense and arguably prohibitive. These inefficiencies are exacerbated by the significant sociopolitical and environmental costs of large-scale hydropower projects.

Policy Directions for the Future

China's overall energy strategy is somewhat confused and uncoordinated—not unlike that of the world's other large consuming nations, including the United States. China has pursued a number of ambitious efficiency goals and conducted a variety of interesting local experiments. These include Beijing municipality's establishment of coal-free zones, Shanghai's maglev train, regional pollution-rights trading programs, a national tax on high-sulfur coal, and municipal efforts to shift public buses over to cleaner burning fuels. This multiplicity of approaches, however, particularly when combined with other national goals that impinge indirectly on energy, creates confusion and unintended consequences. Not unlike approaches to other aspects of institutional reform in China, energy policy has been fragmented, both horizontally and vertically. Numerous experiments, competing standards, and alternative microlevel approaches have been allowed to proliferate. At the same time, at the central level, as in most countries, various aspects of energy policy—or policy areas that impinge on energy issues—end up spread in uncoordinated fashion across a range of administrative organs. Such diffusion and fragmentation make all the more difficult the internalization of the externalities associated with national energy choices.

Whether by default or design, national industrial policy is energy policy. The decision to promote automobile production and consumption has implications for energy demand and urban planning; it also diverts research and development (R&D) resources away from alternative energy projects.

Macroeconomic growth policy is also energy policy. Policies that promote growth and urbanization not only increase demand for energy, they also alter the kinds of energy demanded.

Environmental regulatory policy is also energy policy, to the extent that it shifts the relative costs of fuels and the availability of energy-efficient appliances and materials. Health care policy is also energy policy, for it ultimately must cope with the impact of pollution on people. Finally, given increasing dependence on foreign energy sources, foreign policy is energy policy because ultimately it must be directed toward guaranteeing steady overseas supplies.

Meeting China's energy needs does not necessarily require centralized solutions, such as large-scale regional power-generation projects or nationally integrated power grids. Quite to the contrary, distributed, modularized power arrangements are in many cases better suited to China's highly varied geographic, demographic, and developmental landscape. The point is that given the centrality of energy policy to China's development goals, that centrality demands concerted attention and comprehensive cross-bureaucratic coordination.

By virtue of its market size and rapid rate of growth, China has the ability to make markets. In setting and enforcing tough energy-efficiency standards for consumer appliances and vehicles, the government leaves foreign producers little choice but to comply and innovate. Similarly, to the extent that domestic producers are forced to meet these standards, they develop core competencies in the design, development, and production of energy-efficient products, competencies for which global markets will only grow as energy constraints become more binding on all nations in the future.

As they chart their way to a more sustainable national energy posture, Chinese policy makers face important choices over a wide range of technologies and energy-related sectors. The areas and recommendations listed below are intended to outline the domains across which change is both possible and likely to proceed.

Improving Energy Efficiency

Rather than promoting automobiles or semiconductors as drivers of national innovation, the government should direct industrial policy toward the development of alternative-energy vehicles and renewable energy technologies. A national effort on these fronts not only would address domestic energy supply issues, but also would set up Chinese producers to become key innovators in an increasingly energy-constrained world. In short, China should use its power as a global producer and global consumer to make energy efficiency and energy-related innovation the core of its national industrial competitiveness.

China must deepen its commitment to end-use, energy-efficiency improvements. In many cases, regulations are already in place but not uniformly enforced. As the building of urban commercial and residential space ramps up, it is imperative that the government promote energy-efficient designs and construction materials. By the beginning of 2007, China had become the world's largest construction market, adding roughly 2 billion square meters of floor space every year (Worldwatch Institute 2007). As of the end of 2006, the manufacturing and transport of building materials, the construction of new residential and commercial space, and the heating and cooling of buildings consumed 45 percent of China's total primary energy. The 11th Five Year Plan (2006–10) calls for energy savings of 50 percent in new buildings, but local developers are loathe to pay the higher up-front costs for energy-efficient materials and building systems. Given the potential long-term energy—and, by extension, cost-savings from more-efficient construction techniques and materials—to government needs to enforce its emerging building standards and to educate the public at large about the overall economic and environmental benefits.

It is also imperative that the government enforce the new fuel standards for automobiles that it promulgated in 2004. Particularly given the appeal of its automotive market for global producers, China has every reason to become a global leader in pushing vehicle fuel and emissions standards. The first phase of the new standards went into effect in 2005, and the second phase will commence in 2008. Enforcement has been, and will continue to be, a main challenge in this process. Lax enforcement threatens to vitiate not just the standards but the credibility of the government more broadly.

End-use efficiency enhancement must be coupled with measures to ensure that efficiency gains do not lead to expanded usage, as they have in many countries. Achieving this goal will inevitably involve complex management of domestic tariff structures. In transport, for example, the government will almost certainly have to explore restrictions on automobile access to urban areas (along the lines of London's congestion pricing or Singapore's road-use pricing).

Allowing Market Forces to Operate

It is critical that energy prices be permitted to reflect market forces of supply and demand. For the most part, coal prices in China do reflect current domestic supply and demand conditions, but prices for oil and electricity clearly do not. The current system of setting domestic oil prices based on international levels (through a formula based on monthly averages in Singapore, Rotterdam, and New York) insulates domestic prices from local market guidance and leads to shortages. Oil prices need to be freed up domestically, so that domestic suppliers and consumers can adjust accordingly.

Similarly, retail electricity prices tend to be shielded from market guidance. Prices are kept artificially low, facilitating even more rapid growth in household appliances and unprecedented high peak power loads in major Chinese cities. What results are blackouts and brownouts. Electricity prices must be allowed to reflect basic fuel prices, for coal, oil, or natural gas.

Shifting to Gasification

Although coal will remain the dominant primary energy source, emphasis must shift from combustion technologies to gasification. Such technologies permit the production of cleaner gas and liquid coal-based fuels, alternatives to imported natural gas and petroleum. Gasification and liquefaction also facilitate potentially commercially viable carbon dioxide capture and sequestration, thus addressing the emission not only of sulfur dioxide but also of carbon-related greenhouse gases. These technologies are still experimental today; focused research and development efforts are required to bring down costs and attain commercial viability. Such improvements are arguably more important—and more globally applicable—than anything else China could do today in the area of national industrial policy.

Integrating Renewable Energy Sources on a Large Scale

With the development of more-modular, distributed power systems, the ability to integrate renewable energy sources on a large scale becomes increasingly feasible. As suggested by the government's 2005 National Renewable Energy Law, there is potential for far greater use of wind and solar energy. Using Japan's example to craft a regulatory framework that supports photovoltaic use in urban residential and commercial buildings or Germany's Freiburg model to promote both wind and solar power at the municipal level ("Germany Sets Shining" 2007), China could substantially increase its use of alternative renewables. Large-scale wind farms in the west could be linked to urban centers by high-voltage DC transmission lines. With or without a shift toward hydrogen, China should aim to rely on alternative wind and solar power for 10 percent of its total energy supply by 2020. This would involve using sizable tracts of land not too far from centers of consumption.

Price Reform and Marketization in the Power Sector

It is in the power sector that some of the most dramatic changes in China's energy posture are manifested today. Driven both by industrial and urban household consumption, demand for electricity is soaring in China. As China rushes to meet this demand by building new generation facilities, expanding transmission networks, and securing new sources for key fuels, the ramifications for everything from living standards to overall national security are vast. On the electricity supply side, China faces urgent decisions regarding types of generation technologies and fuel feedstocks to invest in, the location of new generation facilities, and the upgrading of transmission networks to transport power regionally and nationally. On the demand side, equally substantial issues are associated with how, where, and when consumers use power.

The choices made today have monumental consequences for the future. Through these choices, China can launch itself on a path of sustainable energy utilization—a path that will at once foster growth, rising living standards, and stability, both within and beyond China's borders.

Principles of Marketization and Pricing in the Power Sector

Technological innovation and efficiency-promoting regulation in the power sector are important elements of a long-term strategy. But the most fundamental element—the one on which the success of further reforms will hinge—is the issue of price reform and marketization. Prices in any market are essential not just for collecting revenue but also for ensuring sufficient supply and efficient utilization. To the extent that price signals are clear and unrestricted, they indicate to consumers the cost of producing the goods or services consumed; they indicate to producers the willingness of consumers to pay. In theory, the market-clearing price should settle at the intersection of the marginal cost of the last producer and the marginal value to the last consumer. It is through this price that resource allocation should ultimately be determined.

Pricing for power is not so simple. Electricity consumption flows over time in a pattern of wide peaks and troughs. Because electricity cannot be effectively stored in low-demand periods, it must be generated when needed. This fact has several important ramifications for the prices of electricity generation.

First, it makes sense economically to build generating plants of varying technologies and fuel types. Some plants should be able to run all the time at low cost (without being easily be ramped up or down in the short run); others should be able to start and stop on short notice.

Second, as demand rises and falls, certain generating plants will come on- and offline. The determination of the order by which this takes place ("dispatch") should be driven by short-run marginal cost. Through "merit-order dispatch," plants with the lowest marginal costs are brought online first, with those with higher marginal costs brought online in succession as demand rises. In this manner, short-run costs to the system as a whole are minimized.

Third, the price paid by the final customer should be set at the marginal cost of the system as a whole. The marginal cost of a generating system is the running cost of the last (most expensive) generating plant brought online each hour plus the value to the consumer of electricity at times when the system is short of capacity. In other words, output prices for generation should be set at the running costs of the marginal producer for each hour plus—for peak hours—a charge that recovers the investment cost of a peaking plant.

Transmission pricing, in its intermediary position between generation and distribution, has its own complexities. In a marketized electricity sector, one would expect to see a variety of competing generators that are dispatched on merit order. Given current wire-based technologies, however, transmission tends to be a monopoly activity necessitating some sort of regulated price. If the goal were simply to keep the transmission company solvent, one could divide total needed revenues by all the electricity sold, thus creating a "postage stamp" for use of the transmission system. Such a mechanism would ensure cash flow to cover the transmission company's existing cost structure, but it would not provide any pressures or incentives to shift the underlying technologies or management practices driving that cost structure. To achieve the incentive effects needed for efficient resource allocation and utilization, however, a more complex, market-oriented tariff is necessary, for two main reasons.

First, for efficient real-time use of a transmission network, users who at any given time are willing to pay more (and thus value the network more) need to be given priority over those who do not. Prices must ultimately manage congestion, a problem that if left unresolved leads to power outages and instability in the power system. The costs of such strain must be internalized. One mechanism for doing so involves the use of "nodal pricing." In any power system, unique "prices" for electricity can be defined at each node of the transmission system. Such prices vary locationally, depending on the amount of congestion in the system at a given point and the distance from generating plants (because distance drives the amount of electricity lost through transmission). In a marketized system, generators are paid the price at their location, while large consumers and distribution companies pay the price at their location. Congestion rents accumulate when nodal prices diverge. Regulation and supervision is then required to ensure that the transmission company—a local or regional monopoly in most cases—does not grab these rents and thus face incentives to increase congestion.

Second, marketized transmission prices are necessary to guide longer-term location and investment decisions, whether for electricity producers and consumers. Electricity generators generally like to be near their fuels, while major industrial consumers like to be near their markets and customers. Transmission tariffs need to reflect the systemic costs (caused by increased congestion or increased electrical losses) imposed by such decisions. The combination of a "postage stamp" transmission access fee and nodal price transmission tariff can achieve this reflection.

In summary, efficient, sustainable utilization of energy resources depends on myriad interconnected decisions by producers and consumers. The market, operating through the mechanism of price, is the most effective mechanism for guiding these decisions. Given the unique features of the electric power sector, however, marketization can proceed only if certain conditions are met. Because of the differing market structures of generation, transmission, and distribution, these three areas must be separated out in terms of both pricing and ownership. It is not enough simply to aggregate a series of charges related to electricity production and delivery and then divide them by a unit of electricity sold. Rather, to facilitate merit-order dispatch on the generation side—a critical underpinning of market pricing—competition must be permitted among generators.

Moreover, to ensure that dispatch actually proceeds on the basis of marginal cost, ownership of generation must be separated from ownership of transmission. To the extent that transmission entities are permitted to own generators, conflicts of interest inevitably arise, because transmitters favor their own generators in the dispatch ordering process and block the entry of new generators. Furthermore, particularly given the key role of regulation in the less competitive parts of the power sector (transmission and distribution), regulatory power must be separated from ownership.

Although the application of competition and market pricing generally begins in generation, it must not stop there. Particularly for systems facing immediate pressures for physical expansion, transmission pricing must go beyond mere access fees to ultimately reflect the costs of congestion and distance-induced losses. It is only at that point that price will effectively guide the sort of longer-term investment decisions by electricity producers and consumers that deeply affect the efficacy and physical status of the power system as a whole.

Reform and Marketization in the Chinese Power Sector
Market restructuring of the power sector has been a clear policy goal of the government since at least the mid-1990s. The 1996 Electricity Law permitted the entry of nonstate entities into the generating sector, recognized the need for electricity prices to cover producer costs, and acknowledged the need to separate the regulatory function of the government from the ownership role of power producers. This law was followed in 1998 by State Council Document 146, which mandated the separation of ownership of electricity generation from the transmission network, thus providing the means for an unbundling of generation and transmission prices and the means for merit-order dispatch.

State Council Document 5, issued in 2002, pushed the agenda substantially forward by calling for full competition in the power sector, beginning with generation. Market trials permitting generators to sell power directly to large customers were permitted. The document also identified a series of longer-term goals, including (a) the formal separation of generation from transmission in terms of ownership and regulation; (b) the establishment of competitive regional markets for dispatching generators; (c) the establishment of new pricing mechanisms, including mechanisms that take into account environmental impacts; and (d) the development of market-oriented pricing mechanisms for all parts of the electricity supply chain, including not just generation but also transmission, distribution, and retail pricing.

That the government committed itself to this highly ambitious and progressive agenda is both extraordinary and commendable. In at least one area—the freeing up of rules on power plant financing—the successes are indisputable. Changes appear to have been far less dramatic in other areas, although information is anecdotal. Diversification of financing for—and ownership over—power plants has driven a substantial ramping up of generating capacity since 2002.

At the same time, a vast gap remains between these goals and reality on the ground. Several reforms need to be made.

Improve the pricing of electricity. China's system of electricity pricing remains rigid, inefficient, and nonmarket oriented. Those are basically two types of tariffs: one for the purchase of power by provincial or regional power companies from independent power producers and one for the purchase by final consumers from the power company. The first tariff is determined contractually on a generator-by-generator basis. The second tariff is fixed, varying only by class of consumer (industrial versus household, high-voltage versus low-voltage, and so forth). The vast complexity in pricing is based not on time, place, or extent of usage—the factors one would expect market pricing to be based on—but on the nature of the customer. Moreover, these tariffs are unresponsive to shifts in supply and demand.

Unbundle generation and transmission pricing. No clear mechanism exists for passing along efficiency-related cost reductions on the part of generators to consumers, and no clear mechanism has been set for raising the funds needed to construct and upgrade transmission and distribution networks. No mechanism exists for incorporating into the final retail price of electricity the costs arising from system congestion and electricity loss through transmission.

Implement a clear method of market-oriented, merit-based generator dispatch. Dispatch hours (running times) are currently allocated to plants based on the principle of "fair" distribution. Because merit-order dispatch does not occur—and indeed cannot occur, to the extent that generation and transmission prices remain bundled—electricity prices remain fundamentally nonmarket oriented.

Simplify cross-subsidies and increase transparency of differential pricing systems. A substantial portion of electricity consumers—namely, the urban household sector—pay a low price for electricity, which is subsidized by higher-voltage industrial customers and the power generators themselves. Generators find themselves caught between liberalized, rising fuel costs and governmental restrictions on the amount that can be charged for electricity production. Even some of the newer power projects that have power purchase agreements (PPAs) with regional grid companies—which mandate prices higher than national standards—have faced substantial problems. The PPA mandated prices have been overridden by governmental pricing bureaus in the name of fighting inflation. Moreover, in regions where surplus power exists, state grid companies in some cases have refused to abide by the PPA take-or-pay clauses to which they initially agreed.

Implement regulatory restructuring. To the extent that the distinction between transmission company and generator and between commercial operator and governmental regulator remains blurry, real marketization is unlikely to occur. The problems of inflexible tariffs, bundled tariffs, non-market-based dispatch, price subsidies, and regulatory conflicts of interest are deeply intertwined. These problems fundamentally impede the sort of market-oriented price reforms that are absolutely necessary to guide the behavior of commercial producers and consumers as well as long-term investment decisions.

China can and should pursue a variety of means of ensuring energy security for the future. Among these means are regulatory regimes that encourage energy conservation, diversification into new fuels, and development and dissemination of energy-saving technologies. In the near term, however, price reform in the power sector stands out as not just the single-greatest policy challenge but also the one that, if met, will yield the highest near-term returns and have the most profound impact on the behavior of energy producers and the growing numbers of urban consumers alike.

References

APERC (Asia Pacific Energy Research Centre). 2004. *Energy in China: Transportation, Electric Power, and Fuel Markets.* Institute of Energy Economics, Tokyo. http://www.ieej.or.jp/aperc/pdf/CHINA_COMBINED_DRAFT.pdf

"China 2007 Auto Output." http://www.Forbes.com, September 9.

"China's Goal to Increase Nuclear Power Difficult but Unchanged." 2006. Xinhua News Service, June 8.

Deffeyes, Kenneth S. 2005. *Beyond Oil: The View from Hubbert's Peak.* New York: Farrar, Straus and Giroux.

Downs, Erica S. 2004. "The Chinese Energy Security Debate." *China Quarterly* 177 (March): 21–41.

EIA (Energy Information Administration). 2003a. *China: Country Analysis.* U.S. Department of Energy, Washington, DC. http://www.eia.doe.gov.

———. 2006. *China: Country Analysis.* U.S. Department of Energy, Washington, DC. http://www.eia.doe.gov.

———. 2003b. *China: Environmental Issues.* U.S. Department of Energy, Washington, DC. http://www.eia.doe.gov.

———. 2004a. *China's Nuclear Industry.* U.S. Department of Energy, Washington, DC. http://www.eia.doe.gov.

———. 2004b. *International Energy Outlook 2004.* http://www.eia.doe.gov/oiaf/ieo/download.html

Gaulier, Guillaume, Françoise Lemoine, and Deniz Unal-Kesenci. 2006. "China's Emergence and the Reorganisation of Trade Flows in Asia." Centre d'Etudes Prospectives et d'Informations Internationales Working Paper 2006-05, Paris.

"Germany Sets Shining Example in Providing a Harvest for the World." 2007. *Guardian,* July 23.

Hunt, Sally. 2002. *Making Competition Work in Electricity.* New York: Wiley.

———. 2003. *Guiding Principles of Pricing: Jiangsu Power Sector Tariff Study.* World Bank, Washington, DC.

IEA (International Energy Agency). 2003. *Key World Energy Statistics.* http://www.iea.org.

———. 2007a. *Key World Energy Statistics.* http://www.iea.org.

———. 2007b. "Statistics by Country/Region." http://www.iea.org/Textbase/stats/index.asp.

Kroeze, Carolien, Jaklien Vlasblom, Joyeeta Gupta, Christiaan Boudri, and Kornelis Blok. 2004. "The Power Sector in China and India: Greenhouse Gas Emissions Reduction Potential and Scenarios for 1990–2020." *Energy Policy* 32 (1): 55–76.

Landsberg, Mitchell. 2007. "The World: China May Lead in Greenhouse Gases." *Los Angeles Times*, June 21.

Larson, Eric D., Wu Zongxin, Pat DeLaquil, Chen Wenying, and Gao Pengfei. 2003. "Future Implications of China's Energy-Technology Choices." *Energy Policy* 31: 1189–1204.

Manning, Robert A. 2000. *The Asian Energy Factor: Myths and Dilemmas of Energy, Security, and the Pacific Future.* New York: Palgrave.

McGregor, Richard. 2007. "China's Power Capacity Soars." *Financial Times.* February 6.

MIT (Massachusetts Institute of Technology). 2007. *The Future of Coal: Options for a Carbon-Constrained World.* Cambridge, MA. http://web.mit.edu/coal/.

NBS (National Bureau of Statistics). 2006. *China Statistical Yearbook.* Beijing: China Statistics Press.

National Research Council. 2004. *The Hydrogen Economy: Opportunities, Costs, Barriers, and R&D Needs.* Washington, DC: National Academies Press.

Ni, Weidou, and Thomas B. Johansson. 2004. "Energy for Sustainable Development in China." *Energy Policy* 32 (10): 1225–29.

Roberts, Paul. 2004. *The End of Oil.* Boston: Houghton Mifflin.

Rosen, Daniel, and Trevor Houser. 2007. "China Energy: A Guide for the Perplexed." In *China Balance Sheet.* Center for Strategic and International Studies and Peterson Institute for International Economics, Washington, DC.

Shiu, Alice, and Pun-Lee Lam. 2004. "Electricity Consumption and Economic Growth in China." *Energy Policy* 32 (1): 47–54.

Sinton, Jonathan E., and David G. Fridley. 2003. "Comments on Recent Energy Statistics from China." *Sinosphere Journal* 6 (2): 6–11.

Sun, J. W. 2003. "Three Types of Decline in Energy Intensity: An Explanation for the Decline of Energy Intensity in Some Developing Countries." *Energy Policy* 31 (6): 519–26.

UNESCO/Shell Chair in Coal Gasification Technology. 2007. "Report on Applying Coal Gasification Technology in China's Coal Chemical Industry." UNESCO, Beijing.

U.S. Department of Energy. 2005. *National Security Review of International Energy Requirements.* Washington, DC.

U.S. Department of Energy. 2007. "International Data Projections." http://www.eia.doc.gov/oiaf/forecasting.htm.

Victor, David G., Thomas C. Heller, Joshua C. House, and Pei Yee Woo. 2004. "Experience with Independent Power Projects (IPPs) in Developing Countries." Working Paper 23, Center for Environmental Science and Policy, Program on Energy and Sustainable Development, Stanford University, Palo Alto, CA.

Wald, Matthew L. 2004. "Questions about a Hydrogen Economy." *Scientific American* 290 (5): 66–74.

Wang, Xiaohua, and Zhenmin Feng. 2003. "Energy Consumption with Sustainable Development in Developing Country: A Case in Jiangsu, China." *Energy Policy* 31: 1679–84.

Watts, Jonathan. 2006. "Thirsty China Opens Huge LNG Terminal." *Guardian*, June 28.

Worldwatch Institute. 2007. "China Pushing for Energy Efficient Buildings." http://www.worldwatch.ore/node/4874.

Wu, Yanrui. 2003. "Deregulation and Growth in China's Energy Sector: A Review of Recent Development." *Energy Policy* 31 (15): 1417–25.

Yang, Hong, He Wang, Huacong Yu, Jianping Xi, Rongqiang Cui, and Guangde Chen. 2003. "Status of Photovoltaic Industry in China." *Energy Policy* 31: 703–07.

Zhang, Chi, and Thomas C. Heller. 2003. "Reform of the Chinese Electric Power Market: Economics and Institutions." Working Paper 3, Center for Environmental Science and Policy, Program on Energy and Sustainable Development, Stanford University, Palo Alto, CA.

Zheng, Li. 2007. "Energy and China." Paper presented at the MIT Energy Initiative Energy Seminar, Massachusetts Institute of Technology, Cambridge, MA, February 21.

CHAPTER 7

Water and Urbanization

Zmarak Shalizi

The geography, spatial characteristics, and pace of urbanization in China will be powerfully affected by the availability of potable water to urban residents and industry. This chapter examines the evolving water supply situation in China's urban sector; the degree to which water could constrain potential growth and urban development in parts of the country (Bao and Fang 2007); and the scope for enhancing the efficiency with which supplies are used and recycled.

The chapter is divided into six sections. The first section provides an overview of the growing scarcity of water in China. The second section describes patterns and trends of water supply. The third section describes the effect of pollution on water supply. The fourth section assesses the likely trajectory of water demand and its distribution across sectors. The fifth section draws some implications for investment. The final section provides some policy recommendations.

Low per Capita Availability of Water

China's total naturally available water flows (not stocks) from all surface and underground sources are estimated at about 2,812 billion cubic

The author would like to acknowledge the able research assistance provided by Holly Li, Siyan Chen, and Tomoko Okano, as well as comments and inputs provided by Hua Wang, Shahid Yusuf, Kaoru Nabeshima, and anonymous reviewers of earlier drafts.

meters a year, placing China fifth in the world, behind Brazil, the Russian Federation, Canada, and Indonesia (FAO 2007). However, on a per capita basis, China's naturally available annual water flow of 2,114 cubic meters per person in 2003–07 is one of the lowest levels in the world for a populous country, next only to India's 1,150 cubic meters per person (FAO 2007). China's available water per person is one-third the world average (6,794 cubic meters per person), and one-quarter the average for the United States (9,446 cubic meters per person) (World Bank 2007). Thus, in a global context, China's per capita availability of water is exceedingly low, suggesting the potential for water stress as demand for usable water rises with growth in population and per capita income.

Despite the one-child policy introduced in 1979, China's population has been growing steadily, from almost 1 billion in 1980 to 1.19 billion in 1993 and 1.31 billion in 2005 (table 7.1). As a result, annual per capita water availability dropped by 25 percent between 1980 and 2005, from 2,840 to 2,147 cubic meters per person (table 7.2).

Regional Differences in Water Availability

China's low natural availability of water per person masks substantial regional disparities in water availability.[1] Demand for water is growing throughout the country, but total water availability in the north is about one-sixth that in the south (405 billion cubic meters versus 2,406 billion cubic meters (see table 7.2) and one-tenth the world average (Wang and Lall 2002). The 596 cubic meters per person in the north in 2005 qualifies the north as a whole as an area of water scarcity, a condition worse than one of water stress.[2] The north is a very large area and was home to 680 million people (more than the total population of Europe or Latin America) in 2005. Although it accounts for roughly 52 percent of China's population, it has just 14 percent of China's water resources (NBS 2006).

Water scarcity is most acute north of the Yangtze River, particularly in the catchments of the Huai, Hai, and Huang (Yellow) Rivers (the 3-H

---

1 Average annual rainfall is about nine times greater in the southeast (1,800 millimeters) than in the northwest (200 millimeters). More than 45 percent of China receives less than 400 millimeters of precipitation a year (Economy 2004).

2 *Water scarcity* is defined as an annual supply of water less than 1,000 cubic meters per person. *Water stress* is defined as an annual supply of water of less than 2,000 cubic meters per person.

Table 7.1. Population of China, 1980–2005, by Region

| | Population | | | | | | | | Annual growth rate (percent) | | |
| | 1980 | | 1993 | | 2002 | | 2005 | | | | |
Region	Billion	Percent	Billion	Percent	Billion	Percent	Billion	Percent	1980–93	1993–2005	1980–2005
North[a]	0.52[b]	52.5	0.62	52.1	0.65	51.0	0.66	50.4	1.4[b]	0.5	1.0[c]
South[a]	0.48[b]	47.5	0.57	47.9	0.63	49.0	0.65	49.6	1.3[b]	0.1	1.2[c]
Urban	0.19	19.2	0.33	27.7	0.50	39.1	0.56	42.8	4.3	4.5	4.4
Rural	0.80	80.8	0.85	71.4	0.78	60.9	0.75	57.3	0.5	−0.01	−0.3
Total[c]	0.99	100.0	1.19	100.0	1.28	100.0	1.31	100.0	1.4	0.8	1.1

Source: NBS 1981, 1994, 2003, and 2006.

a. The north–south split is based on World Bank 2001a and IIASA 1993. North is defined as the Huai, Hai, and Huang River basin provinces (Beijing, Tianjin, Hebei, Shanxi, Inner Mongolia, Jiangsu, Anhui, Shandong, Henan, Shaanxi, Gansu, Qinghai, and Ningxia) and the three provinces in the northeast (Liaoning, Jilin, Heilongjiang). South is defined as the rest of China.

b. Figures are from NBS 1981 for 1981, and the population of south China does not include Hainan Province.

c. Excludes Hong Kong, Macao, and Taiwan.

Table 7.2. Gross Water Availability per Capita, in North and South, 1980–2005

	Gross water availability[a]		Water availability per capita (cubic meters)			
Item	Billion cubic meters	Percent of total[b]	1980	1993	2002	2005
Total	2,812	100	2,840	2,363	2,197	2,147
Surface	2,712	96 (76)				
Aquifer	829	29 (23)				
North	405	14	779	653	623	614
Surface	334	12 (10)				
Aquifer	169	6 (5)				
South	2,406	86	5,015	4,223	3,819	3,702
Surface	2,377	85 (67)				
Aquifer	678	24 (19)				

Source: IIASA 1993; table 7.1.
a. The sum of surface and aquifer water exceeds the total water resource by the amount of overlap between them.
b. The figures in parentheses are adjusted to account for the overlap.

rivers).[3] Since the 1980s, the magnitude and frequency of water shortages have been growing, generating severe economic losses.[4] Total water shortages in 2000 were calculated at 38.8 billion cubic meters; unless measures are taken to reduce demand and augment supplies, they are projected to reach 56.5 billion cubic meters by 2050. These shortages are estimated to cost the Chinese economy Y 5.0–Y8.7 billion a year (US$620 million–US$1.06 billion) (Economy 1997; Economy 2004).[5]

The problems in Beijing and the Hai River basin are well known but not unique. In the relatively dry regions in the north, northwest, and northeast, there are many large urban centers, including seven cities with populations of more than 2 million each and 81 cities with populations of 200,000–500,000 each. In many of the major cities, urban water use has increased, as mayors have embarked on beautification campaigns to

3 In the densely populated Hai River basin, for example, industrial output is growing rapidly, and the basin is intensively cultivated. However, water availability per capita is only 343 cubic meters a year. Residents in the Pearl River basin in the south have nine times more water available per capita.
4 Agriculture is the most water-intensive activity, followed by food processing, paper, and textiles (Guan and Hubacek 2007). It takes 1,000 tons of water to produce 1 ton of grain. The water-scarce north exports agricultural products to other regions, using 7,340 million cubic meters of water, of which 4,284 million cubic meters is from surface water resources and the rest from rainfall. This amounts to a net export of 5 percent of water resources from the north to other regions of China. In contrast, Guangdong, relatively water-rich province, imports water-intensive goods (about 445 million cubic meters) and produces or exports electric components and various commercial and social services, which are not water intensive (Guan and Hubacek 2007).
5 These numbers were calculated for all China as of 1997.

plant trees, shrubs, flowers, and grass along roadways and in municipal parks (USDA 2000), in part to attract new investments and skilled labor and in part to combat locally the effects of dust storms associated with the depletion of surface and aquifer water elsewhere. These large cities compete with agriculture for scarce water resources. The problems are emerging in an acute form in other metropolitan subregions experiencing very rapid growth, because the elasticity of water demand with respect to urban population growth is greater than one (Bao and Fang 2007). More than 400 of China's 600 cities are believed to be short of water, and about 100 face serious water shortage problems (Wang and Lall 2002).

To compensate for surface water scarcity, China uses a growing reliance on groundwater in the north and desalinated water in coastal areas.[6] Groundwater is being depleted at a faster rate than it is being replenished, leading to "mining" of aquifers. When aquifers are mined, they are not available as insurance in drought periods, compromising sustainable use of the resource for current as well as future generations. In 2006, 30 percent of arable land in Sichuan Province was expected to yield no output because of the drought ("Still Poor" 2006).[7] In some areas, the overuse of underground water is contributing to severe aridity and increasing migration away from fragile lands.

The extent of the mining of groundwater is severe. Sustainable groundwater flows in the Hai River basin have been estimated to be on the order of 17.3 billion cubic meters a year, while 1998 withdrawals were 26.1 billion cubic meters a year, indicating overextraction of as much as 8.8 billion cubic meters annually. As a result, groundwater

---

6 China is also investing heavily in desalination plants. The second-largest plant in the country, which can process more than 100,000 tons of water a day, will be built in Zhejiang, at a cost of Y 1.1 billion. Its production will enable it to supply industrial users and 500,000 people across the coastal Xiangshan county. More than 20 desalination plants process 120,000 cubic meters of seawater a day. By 2010 this will increase to 800,000–1 million cubic meters a day. The State Development and Reform Commission forecasts that desalinated water will account for 16–24 percent of water used in coastal areas in the future ("China Turns" 2007).

7 Rainfall in Guangdong Province was down 40 percent in 2005 (MacBean 2007). The worst drought in 30 years hit Liaoning in 2007, drying up 88 small and medium-size reservoirs and leaving 1.2 million people short of drinking water ("Drought Leaves" 2007). Water scarcity and climate change could reduce China's agricultural output by 5–10 percent by 2030. However, China is still aiming to achieve the target of producing 95 percent of its grain consumption domestically ("China to Keep" 2007). In addition to water shortages, air pollution reduces agricultural productivity. Almost 70 percent of the crops planted in China cannot attain optimal yields, primarily because of the haze from pollution (MacBean 2007; Shalizi 2007).

tables have dropped by as much as 90 meters in the Hai plains (World Bank 2001a). The groundwater table in Beijing is estimated to have dropped 100–300 meters. Anecdotal evidence suggests that some deep wells around Beijing now have to reach 1,000 meters to tap usable quantities of water, dramatically increasing the cost of water supply and the risk of contamination from arsenic and other contaminants.

The removal of underground water domes has many adverse consequences. It has resulted in saltwater intrusion along coastal provinces in 72 locations, covering an area of 142 square kilometers, according to one estimate (World Bank 2001a). It is also leading to subsidence in coastal and noncoastal areas. The subsidence is up to several meters in cities such as Beijing, Shanghai, Shijiazhuang, Taiyuan, and Tianjin, causing damage to buildings and bridges and even leading to their collapse. Subsidence of land as water is extracted is also diminishing flood protection and exacerbating water logging in urban areas, because drainage is less effective (World Bank 2001a).[8]

Contribution of Pollution to Water Shortages

Many of China's water bodies are polluted, some heavily so. Surface and groundwater pollution now represent a major problem for both public health and the environment. Pollution-degraded water exacerbates the shortage of water resources downstream. It also makes it difficult to recycle water where it is scarce. As such, pollution represents a growing constraint on national development objectives in China.

In 2003, 38 percent of China's river waters were considered to be polluted, up from 33 percent a decade earlier. According to the 2003 annual report of the State Environmental Protection Administration (SEPA), more than 70 percent of the water in five of the seven major river systems—the Huai, Songhua, Hai, Yellow, and Liao—was grade IV or worse, meaning it could not be used for of any designated beneficial uses. In the Hai and Huai River systems, 80 percent of the water was unusable (EIA 2003; SEPA 2003). Even the majestic Yangtze River suffered a sharp decline in water quality, more than doubling the percentage of its water not suitable for human contact to 48.5 percent in 2002 (Economy 2004).

Half of all water pollution is caused by nonpoint sources in rural areas, including fertilizer runoff (which increases the flow of nitrogen

---

8 Such environmental damage can be reduced with better management of groundwater extraction. See the example in Zhengzhou (Gong, Li, and Hu 2000).

and phosphorous into water bodies [see Palmer 2001]), pesticides; and waste from intensive livestock production. These problems, especially in certain rural areas close to cities, can be expected to worsen in the near future. With growing urban demand, livestock production has increased its contribution to the gross value of agricultural output from 14 percent in 1970 to 31 percent in 1998. Horticultural production for urban centers is also rising steeply. These trends are expected to continue, as urbanization increases, disposable incomes rise, and food distribution systems in rural areas improve. Rural sources of pollution, such as livestock operations, rural industry, and towns and villages, remain essentially uncontrolled and unaccounted for by current government management programs (Wang 2004).

The remaining half of water pollution comes from industrial and municipal wastewater discharges and the leaching of pollutants from unlined solid waste sites into surface or below-ground water bodies (World Bank 2004). The rapid growth in urban populations and industrial activities is adding to the pollution of China's waterways from phosphorous, indicator bacteria, metals, and solvents. In the absence of sufficient water treatment plants, large volumes of raw sewage are dumped into local streambeds daily, and industrial water is often untreated. Only 56 percent of urban wastewater was treated in 2006. The target is to reach 70 percent for cities with populations of more than 500,000 ("Strong Growth" 2007). When upstream water is returned to the stream polluted, water quality downstream is degraded. In some cases, polluted water in the streams has seeped into the groundwater (USDA 2000). Government monitoring and enforcement programs are having only limited impact, because of selective application of the laws and low levels of fines at the provincial and central levels, combined with weak enforcement of rules at the local level, which diminish the deterrence value of regulations. Regulations are also incomplete insofar as load-based standards are absent and the standards that are set are not achievable given China's current technological capabilities. For these reasons, "more than 75 percent of the water in rivers flowing through China's urban areas is unsuitable for drinking or fishing. Only 6 of China's 27 largest cities' drinking water supply meet State standards . . . [and] many urban river sections and some large freshwater lakes are so polluted that they cannot even be used for irrigation" (Economy 2004; see also ABS Energy Research 2006).

In 2000 the major water pollutant—chemical oxygen demand (COD) discharge—was split almost evenly between industrial and municipal sources.[9] Industrial sources, mostly in urban areas, contributed about 7.40 million tons, while municipal sources, from commercial, residential, and public amenities, contributed about 7.05 million tons of COD. Municipal wastewater and COD discharge has been growing (at 3.1 percent a year in the 1990s) relative to industrial wastewater discharge; by 2000, municipal wastewater discharge (at 22.1 billion tons) was 14 percent (2.7 billion tons) more than industrial wastewater discharge (Wang 2004). The costs of benefits forgone by not treating wastewater were estimated at Y 4 billion in 2000 rising to Y 23 billion in 2050 in the Hai and Huai basins (World Bank 2001a).

Disaggregating the total industrial discharge into sectors shows that six sectors (pulp/paper, food, chemicals, textiles, tanning, and mining) account for 87 percent of total industrial COD load but only 27 percent of the value of gross industrial output. Toxic pollution loads (principally metals and solvents) are undocumented but estimated to be about 1.7 percent of total COD loads, representing a significant threat to public health and aquatic systems. High pollution loads in the water seriously affect the pollution of coastal zone waters, which do not meet coastal zone standards for marine aquatic life (Wang 2004).

Recent Trends in Water Demand

Water use in China is sometimes disaggregated into four categories. Two reflect production-related demand by farms and factories (agriculture and industry), and two reflect consumption-related demand by households (rural and urban) (table 7.3).

Production-Related Demand

Agriculture remains the largest user of water in China, accounting for about 64 percent of the total in 2005 (NBS 2006), even though annual water use for agriculture decreased by 3 percent between 1980 and 2005 (from 370 billion to 358 billion cubic meters), as industrial and urban needs preempted agricultural needs, and productivity (efficiency) of water use in agriculture increased.

Industry, which has sustained double-digit growth rates since the early 1980s, is the second-most important source of demand for water.

---

9 COD measures the oxygen needed to decompose organic matter. The United States uses the five-day biochemical oxygen demand criterion (the amount of oxygen required by bacteria to break down organic matter over five days). The modeling of water quality and the factors influencing the level of dissolved oxygen are described by Palmer (2001).

Table 7.3. Water Use, by Sector, 1980–2005

	Water use										Annual growth rate (percent)		
	1980		1993		1997		2002		2005				
Sector	Volume (billion cubic meters)	Percent of total	Volume (billion cubic meters)	Percent of total	Volume (billion cubic meters)	Percent of total	Volume (billion cubic meters)	Percent of total	Volume (billion cubic meters)	Percent of total	1980–1997	1997–2005	1980–2005
Production	416	94	471	91	504	91	488	89	487	87	1.1	-0.4	0.6
Agricultural	370	83	383	74	392	70	374	68	358	64	0.3	-1.1	-0.1
Industrial	46	10	89	17	112	20	114	21	129	23	5.4	1.8	4.2
Domestic	28	6	47	9.1	53	9	62	11	68	12	3.7	3.2	3.6
Urban	6.8	1.5	24	4.6	25	4.4	32	5.8	n.a.	n.a.	7.9	5.3[a]	7.3[b]
Rural	21.3	4.8	23	4.4	28	5	30	5.4	n.a.	n.a.	1.6	1.4[a]	1.6[b]
Total	444	100	519	100	557	100	550	100	563	100	1.3	0.1	1.0

Source: IIASA 1999; NBS 2003, 2006.
n.a. Not available.
a. Figures are for 1997–2002.
b. Figures are for 1980–2002.

Between 1980 and 2005, water use in industry increased from 46 to 129 billion cubic meters, an increase of 280 percent. In 2005 industry accounted for 23 percent of total water consumption (NBS 2006).[10] Together, the production sectors—agricultural and industry—are responsible for 87 percent of water demand in China.

Some observers believe that water demand by industry may be decelerating, as industries are becoming more water efficient or shifting toward subsectors with lower water requirements (University of British Columbia 2004). The evidence for this, however, is still anecdotal. Even if a shift is occurring, as recently as the late 1990s, industry in China was consuming 4–10 times as much water as industry in more-industrial countries (Wang and Lall 2002). China uses six times more water per unit of GDP than the Republic of Korea and 10 times more than Japan ("Still Poor" 2006).

Consumption-Related Demand

Urban residential water demand was insignificant in 1980, at 1.5 percent of the total. By 2005, the number of residents in China's cities had more than doubled, from 191 million in 1980 to an estimated 562 million in 2005 (see tables 7.1 and 7.3), and their per capita income increased even more rapidly. As a result, between 1980 and 2002, urban residents' share of total water use quadrupled to almost 6 percent, with urban water consumption increasing from 7 billion to 32 billion cubic meters (see table 7.3). This increase reflects the rising standard of living in urban areas, which allowed urban residents to purchase washing machines and move into apartments with flush toilets and individual showers.[11] Urban areas experienced the largest increase in water use of any sector in the past two decades. The increase was accompanied by the rising discharge of black, yellow, and grey waters.

Per capita water use in cities varies greatly by region. Annual domestic demand in Beijing rose from 552 million cubic meters a year in 1993 to 829 million cubic meters in 2000. In contrast, in Tianjin, in the dry Hai River basin, residents still use only 135 liters of water a day—less than 40 percent of the 339 liters a day used by residents in the wet urban areas in the southern province of Guangdong (USDA 2000).

---

10 The growth of industrial water use in China is commensurate with its stage of development: water withdrawals for industry average 59 percent of total water use in high-income countries and just 8 percent of total water use in low-income countries (UNESCO 2003).

11 Domestic household consumption per capita rose tenfold in the past five decades, to 240 liters a day per person in 2000 (University of British Columbia 2004).

Future Demand Projections

Agriculture remains the largest consumer of water in China, but growth in demand has been greatest in urban and industrial use. In 2005, China consumed about 563 billon cubic meters of water, of which 64 percent was used for agriculture, 23 percent for industry, and 12 percent for household purposes. Demand for water grew at an annual rate of 7.3 percent for urban households and 4.3 percent for factories between 1980 and 2002, with water demand by rural households and farms remaining almost unchanged.

In the absence of a detailed and calibrated China-wide simulation model, it is difficult to analyze the implications of different scenarios for water demand. However, some aspects of future water demand can be analyzed with the aid of a simple simulation model (Shalizi 2006). The model is used as a broad-brush illustrative exercise to understand the key drivers of water demand. It cannot be used to identify location-specific policy priorities or planning targets.

The key variables in the model are population forecasts and changes in (a) the urban–rural composition of the population; (b) per capita water demand by rural and urban households; and (c) the composition of production by primary (agriculture), secondary (manufacturing), and tertiary (services) activities. These variables can be used to project the sensitivity of the aggregate demand for water to different average GDP growth rates through 2050, assuming that water demand per yuan of output in the various subsectors does not change significantly. The projections provide a backdrop for comparing actions to aggressively increase the efficiency of water use in subsectors versus actions to aggressively increase water supplies, recognizing that the composition of the portfolio of feasable actions will vary by region, river basin, and even locality.

The projections use two scenarios for population in 2050. The first is the United Nations' medium-term projection, which assumes a growth rate of 0.2 percent a year, with the population peaking and then leveling off at 1.4 billion people by 2050. The second is the figure of 1.6 billion in 2050, which was used in the World Bank's water strategy for North China (World Bank 2001a) and implicitly assumes a 0.45 percent annual growth rate. The model assumes the same urban–rural split and GDP structure for 2050 used in the water strategy study of the World Bank. It also assumes that demand for water of rural and urban households will continue to grow at either a slow rate (similar to that during 1997–2002) or a fast rate (similar to that during 1980–97).

Using these very simple assumptions, the model projects that a doubling of the population growth rate from 0.2 to 0.45 percent a year has a negligible impact on water demand. The increase in the urban share of the population, however, is more significant, particularly if average demand for water by urban households continues to grow rapidly. These changes in demand—not excessive in their own right—will be more difficult to accommodate if there is not also a substantial deceleration, and possibly even a decline in water demand by agriculture and industry.

Even though the share of agriculture and industry in GDP is decreasing, if per unit water consumption patterns in the production sectors do not change significantly, water shortages will continue to grow, constraining the economy's ability to grow at an average rate of more than 5 percent a year over the next 50 years. Even a 4 percent annual growth rate through 2050 could generate the need to more than double water supply in many areas.

To put this required increase in water in perspective, aggregate water demand grew only 27 percent during the explosive growth period of 1980 to 2005, rising from 444 billion to 563 billion cubic meters. This increase put acute strain on supplies in the 3-H river basin. Key metropolitan regions began experiencing so much water shortage that they had to resort to diverting water from downstream rural users and estuaries and to pumping aquifers at a rate faster than replenishment, a strategy that is unsustainable.

Policy and Investment Implications

Generalizations and "one size fits all" recommendations are likely to be inappropriate in China, because of its size and complexity. But solutions tailored to location-specific problems are difficult to summarize and tedious to enumerate. Moreover, some of the information necessary to evaluate proposed solutions is not easily obtainable in public documents or consistent across sources (in part because information sources vary in their definitions and coverage and are rarely complete).[12]

Many of the problems cited in this chapter are well known to Chinese authorities, who have initiated a wide range of programs to cope with

---

12 Many instances of water scarcity are highly localized and are not reflected in national statistics. In addition, the accuracy and reliability of information vary greatly across subnational regions and categories of information, as does the year in which the information was gathered. As a result, establishing consistency between different variables within and across time periods is difficult. All data should therefore be considered as estimates.

them.[13] In addition to the comprehensive overview of China's water needs completed by the Ministry of Water Resources in 2002, the World Bank prepared a strategy document in 2002 that outlines key actions (World Bank 2002a). Neither of these documents provides a quantitative assessment of how much of the various problems will be resolved by the actions proposed, and neither fully costs or sequences the actions. The documents nevertheless provide an excellent array of actions to be implemented.

China has been very successful in investing in physical infrastructure to control flooding, restore forested watersheds, and improve water supply and wastewater treatment. It has been far less successful in managing demand through better pricing and conservation policies, or in achieving better institutional coordination of integrated water management programs at different jurisdictional levels, although there have been some successes that have not yet been generalized (as in the Tarim River basin [World Bank 2004]). Where water is not being used efficiently, expanding water supply at increasing marginal costs will only increase the drain on public resources. Such a strategy is also not sustainable.

Expanding the role of markets and market price signals as a feedback mechanism in allocating water would go a long way toward helping conserve the resource and allocate it to the highest economic use; doing so would also send signals on priority investment requirements. Expanding the role of water markets and prices is a corollary of expanding the role of markets in the production of private goods and services (Yaozhou 2000). However, the expansion of water markets and prices presupposes progress in establishing the institutional framework for water rights/entitlements, valuation, and appropriate measurement, efforts that are still incomplete.[14]

---

13 The *Water Resources Report* (MWR 2003) summarizes the implementation status of these programs.

14 Tradable water rights are one potentially important route to improving institutions for the allocation and use of water. This calls for designing and implementing mechanisms that will facilitate the functioning of a system of tradable water rights. As noted in a recent World Bank report (2004: 3–4). "Such a system would make a major contribution to increasing the value of production per unit of water consumed in irrigated agriculture areas and to the reallocation of water from agriculture to priority uses. A significant amount of informal water trading already goes on in China. Chinese water law includes provisions for the issuing of water licenses, but the issuing and enforcing of water licenses in irrigation areas is not widespread. At each point of water measurement, a corresponding water right should be issued that includes a flow rate, a total volume of allowable annual delivery per extraction, and a total volume of allowable annual consumptive use. The sum of all of the consumptive use rights for a river basin or aquifer should not exceed the allowable total consumptive use in the basin or aquifer in order to have sustainable water resources use and management. Once the

Imposing taxes and subsidies, as well as educating farmers, firm managers, and households in water conservation options, will be required to augment the role of water pricing where market prices provides insufficient information and incentives for the correct allocation of water.

Demand-management strategies, including conservation measures, are essential not just to reduce water wastage but also to reduce the need for costly interbasin water transfers. With some important exceptions, encouraging urbanization (and new infrastructure development) in areas that are not currently water scarce or likely to become water scarce may be an efficient long-term strategy. There was a dramatic demographic shift from rural to urban areas between 1980 and 2005. Net-rural-to urban migration was about 310 million people in the 25-year period 1980 and 2005. As a result the urban share of the national population increased from 19 to 43 percent (see table 7.1).[15] This shift was associated with a quadrupling of the urban share in total water demand. However, during this 25-year period, there was a negligible net demographic shift from north to south of approximately 20 million migrants.[16] As a result, the relative shares of the two zones remained almost constant, at 52 percent for the north and 48 percent for the south, despite growing water scarcity in the north.[17] This anomaly requires further analysis, but lack of adequate price signals on the real economic costs of water could be one factor.

Allowing or encouraging continued urbanization also requires that the collateral damage associated with expanding urban water demand be

---

consumptive use water rights issued equal the allowable total consumptive use rights in a basin, no further water rights should be issued. No water diversion or well drilling and pumping should be permitted without a corresponding water right. Once a complete system of water rights per measurement is operational, then a system of tradable water rights could begin to function. To ensure maintaining a water balance and no negative impacts on third parties, the consumptive use right is the right that should be traded. All water rights trades should be registered and approved by the government authorities ensuring no effect on third parties. Without a complete system of consumptive use water rights and measurement, tradable water rights will not be able to aid in the reallocation of water within a sustainable water resources management system; therefore, trading in water rights should be restricted."

15 If the urban share of the national population had been the same in 2005 as it was in 1980, the urban population would have been 310 million less than it was.

16 If the northern share of China's population had been the same in 2005 as it was in 1980, the population in the north would have been 22 million less than it was.

17 One caveat is the possibility that official data underestimate the extent of migration of the population from the north to the south. This problem is analogous to the difficulty of measuring the population in urban areas, which include unregistered (non–hukou) migrants, as noted in chapter 3.

reduced. Using fresh water would be less consequential if water abstracted upstream could be returned to river flows in good condition to be used again downstream. This can be done only if water polluted through urban and industrial use is treated appropriately first, which will require significant new investments. For example, despite its 1,179 operational industrial wastewater primary treatment plants, which have the capacity to treat 1.13 billion cubic meters of industrial wastewater, Chongqing, a center for heavy industry, treats only about 57 percent of its industrial wastewater and 54 percent of its household wastewater (Okadera, Watanabe, and Xu 2006). Because Chongqing is situated upstream of the Changjiang River, the polluted water flows through the Three Gorges Dam to urban and rural areas downstream. An additional US$122 million of investment is required to fully treat the water in Chongqing (Okadera, Watanabe, and Xu 2006).

Overall, about half of China's urban wastewater is treated. Even in Beijing, only 50 percent of wastewater is treated, despite the increase in wastewater treatment capacity from 50 million tons in 1990 to 517 million tons in 2003; the goal is to treat 70 percent by 2010 (Yang and Abbaspour 2007). Some 278 cities have no treatment facilities ("Drip, Drip, Drip" 2006). Thus, in addition to higher water prices in urban areas, charges for wastewater discharges and other pollutants must rise. Better monitoring, information disclosure, and enforcement of appropriate standards are also needed.

Pollution from urban municipal sources could be managed by the use of updated municipal sewerage systems, including collecting sewers and treatment plants designed to receive industrial wastewater. This combined use would yield large savings, both to the municipality and to industries, because of economies of scale in removing degradable organics (with the provision that participating industries would first remove toxic and other harmful substances using in-plant treatment before discharging into the municipal system). To the extent practicable, the treated municipal effluent would be reused as water supply for irrigation and industry. Municipal systems would also include provisions for effective use of on-site excreta disposal units for homes and buildings not connected to municipal sewers (the same provision would apply to rural homes), so that these wastes are not left unmanaged and subject to being flushed into waterways by surface runoff.

Public disclosure of information on water quality and community consultation could improve feedback and facilitate better monitoring. Research by Jiangsu Province, SEPA, and the World Bank on pilot versions

of community consultation and feedback processes, as well as public disclosure of information (Wang and others 2004), have determined that
they are effective and have the potential to be scaled up (Lu and others
2003; Jiangsu Environmental Protection Bureau 2007).

Reducing the Cost of Wastewater Treatment and Improving Its Monitoring

Increasing wastewater charges (specially the rate by which charges increase)
will be easier if there is better monitoring and information disclosure
and if more wastewater is treated for reuse. Increasing the amount of
wastewater treated for reuse requires that increases in wastewater charges
be complemented by declines in the cost of investment in wastewater
treatment plants.[18]

More than 1,000 wastewater plants were built between 2000 and
2006 ("Strong Growth" 2007), but the utilization rate is only 60 percent.
About 50 plants in 30 cities are operating at below 30 percent capacity,
and some are left idle, mainly because of inadequate wastewater collection
facilities ("Strong Growth" 2007; Yang and Abbaspour 2007) and because
revenues collected from customers are transferred to the general city
budget and not used to ensure that treatment plants have the resources
needed to operate.[19]

Operational efficiency is also low, mainly because plants carry out only
primary treatment. Even in Shanghai the efficiency is only 10–30 percent
(Okadera, Watanabe, and Xu 2006). Moreover, investment coordination
across metropolitan regions is inadequate. There are economies of scale
and optimal sizes for wastewater treatment plants. Despite this approach,
many small, adjacent municipalities respond to national directives by implementing their own suboptimal wastewater treatment plants, increasing
the overall national costs of wastewater treatment.

Widening the options for wastewater investment decisions can help
contain costs. As noted in the *World Development Report 2003* (World
Bank 2002b), New York City found it cheaper to repurchase land along
part of its watershed that had been sold for development than to build

---

18 At the current low rate for wastewater collection, private sector participation is difficult to imagine. Until these rates are increased, the public sector will have to shoulder
the needed investment costs associated with increasing wastewater treatment capacity
to reduce water pollution in urban areas. One estimate puts the figure as US$30 billion
between 2006 and 2010 (Zhong, Wang, and Chen 2006).

19 This information is based on informal communications with the author of an ongoing
"City Development Strategy" in 11 cities in China.

an expensive water treatment plant. Doing so was possible because the topography provided for a natural filtration process that was very effective. This option will not be an appropriate in all cases, but it may be in some cases. More important, widening the array of options to be reviewed and evaluated, when undertaking cost-benefit or feasibility studies, may help identify new cost-effective solutions. Restricting land development and restoring local watershed filtration capacities may reduce the amount of water requiring treatment, thereby reducing the cost of wastewater treatment in China.

Augmenting the Water Supply

Demand-management policies through market prices or new institutional arrangements may not be sufficient to deal with the full range of environmental water problems facing China. It is easier to introduce water charges when scarcity has emerged but critical thresholds have not yet been crossed. It is more difficult to introduce water pricing and wastewater charges when implicit rights to subsidized or free water resources have been acquired and critical thresholds crossed.

Two such thresholds are important in China. The first is the lack of adequate water in rivers to ensure year-round flows to flush the rivers, transport silt to the delta, and avoid ecosystem damage downstream, all of which are already occurring. The second is the need to restore some, if not all, of the groundwater that has been overpumped in the recent past. In both cases, more water flow has to be restored to the ecosystem and aquifers.[20]

It may be possible to restore water flows to natural systems by setting the price so high that existing users voluntarily renounce some of their water claims. But in the absence of water markets and well-defined water rights, it may not be possible to fully restore the minimum requisite water abstracted from rivers that now run dry. More important, ecosystem needs are public goods and by definition difficult to include in water markets (when flows in rivers are low, for example, water for environmental

---

20 In the case of aquifers, one study (Gunaratnam 2004) provides a clear set of actions to be implemented: "The key actions required by the action plan are (a) definition of groundwater management units with determination of sustainable yields; (b) preparation of groundwater management plans; (c) allocation of licensing linked to sustainable yield and undertaken by one department only; (d) licensing of well construction drillers; (e) development of a national groundwater database; and (f) preparation and implementation of a groundwater pollution control strategy, including provision in selected cities for recharging of groundwater by spreading of treated wastewater effluents or of floodwaters on permeable spreading areas, and for the injection of treated effluents to establish groundwater mounds to prevent salinity intrusion into freshwater aquifers."

needs must come from a reduction in irrigation). Ensuring that public goods, such as ecosystem water requirements, are handled appropriately will require institutional reforms, as noted earlier.

Investment in catchment reservoirs and watershed management in catchment basins through reforestation, to stabilize damaging unevenness in water flows over time, are other examples of supply-oriented interventions that need to complement demand-management policies, particularly where externalities and public goods are involved. For the future, some augmenting of existing supplies—through interbasin transfers and the reuse of wastewater, for example—will be required.[21] One such interbasin transfer is the South-to-North Water Transfer Project.[22] This scheme entails transferring 19 billion cubic meters a year initially and eventually up to 45 billion cubic meters of water a year from the Yangtze River, at a cost of US$60 billion. The crucial component of the project, including that which supplies Beijing, was completed in July 2006; the entire project will not be completed until 2050 ("China: A Five-Year Outlook" 2004; "Still Poor" 2006; Wu 2006).[23] Depreciating these costs and adding operating costs will likely require prices well in excess of those currently prevailing of less than one yuan per cubic meter. (World Bank 2001b) However, even with the south–north transfer, water use in irrigated agriculture in the 3–H basins will need to be reduced by 20–28 billion cubic meters from current levels by 2020.

Gunaratnam (2004) points out that in industrial countries, treated municipal wastewater represents a very valuable source of supplemental water for the industrial raw water supply and for irrigation of farming and urban green zones. The use of treated municipal wastewater for urban green zones may even be the preferred use, because of the lower quality requirements and relatively low infrastructure costs (Yang and Abbaspour 2007).[24] Hence, future plans for meeting urban needs should incorporate provisions for municipal sewerage systems to facilitate reuse. Using the price of fresh water in 2003 as an opportunity cost, the net economic benefit of reusing wastewater in Beijing is Y 134–Y 298 billion a year

---

21 Interest in reusing water is not new. See the case study of water reuse project in Changzi city by Peng, Stevens, and Yiang (1995).

22 The concept of south–north water transfer was first aired by Mao Zedong, in 1952. Three channels (western, middle, and eastern routes) with a total length of 1,300 kilometers will link four major rivers of China: the Yangtze, Yellow, Huaihe, and Haihe ("China: Moving Water" 2003). See Gao and others (2006) and Wu and others (2006) for details on the western and middle routes of the South-to-North Transfer Project.

23 Initially, the capital costs of the south–north transfer of 18 billion cubic meters was estimated to be Y 245 billion (World Bank 2001b).

24 Wastewater can also be used to replenish the groundwater (Yang and Abbaspour 2007).

(19–43 percent of Beijing's GDP in 2005). Beijing now requires new residential buildings with construction areas larger than 30,000 square meters to have on-site wastewater reuse facilities (Yang and Abbaspour 2007).[25] Such planned reuse would have to be subject to regulatory control through permits to ensure that public health needs are protected.

Conclusions

China's rapid urbanization increases the urgency of decisively tackling the growing scarcity of water, a constraint that can only tighten as the climate warms and glaciers feeding the major river systems and aquifers disappear in the coming decades. Urban development and the geography of urbanization will need to be coordinated with policies aimed at managing demand in urban as well as rural sectors and by measures to augment or recycle the usable supply of water.

Despite growing water scarcity in the north, there has been no noticeable demographic shift from north to south. This anomaly requires further analysis; lack of adequate price signals on the real economic costs of water could be one factor. With some important exceptions, encouraging urbanization (and new infrastructure development) in areas that are not currently water scarce, or likely to become water scarce, may be an efficient long-term strategy.[26]

Among the actions discussed in this chapter, four stand out as most significant from the perspective of urban development:

- Allocate water for public uses (such as estimated ecosystem water needs) first, before allocating it to private uses (industry, residential, and agriculture as residual claimants), through either markets or administrative arrangements.[27] In either case, water use must be regulated to protect public health and the environment.
- Shift from administrative to price-based allocation of water, initially through better technocratic analysis, eventually complemented through water markets based on the fair and transparent allocation of property rights in water. Water markets cannot totally replace administrative

---

25 Onsite treatment is often economically unviable; treatment should be centralized (Yang and Abbaspour 2007).

26 This is a broader strategy than the informally discussed possibility of moving China's capital out of Beijing to a less water-stressed area.

27 The South African Water Act of 1997 considers its water resources as a public good, a resource for all under state control and licensed (http: www.thewaterpage.com/Solanes Dublin.html). China's water laws have been revised recently to address some of the public goods issues raised above (Xiangyang 2004).

(quota) allocations of water, for reasons that are well known and implicit in the previous recommendation regarding public/private use of water. The balance between the two allocation mechanisms (administrative versus market) will be determined politically, though good technocratic analysis can inform the political debate.

- Improve the institutions involved in water management, not only at the metropolitan level but also at the river-basin level, including through better coordination of water use through invigorated river basin/watershed management commissions, and greater involvement of communities in joint monitoring and enforcement through public disclosure schemes.
- Increase urban water recycling through more reliable and cost-effective wastewater and sewerage treatment, and more appropriate sewerage and wastewater charges.

The greatest challenge is for national and local/urban governments to craft policies and rules within China's complex cultural and legal administrative system that provide incentives for users to increase efficiency of water use and for polluters to clean up the water they use and return clean water to stream flows. Using a standard public economics framework, water requirements for public goods, such as ecosystem needs, should be set aside first, before allocating property rights in water (to enable water markets to function and generate efficient allocation signals). Even then, water markets will have to be regulated to ensure that public goods, such as public health, are not compromised. Until water markets are implemented, staying the course on increasing the water and sewerage or the wastewater prices administratively and encouraging water conservation is necessary to reduce the wasting of currently scarce water resources as well as the new water supplies to be provided in the future. Investments in supplying water for rapidly growing urban areas and treating urban sewerage and wastewater will be more effective when combined with more-vigorous demand-management policies and institutional reform.

References

ABS Energy Research. 2006. *Water and Waste Utilities of the World.* London:

Bao, Chao, and Chuang-Lin Fang. 2007. "Water Resource Constraint Force on Urbanization in Water Deficient Regions: A Case Study of the Hexi Corridor, Arid Area of NW China." *Ecological Economics* 62 (3–4): 508–17.

"China: A Five-Year Outlook." 2004. *Oxford Analytica*, March 31.

"China: Moving Water and People." 2003. *Business China*, March 31.

"China to Keep Grains Goals despite Climate Change." 2007. *Reuters News*, June 19.

"China Turns to Desalination to Keep Taps Flowing." 2007. *Straits Times*, June 14. http://app.mfa.gov.sg/pr/read_content.asp?View,7452.

Chinese Academy of Science. 2003. *China Country Report on Sustainable Development: Water Resources*. Committee of Sustainable Development Strategy, Beijing.

"Drip, Drip, Drip." 2006. *Business China*, September 27.

"Drought Hits Northern China" 2007. AP Newswires. June 19.

"Drought leaves 1.2 million short of drinking water in NE China." 2007. *Xinhua News*. July 19. http//www.chinadaily.com.cn/china/2007-06/19/content_897742.htm.

EIA (Energy Information Administration). 2003. "Country Analysis Briefs." U.S. Department of Energy, Washington, DC.

Economy, Elizabeth. 1997. "The Case Study of China." http//www.library.utoronto.ca/pcs/state/china/chinasum.htm.

Economy, Elizabeth. 2004. *The River Runs Black*. Ithaca, NY: Cornell University Press.

FAO (Food and Agricultural Organization). 2007. "AQUASTAT." Rome. http://www.fao.org/nr/water/aquastat/dbase/index.stm.

Gao, Yanchun, Changming Liu, Shaofeng Jia, Jun Xia, Jingjie Yu, and Kurt Peng Liu. 2006. "Integrated Assessment of Water Resources Potential in the North China Region: Developmental Trends and Challenges." *Water International* 31 (1): 71–80.

Gong, Huili, Menlou Li, and Xinli Hu. 2000. "Management of Groundwater in Zhengzhou City, China." *Water Research* 34 (1): 57–62.

Guan, Dabo, and Klaus Hubacek. 2007. "Assessment of Regional Trade and Virtual Water Flows in China." *Ecological Economics* 61 (1): 159–70.

Gunaratnam, Daniel. 2004. "China Water Resources Issues and Strategy." World Bank, Washington, DC.

IIASA (International Institute for Applied Systems Analysis). 1993. IIASA databases. http://www.iiasa.ac.at/Research/LUC/ChinaFood/data/water/wat_8.htm, http://www.iiasa.ac.at/Research/LUC/ChinaFood/data/water/wat_11.htm, http://www.iiasa.ac.at/Research/LUC/ChinaFood/data/water/wat_7.htm.

Jiangsu Environmental Protection Bureau. 2007. "Jiangsu Carried Out Round Table Dialogue Pilot Project." January. http://www.jshb.gov.cn/jshb/xwdt/showinfo.aspx?infoid=5e25a4db-df0b-474b-a34a-2e5fa3ee901e&categoryNum=002001&siteid=1.

MacBean, Alasdair. 2007. "China's Environment: Problems and Policies." *World Economy* 30 (2): 292–307.

MWR (Ministry of Water Resources). 2002. China *Water Resources Statistics Report Beijing.* http//gks.chinawater.net.cn/cwsnet/CWSArticle_View.asp? CWSNewsID=14983.

MWR (Ministry of Water Resources). 2003. *Water Resources Report.* Bejjing:

NBS (National Bureau of Statistics). Various years. *China Statistical Yearbook.* Beijing: China Statistics Press.

Lu, Genfa, Yuan Wang, Yu Qian, Jun Bi, and Gangxi Xu. 2003. "Application of Corporation Environmental Performance Disclosure in Environmental Management." *Chinese Practice.* Vol. 1, No 1, 2003, March. Available at: http://www.chinaenvironment.net/pace/perspectives/print.php?id=7_0_6_0

Okadera, Tomohiro, Masataka Watanabe, and Kaiqin Xu. 2006. "Analysis of Water Demand and Water Pollutant Discharge Using a Regional Input-Output Table: An Application to the City of Chongqing, Upstream of the Three Gorges Dam in China." *Ecological Economics* 58 (2): 221–37.

Palmer, Mervin D. 2001. *Water Quality Modeling.* World Bank, Washington, DC.

Peng, Jian, David K. Stevens, and Xinguo Yiang. 1995. "A Pioneer Project of Wastewater Reuse in China." *Water Research* 29 (1): 357–63.

SEPA (State Environmental Protection Agency). 2003. *State of the Environment in China.* Beijing:

Shalizi, Zmarak. 2006. "Addressing China's Growing Water Shortages and Associated Social and Environmental Consequences." Policy Research Working Paper 3895, World Bank, Washington, DC.

———. 2007. "Energy and Emissions: Local and Global Effects of the Giants Rise." In *Dancing With Giants: China, India, and the Global Economy.* Singapore: World Bank and Institute of Policy Studies.

"Still Poor and Now Thirsty, Too." 2006. *Business China,* September 11.

"Strong Growth Seen in China's Water Sector." 2007. *Business Times Singapore,* June 18.

"The Case of China." 1997.

UNESCO (United Nations Educational, Scientific, and Cultural Organization. 2003. *Water for People, Water for Life.* http://unesdoc.unesco.org/images/ 0012/001295/129556e.pdf.

University of British Columbia. 2004. "Introduction to Beijing-Tianjin." Center for Human Settlement, Vancouver. http://www.chs.ubc.ca/china/introbeijing.htm.

USDA (U.S. Department of Agriculture). 2000. *Agricultural Outlook January– February 2000.* Washington, DC: Economic Research Service.

Wang, Hua. 2004. "China Water Issues." World Bank, Development Research Group, Washington, DC.

Wang, H., J. Bi, D. Wheeler, J. Wang, D. Cao, G. Lu, and Y. Wang. 2004. "Environmental Performance Rating and Disclosure: China's Greenwatch Program." *Journal of Environmental Management* 71 (2): 123–33.

Wang, Hua, and Somik Lall. 2002. "Valuing Water for Chinese Industries." *Applied Economics* 34 (6):759–65.

Water Resources and Electric Power. 1997. *Use of Water Resources in China.* Beijing:

Woodrow Wilson Institute. 2004. "Water Conflict Resolution in China." Summary of Environmental Change and Security Program, January 28, Washington, DC: http://www.wilsoncenter.org.

World Bank. 1997. *Clear Water, Blue Skies.* New York: Oxford University Press.

——. 2001a. *Agenda for Water Sector Strategy for North China,* vol. 1. Washington, DC: East Asia and Pacific Region, World Bank.

——. 2001b. *Agenda for Water Sector Strategy for North China,* vol. 2. Washington, DC: East Asia and Pacific Region, World Bank.

——. 2001c. *China Air, Land, and Water Environment Priorities for a New Millennium.* Washington, DC: East Asia and Pacific Region, World Bank.

——. 2002a. *China: Water Resources Assistance Strategy.* Washington, DC: East Asia and Pacific Region, World Bank,

——. 2002b. *World Development Report 2003.* Washington, DC: World Bank.

——. 2004. "11th Plan Water Note." World Bank, Washington, DC.

——. 2007. *The Little Green Data Book.* Washington, DC.

Wu, Xianfeng, Changming Liu, Guilian Yang, and Qing Fu. 2006. "Available Quantity of Transferable Water and Risk Analysis: Western Route Project for South-to-North Water Transfer in China." *Water International* 31 (1): 81–86.

Xiangyang, Xiong. 2004. "The Revision of Water Law of P.R.C. and the Efforts for Remedying the Dry-Up Problems of Yellow River." Beijing: Ministry of Water Resources.

Yang, Hong, and Karim C. Abbaspour. 2007. "Analysis of Wastewater Reuse Potential in Beijing." *Desalination* 212 (1–3): 238–50.

Yaozhou, Zhou, and Wei Bingcai. 2000. "Pricing Irrigation Water in China." In *Pricing Irrigation Water,* ed. Yacov Tsur. Washington, DC: Resources for the Future.

Yusuf, Shahid, and Kaoru Nabeshima. 2006. "China's Development Priorities." World Bank, Development Research Group. Washington, DC.

Zhong, L., X. Wang, and J. Chen. 2006. "Private Participation in China's Wastewater Service under the Constraint of Charge Rate Reform." *Water Science & Technology: Water Supply* 6 (5): 77–83.

CHAPTER 8

The Changing Role of Urban Government

Tony Saich

The economic reforms of the past three decades have necessitated significant changes in the role of the governing apparatus, especially at the local level. While the challenges are many, this chapter focuses on urban governance and welfare provision.

For urban China the shedding of welfare responsibilities by state-owned enterprises (SOEs) and the intention to move millions of people from rural areas to cities by 2020 have brought new responsibilities to and put new pressures on local urban governments. This population creates new challenges as China's towns and cities strive to knit fragmented social welfare provision into a more coherent framework of support. At the same time, urban governments have responsibilities for job creation, public safety, and basic physical infrastructure. Far greater responsibility lies with local governments than is the case in most other countries.

Meeting the urbanization goals will present major challenges for the government in terms of investment in urban infrastructure and planning. It will also present significant challenges for job creation. Infrastructure programs will create some employment opportunities, but whether the service industry can be expanded sufficiently to accommodate the estimated 150–200 million surplus workers in rural China remains to be seen.

Urbanization is seen as the best long-term solution to the problems of inequality in service provision, which primarily reflect urban–rural differences. Yet the current leadership is concerned about the consequences. It is therefore seeking to restrict the expansion of large cities while encouraging the growth of small towns. In 2006, General Secretary Hu Jintao and Premier Wen Jiabao bundled policies to "build a new socialist countryside" that seek to improve conditions for those who remain behind in order to reduce the pressures of urbanization. In addition, they have promoted policies to improve the lot of urban migrants and to push more integrated social welfare programs to help those who have been disadvantaged by reforms to date, such as workers laid off from SOEs and elderly people who lack family support (see chapter 4).

It is primarily local urban governments that are charged with finding the solutions and supplying most of the funding for the promises made by the central government. The challenge is how to get better local government performance with constrained resources and competing demands.

This chapter first looks at how the role of local government has changed under reform and the incentives that shape the behavior of local government in China. It then provides some preliminary evidence on how Chinese citizens view the performance of urban government. It closes by considering alternatives for providing more effective public goods and services.

The Changing Role and Incentives of Local Government

Reforms have changed the role of local urban government in terms of economic and fiscal management, the provision of public goods and services, and the strength and structure of local administrative units. During the Mao years and the earlier phase of reforms, the capacity of local administrative units to provide public services was weak. These units primarily served people who were not employed by government agencies or SOEs and their dependents. As reforms have progressed, local governments have acquired a number of real administrative powers over planning and land use, public works, local foreign trade, and the provision of social welfare.

Local government has received greater powers over investment approval, entry and exit regulation, and resource allocation (Lin, Tao, and Liu n.d.). Perhaps the strongest expression of this increase in power was the formation of Special Economic Zones, which led to an expansion of economic decision-making powers for many coastal cities and then to other cities inland. In addition, since the 1980s, the authority over many

SOEs was delegated to municipal governments. This meant that local governments were faced with fixed asset spending on these enterprises as well as on the wide range of welfare services they provided. While this devolution of powers offered the potential to raise revenues, it added a significant and rising fiscal burden, in the form of expenditure assignments on local government, that many found hard to carry in the 1990s.

As the main providers of public services, subprovincial levels of government have had to shoulder expenditure responsibilities that are out of line with international practice (World Bank 2002). The central authorities have transferred a much larger percentage of expenditure responsibilities to local government than is normally the case. The Maoist notion of "self-reliance" reinforced the idea that each locality should minimize "dependence" on support from higher levels. In fact, with the introduction of fiscal contracts in 1988, the central government formally ended its responsibility for financing local expenditures, expanding the role of local government from simply providing services to also financing them. The move delinked expenditure assignments from revenue-sharing considerations, later regularized in the Budget Law (World Bank 2002). Unlike in many other countries, in China these transfers do not play an equalizing role; richer areas often receive proportionately larger transfers (Mountfield and Wong 2005).[1] The local level of government retains primary responsibility for financing infrastructure and providing social welfare.

This division of fiscal responsibility in China differs from that in other countries in the region (table 8.1). As a share of total public spending, subnational expenditure is much higher in China (69 percent) than in Vietnam (48 percent), Indonesia (32 percent), or Thailand (10 percent) (Mountfield and Wong 2005).

Under the 1995 Budget Law, local governments are allowed to run deficits; they are not, however, allowed to issue bonds. Unable to raise adequate resources through measures such as a property or vehicle users tax, local governments are excessively reliant on inadequate central transfers (general or earmarked) for funding, supplemented by off-budget revenues and relying on nongovernment institutions to provide many public goods and services.

---

1 For China as a whole, expenditures were distributed as follows in 1999: 28.2 percent at the provincial level, 30.2 percent at the prefecture level, and 41.5 percent at the county and township level. For revenues the figures were 21.2 percent at the provincial level, 35.4 percent at the prefecture, and 43.4 percent at the county and township level.

Table 8.1. Subnational Expenditure Shares and Functional Allocations in Selected Asian Countries

Country	Subnational expenditure (percent of total)	Functional allocation		
		Education	Health	Social welfare
China	69	Local	Local	Local
Indonesia	32	Local	Local	Local
Thailand	10	Central, provincial	Central, provincial	Central, provincial
Vietnam	48	Provincial, local	Provincial, local	Provincial, local

Source: White and Smoke 2005.

The funding environment became even tougher for local governments after 2004, when the Ministry of Finance shifted its macroeconomic policy to ensure greater fiscal restraint and less reliance on borrowing (Su and Zhao 2006). Borrowing had risen to cover about 30 percent of the costs of infrastructure development, from about 2.5 percent in the mid-1980s.

Most cities have set up a Municipal Development and Investment Company to deal with the funding and operation of infrastructure projects. With local governments technically prohibited from borrowing, these nominally independent companies borrow and use funds on the government's behalf (see chapter 5; Su and Zhao 2006). In addition, many cities contract out services or spin off government departments as quasi-private entities.

One emerging imperative shared by economically developed and more resource-constrained localities is the increasingly acute need each feels to enhance its own sources of revenue. The resultant fiscal inequalities that arise from this system have led to significant inequality in the provision of public goods and services. In 2005, the per capita fiscal revenue of the Shanghai municipal government (Y 7,972) was more than 16 times that of Guizhou (Y 489), a gap that is widening. Per capita fiscal expenditures also show significant inequality, with Shanghai spending Y 9,259 and Guizhou Y 1,396. Provinces such as Guizhou rely on external funding to provide services (NBS 2007).

Political incentives and the demands of higher-level local government agencies are also important in understanding local government performance. Popular expectations and those of higher administrative levels about the range and kinds of services they should provide have not declined. Financial pressures lead to the preference for a development plan that maximizes short-term revenue over longer-term needs and that pays too little attention to distributional and welfare priorities. The main concern of government at all levels is increasing revenues rather than defining the correct role of government. The concern with revenue generation is exacerbated by the fact that despite fiscal decentralization, the central government has retained control over the policy agenda. While localities do not always carry out central policy, the center still mandates many tasks that must be carried out and imposes burdens on lower levels of government. Most of these are unfunded mandates. Cities at the prefecture and county levels are supposed to cover all expenditures on unemployment insurance, social security, and welfare. In contrast, in most other countries, the central government covers social security and welfare, and responsibility for education and health is shared by lower levels of government and the center.

The expenditure responsibilities for townships are similar, although townships often have a weaker financial base and carry the heaviest load for social spending. Together, counties and townships account for 70 percent of budgetary expenditures for education and 55–60 percent for health (World Bank 2002). Yet the township and county levels account for only 30 percent of subnational fiscal revenue. In Xiangyang County, Hubei in 2002, budgetary contributions to education finance amount to 40.6 percent of total expenditure. Of the government contribution, townships provide 84.6 percent and counties provide 15.2 percent, with the rest coming from provinces (Han 2003). Before 1984, the equivalent of the township did not raise revenue independently.

The need to finance expenditure drives local leadership and townships to seek various off-budget revenues, from user fees and other unsanctioned levies. For example, in three counties surveyed by the Development Research Centre of the State Council, expenditures exceeded revenue, increasing the need to raise off-budget revenue (Han 2003). Nationwide, extrabudgetary funds may total 20 percent of GDP; in the three counties surveyed, they ranged from 30 percent of total income (Xiangyang, Hubei) to 69 percent (Taihe, Jiangxi). The use of these extrabudgetary funds and self-raised funds (*zichou zijin*) has clearly been rising and the 1994 tax reforms have heightened the problem.

Despite the rapidly rising social welfare demands, the two major causes of growth in government expenditures are capital spending and administrative outlays. The Organisation for Economic Co-operation and Development (OECD 2006) has calculated that between 1998 and 2003, capital expenditure contributed 31 percent of total growth in expenditure and administrative outlays contributed 21 percent. The burden of the increase in expenditure and administrative outlays falls most heavily on local governments, which provide 82 percent of administrative spending (and less than 56 percent of capital investment) (OECD 2006).

Even in major cities, local governments have difficulty meeting their administrative expenses. Beijing and Shanghai (each of which bears 89 percent of these expenses) and other major municipalities come closest to supporting their needs from their own revenue.

This situation has led to a constant search by local governments for stable revenue sources, with Street Offices, for example, setting up small commercial ventures, and even joint ventures and services being contracted out.[2] In the 1980s and 1990s, financial pressures contributed to the expansion of locally owned enterprises, especially township and village enterprises (TVEs), which were seen as the most-stable sources for local income (see chapter 2). By the mid-1990s, however, TVEs had become a burden for many local governments, and large-scale privatization began.

Still needing funds, many local governments introduced a wide range of sanctioned and unsanctioned fees and levies to cover the funding gap. This practice has come under increasing scrutiny from the central government and has induced local governments to rely on the sales of land under their jurisdiction to raise more revenue, often by converting agricultural land to commercial or residential land use.

These constraints limit long-term strategic planning and investment in social development. They also force local governments to focus on short-term revenue generation, something that is encouraged further by the political contracting system.

Far more needs to be learned about the political demands placed on local officials by higher-level agencies to complete the picture of the forces shaping local government. In some areas, reforms have clearly given local officials greater financial freedom from higher levels and reduced their dependence on higher-level approval for career advancement and economic reward. However, the appointment system leaves most officials dependent on the approval of their superiors for career advancement. A number of researchers have argued persuasively that a pure political economy approach that views state agents as revenue maximizers should be complemented with an understanding of the political incentives generated by the cadre responsibility system, the political contracting system, and the performance contracts (*gangwei mubiao zerenshu*) that govern the work of local governments and officials (Rong and others 1998; Edin 2000; Whiting 2001).

---

2 Street Offices supervise and allocate the budgets of residents' committees and community residents' committees. China had 6,152 Street Offices at the end of 2005.

Meeting performance contracts does not discourage economic development—far from it. They are just one of a complex set of tasks that local officials are required to carry out. Other tasks include maintaining social order, delivering taxes to higher levels of government, and maintaining family planning quotas. Multiple principle-agent relationships operate between different levels of government. These relationships must be understood better in order to improve analysis of the local state, its functioning, and the incentive structure for local officials.

One problem arising from this system is that it weakens the capacity of county, district, and township governments to provide comprehensive development. The resultant system has been called a pressurized system (*yalixing tizhi*) that provides material rewards for lower-level agencies for developing the economy and meeting targets set by superiors (Rong and others 1998).

Priority targets are set nationwide and are usually political or policy oriented in nature. They include, for example, the maintenance of social order and the meeting of family-planning quotas. Hard targets primarily concern economic outputs set by counties for townships. They include meeting tax revenues and attaining or exceeding predetermined growth levels. Soft targets tend to cover social development, such as provision of health and education and protection of the environment. Meeting hard and priority targets is critical, as failure will mean that success elsewhere will be discounted and no promotions, titles, or economic rewards will be distributed.

This system produces a number of perverse outcomes and explains why officials often pursue unpopular policies with such zeal. Performance contracts focus on both quantitative targets and the speed of task completion. This means that less attention is paid to the quality of the finished product. The reward system encourages shoddy building and infrastructure, which has been part of China's urban and rural building boom.

The political contracting system also provides perverse outcomes for officials and lower-level governments when dealing with performance evaluation. For example, there is great pressure to juggle statistics, which are altered to match or even exceed targets. Distorted reporting is best combined with the cultivation of good social and political relations with one's superiors, who carry out evaluations. This is especially important if key targets are going to be missed. The resultant system and incentives suggest that political and vertical networks remain more important than many proponents of "market transition" would suggest.

The system does offer the potential for refocusing incentives should the leadership so desire. A new nationwide performance appraisal system is being developed that has been tested in Qingdao, Shandong Province.

The system tries to shift evaluation away from just measuring whether local officials are satisfying the demands of higher authorities to look at whether public service goals are being attained ("33 Indexes" 2004).

Citizen Satisfaction with Government

Economic reforms, distorted incentives, and ineffective administrative structures have created problems in maintaining effective mechanisms for delivering public goods and services. The costs of reform for the social transition have been higher than expected; some problems, such as sharply increased inequality and long-term unemployment, cannot be resolved by growth alone. Under Hu Jintao and Wen Jiabao, the leadership is trying to address the inequities of reform and the new challenges of providing welfare under their slogan of "building a harmonious society." There has been a shift from immediate to long-term structural concerns. A coherent policy framework and administrative structure need to be developed that can identify and protect vulnerable groups.

To date, the main approach to resolving the challenges of local government service provision has been to improve the revenue stream. In addition to adjusting incentives for officials, this measure is important, but it is insufficient. What is needed is a thorough reappraisal of the role of government in providing services and the kinds of partnerships that can be formed to meet policy objectives.

This section discusses how urban citizens view the performance of their government. A better understanding of how citizens view government, what kind of services they expect, and how they prioritize them will clarify thinking about the changing role of government.

Like most countries, China had adopted a supply-side approach to the provision of public services. The central government sets public policy goals, such as providing nine years of compulsory education, reviving some kind of collective health system for rural areas, and providing a financial floor for urban families in distress, as noted in chapter 4. These are laudable goals, but they represent unfunded mandates, with the burden of implementation falling on local governments. Many local governments have neither the finances nor sufficient incentives to implement such policy directives effectively. The central government has begun to allocate more funding (through transfers) for its favored policies, but funding still remains far from adequate.

What do citizens think about government in general and the provision of particular public goods by local governments and how they prioritize different needs? To find out, the author and the Horizon Research Group conducted three nationwide surveys to understand which areas of government service citizens approve of and which frustrate them (box 8.1). A simple matrix was devised that correlates the level of importance citizens attached to certain services with the level of satisfaction with local-government service provision (figure 8.1). The results suggest that continued urbanization would improve governance, as in virtually all categories, citizens in major urban areas are more satisfied than those living in small towns, townships, or villages.

Box 8.1

The Survey on Citizen Satisfaction with Government

In 2003, 2004, and 2005, the author and the Horizon Research Group conducted a purposive stratified survey of about 4,000 people, about 80 percent of whom responded.[a] Respondents age 16–60 were selected at three administrative levels: the city, the township, and the village. At the city level, seven sites were chosen, based on their geographic location, average per capita income, and population. The sites varied in all three variables, representing lower-middle-income, middle-income, and upper-income individuals, as well as individuals from western, eastern, northern, and southern China. Within cities, respondents were randomly selected through the household registration lists using the Kish method.[b] Because of the large average size of families, respondents at the township and village levels were selected randomly using the closest-birthday method. At least 250 respondents were identified for each city (1,850 total), 150 for each town (1,050 total), and 100 for each village (800 total). Consequently, the sample has an urban bias, resulting in respondents with higher age ranges and, in some cases, higher income levels than the corresponding regional averages. In the analysis stage, the results were weighted to compensate for both urban bias and relative population size. Thus, the final weight for cities was 0.5008. With the exception of respondents 16–19, the demographic profile mirrors reasonably well the national range.

By design, the sample does not include migrants or most ethnic minorities. Using the household registration system does not capture migrant communities. Moreover, migrants lack legal access to public goods and services; their responses therefore create bias in the survey findings. Similarly, ethnic minorities residing in autonomous regions live under varying policy frameworks, rendering a

(continued)

comparison of government performance between regions difficult at best and misleading at worst.

The questionnaire was conducted in the municipalities of Beijing and Shanghai and the cities of Chengdu, Guangzhou, Shenyang, Wuhan, and Xi'an, with Nantong (Jiangsu) added in 2005. Seven small towns (districts or counties) were covered: Beining in Jinzhou (Liaoning Province), Changle in Fuzhou (Fujian Province), Linxiang in Yueyang (Hunan Province), Pengzhou in Chengdu (Sichuan Province), Xingping in Xianyang (Shaanxi Province), Xinji in Shijiazhuang (Hebei Province), and Zhuji in Shaoxing (Zhejiang Province). Seven villages under these small towns were chosen, as well as Feng Shuling village, under the jurisdiction of Wuhan (Hubei Province), making eight villages in total.

a. Unless otherwise stated, the details for the 2004 and 2005 surveys are the same. All surveys were conducted in the fall.
b. Under this method, household area sampling is based on a "face sheet" or table with fractional representation of each adult (Kish 1949).

Figure 8.1. Government Service Satisfaction/Importance Matrix

Area D	Area A
High level of importance, low level of satisfaction (Work is of poor quality and urgently needs improvement.)	High level of importance, high level of satisfaction (Work is of good quality and should remain a policy priority.)
Area C	**Area B**
Low level of importance, low level of satisfaction (Work is of poor quality but does not require immediate attention.)	Low level of importance, high level of satisfaction (Work is of good quality but is of limited importance.)

Source: Author.

Across categories, citizen satisfaction with government declines as one moves down the institutional hierarchy (figure 8.2).[3] This finding is important, because it is distinct from many developed economies, where satisfaction levels tend to rise as government gets closer to the people (see, for example, Pew Research Center 1998).

---

3 These figures include respondents who are extremely satisfied and those who are relatively satisfied with government performance.

Figure 8.2. Citizen Satisfaction with Different Levels of Government, 2003–05

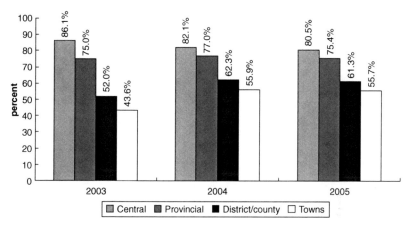

Source: Survey conducted by author and Horizon Research Group.

Local governments in China provide almost all public services. The fact that satisfaction levels decline as government gets closer to the people is therefore a worrisome sign. The percentage of respondents indicating that they were "very satisfied" or "relatively satisfied" with central government service and performance was high, although it dropped slightly between 2003 and 2005, from 86.1 percent to 80.5 percent. Satisfaction with each lower level of government was lower, but satisfaction with the county/district level and the village or residents committee rose between 2003 and 2005. The same trend is evident among urban respondents. In 2005, 83.6 percent of urban residents expressed satisfaction with national government, while just 66.9 percent expressed satisfaction with residents committees. Respondents with higher and lower income levels tend to be the least satisfied (figure 8.3).

Satisfaction with government competence rose between 2003 and 2005. In 2005, 72.2 percent of respondents from municipalities viewed their local government as very competent in implementing policy (up from 64.0 percent in 2003), while only 9.9 percent found it incompetent (down from 14.9 percent in 2003) (table 8.2). In addition, 60.7 percent viewed local officials as friendly (up from 50.0 percent in 2003), while 23.8 percent found them cool and indifferent (down from 33.1 percent in 2003). The new policies of the government and attempts to encourage local governments to be more responsive and take care of those in need may be having an effect, as indicators across the board have improved.

Figure 8.3. Citizen Satisfaction with Different Levels of Government, by Income Level, 2003

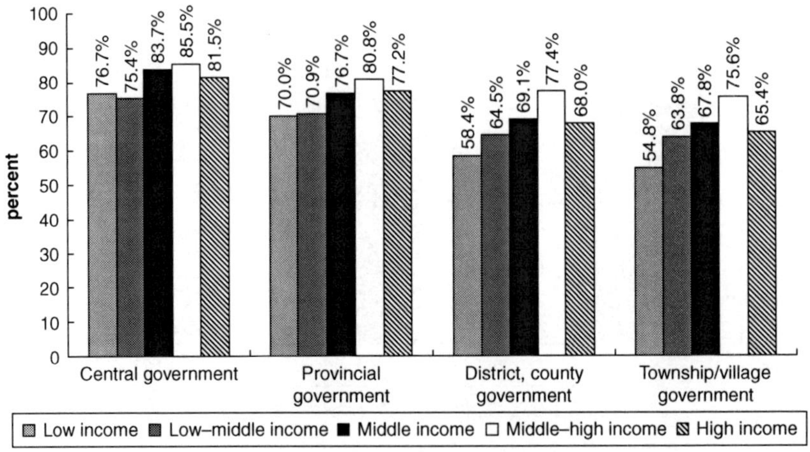

Source: Survey conducted by author and Horizon Research Group.

Table 8.2. Urban Residents' Attitudes toward Government Behavior, 2005

Issue	Number of respondents	Percentage of respondents
Concern for ordinary people		
Raise fees in line with the law	553	56.9
Adopt the method of helping the masses	470	48.4
Care about masses in hardship	458	47.1
Solve real problems	426	43.9
Bring benefits to ordinary people	417	42.9
Think about looking after the masses	406	41.8
Bureaucratic behavior		
Act in line with slogans	389	40.0
Move close to their superiors	373	38.3
Remain aloof from the people	340	35.0
Take care of their own interests	336	34.6
Close to those with money	332	34.2
Raise fees in an arbitrary manner	193	19.8

Source: Survey conducted by author and Horizon Research Group.

While indicators improved, respondents' attitudes about the way local governments implement policy should still raise concern. Irrespective of place of residence, the general view is that when implementing policy, many local officials and governments are concerned with their own interests; are more receptive to the views of their superiors than those of ordinary people; favor those with money; and implement policies formalistically rather than dealing with actual problems. Among rural dwellers, majorities of respondents had negative perceptions in all categories; even in major cities, about a third held negative views of the ways local governments implement policy (table 8.2). The one exception was whether local governments raise levies in accordance with law: only 19.8 percent of respondents felt that local government officials raised fees arbitrarily.

In 2003, only in one category—whether officials helped the masses as opposed to remaining aloof—was there a majority of respondents in favor: 42.4 percent against 41.9 percent. In 2005, there were positive views on all comparisons, but in no category did those replying favorably top 50 percent. The urban respondents who felt that government behaved bureaucratically dropped from 40.7 percent in 2003 to 33.7 percent in 2005, while those who felt government showed concern for the people rose from 40.3 percent to 46.8 percent. Among respondents from small towns and townships, the respondents who indicated that government behaved bureaucratically dropped from 45.1 percent to 38.6 percent; the respondents who indicated that government showed concern for the people rose from 27.3 percent to 34.8 percent.

Satisfaction among urban citizens with the provision of certain public services provides some insights that are helpful for thinking about the changing role of local government. The five areas of local government work that received the highest ratings among residents of municipalities in 2003 were family planning, water and electricity supply, oversight of religious worship, road and bridge construction, and attracting business and investment (table 8.3). In 2005, traffic management and middle and primary school management replaced religious belief and attracting business and investment. However, respondents rated their satisfaction with only one of these services in 2003 and three in 2005 as at least "somewhat satisfied." These services relate to the provision of physical infrastructure and key state priorities; few relate to pressing social policy concerns. In contrast, the five areas of government work that caused the greatest dissatisfaction in 2003 were dealing with corruption, job creation, unemployment insurance, hardship family relief, and social safety. In 2005, tax management replaced social safety. These areas of dissatisfaction relate much more directly to household economic and social concerns and they derive from the new problems and social challenges the reforms have brought with them.

Table 8.3. Highest- and Lowest-Rated Categories of Government Service by Urban Residents, 2003 and 2005

	Highest				Lowest			
	2003		*2005*		*2003*		*2005*	
Service	Satisfaction index	Service	Satisfaction index	Service	Satisfaction index	Service	Satisfaction index
Family planning	3.07	Family planning	3.06	Punishing corruption	2.45	Punishing corruption	2.09
Water/electricity supply	2.98	Water/electricity supply	3.04	Job creation	2.60	Unemployment insurance	2.32
Religious belief	2.96	Road and bridge construction	3.01	Unemployment insurance	2.62	Job creation	2.38
Road and bridge construction	2.96	Traffic management	2.91	Aid for hardship families	2.59	Tax management	2.45
Attracting business and investment	2.87	Management of primary/middle school education	2.91	Medical insurance	2.74	Aid for hardship families	2.47

Source: Survey conducted by author and Horizon Research Group.
Note: Very satisfied = 4; somewhat satisfied = 3; not very satisfied = 2; very unsatisfied = 1.

When the level of importance people attach to a particular service is correlated with satisfaction with government work, the list is much more closely related to the social and economic problems faced by households (figure 8.4). Areas identified where government work is poor and that urgently need improvement are job creation, unemployment insurance, hardship family relief, medical insurance, public sanitation, medical services, and market management. Family planning and religious belief evoke the highest level of satisfaction and the lowest level of importance. In the 2005 survey, the topics of corruption, social safety, and environmental governance evoke the lowest satisfaction and the highest level of importance, while market management drops out of this category. Among people living in towns and townships, corruption, employment, hardship family relief, unemployment insurance, medical insurance, medical and drug services, and social safety all fall in the category of lowest satisfaction, although they are the items to which citizens attach the highest level of importance.

These findings suggest that citizens want government to concentrate on creating jobs and providing basic guarantees to protect against the shocks of the transition to a market economy. Unemployment and medical insurance are high priorities for all residents.

Given that it is unlikely that governments will be able to raise significantly more revenue to finance the provision of public services, it is necessary to reduce costs and focus more clearly on the kinds of services local government can and should provide. The survey reveals that 55.4 percent of respondents in 2005 would not be willing to pay higher taxes in order to receive improved public services; 23.1 percent would be willing to pay more, while 60.2 percent in major municipalities would like to see a reduction in their taxes (up from 44.0 percent in 2003).

Complementing the Role of Urban Government

Local governments alone will not be able to provide the necessary services. To satisfy citizens' needs, government needs to facilitate the further development of alternate service providers and form new partnerships, as noted in chapter 4.

The survey findings highlight a key problem. Generally, citizen satisfaction is highest with the provision of physical infrastructure and lower with the provision of economic and social services that affect households. However, it is precisely physical infrastructure services, such as road and bridge maintenance and the supply of water and electricity,

Figure 8.4. Urban Respondents' Rating of Satisfaction with and Importance of Various Government Functions, 2003

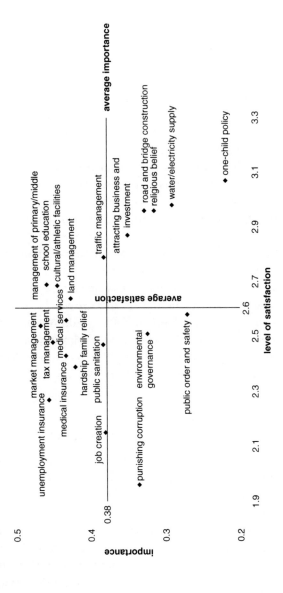

Source: Survey conducted by author and Horizon Research Group.

196

that can be—and already are—most easily contracted out. They are also the kinds of projects for which more funds are available from higher levels of government.

Citizens view local government as less adept at providing the kind of social support that needs to accompany economic transition. To resolve the problems of service provision, government will have to make more-effective use of the market and not-for-profit organizations. This need by government and the impact of reforms have also led to the need for administrative restructuring in urban areas to deal with new challenges, such as the influx of migrant workers or those laid-off from SOEs.

In recent years, pluralism of service delivery has expanded, with voluntary organizations supplementing state provision of basic services and private education and health institutions expanding. The shift resulted primarily from the adoption of cost recovery as the main principle in determining service provision (Flynn, Holiday, and Wong 2001). China has moved farther down the road of privatization under its slogan of socialization (*shehuihua*) than most OECD countries that have adopted policies to boost the role of markets in service provision. It has shifted from an emphasis on equality in social welfare provision to one based on efficiency and cost recovery, something that the current leadership, under Hu Jintao and Wen Jiabao, is trying to address. Those efforts have resulted in further delegation of responsibility to local governments and communities to provide welfare, as well as an acquiescence regarding the emergence of alternate service providers. Effectively, those who can afford it enjoy greater choice, while others have to make do with reduced services or no help at all beyond the family (Saich 2003, 2006).

A public discussion needs to be pursued regarding the kinds of public goods government should supply and those services that should be treated as private goods that need not be funded out of public revenues. One example of a private good is urban housing. It has been treated as a public good in China, with SOEs and other state agencies providing housing at highly subsidized rates. The privatization of housing should be continued, with the profits raised used to reinvest in low-cost housing.

Individual responsibility and the reduction of state provision have also occurred in education and health care. In these sectors, the picture is more complex, and government must play a more active role. There is much to be gained from market-based provision of services, but change has come mainly by default rather than design. Change has also produced unexpected outcomes, with a clear shift from preventive to curative care.

In part, the shift to more-expensive curative care is understandable, as, with the exception of HIV/AIDS, communicable diseases have declined significantly and earlier immunization programs have been successful. With the population now living longer, the diseases to be confronted are beginning to resemble more closely those of the urbanized and industrialized economies. Better regulation of the health sector is needed, together with adequate government funding for preventive care and support of the poor.

There have been interesting experiments to increase citizen choice and the role of markets with the use of education vouchers. However, unlike in the United States, where experiments have sought to improve accountability by allowing citizens to exert their influence directly on suppliers, experiments in China have used vouchers to deal with the issue of equity in education access by targeting vulnerable groups or sectors of education. This is the case in Changxing County, Zhejiang Province, which introduced education vouchers in May 2001. Vouchers have prevented children there from dropping out of school because of financial reasons, and they have guaranteed full attendance at the primary-school level. Some 40 counties in Zhejiang are now using vouchers, which the provincial education bureau is promoting (Center for Comparative Politics and Economics 2006).

One of the distinctive features of reform has been the expansion of social organizations and civilian not-for-profit institutions (see Saich 2000 and chapter 4 of this volume). By the end of 2006, China had some 192,000 registered social organizations (defined as community groups composed of a social group with common intentions, desires, and interests) (Ministry of Civil Affairs 2007). Many of these organizations (95,263) were registered at the county level (Ministry of Civil Affairs 2006). In addition, enterprises, social groups, and individuals had set up about 700,000 not-for-profit institutions to provide social services. This category includes private schools, hospitals, community service centers, vocational training centers, research institutes, and recreational facilities.

Ambivalence about development of the NGO sector remains. The framework for development remains highly restrictive, but leaders are aware that the next phase of reforms will shrink the role of the state in people's lives even farther. As a result, they prefer that the sector be dominated by organizations in which the government plays a strong role. The state is unable to meet many of the obligations that it claims for itself. In urban areas, the lack of state funding has led to efforts to develop service providers that can mobilize local resources and partner with nongovernmental organizations (NGOs) and local communities. With greater recognition and acceptance, the role of NGO contributions is increasingly appreciated. In March 2004, Premier Wen Jiabao vowed to turn over responsibility for more activities in which the government should not be engaged to enterprises, NGOs, and intermediary organizations ("NGOs, can become," 2004).

For alternate service providers to play an effective role, substantial changes must be made in government attitude and practice. Public awareness of the NGO sector and its potential role also needs to increase. The survey results indicate that in 2005, only 36.8 percent of urban residents had heard of NGOs, although 47.5 percent thought that it was appropriate for NGOs to be involved in social welfare work. Without state provision and with an insufficiently developed civil society, increased use of the market to resolve problems is becoming common, not always with positive results. The survey results indicate that 34.6 percent of respondents had no medical coverage in 2005; and there is a marked increase in the use of commercial insurance in one form or another. Although only 13.4 percent of respondents had purchased commercial insurance in 2005 (9.2 percent in 2003), 6.1 percent had jointly purchased such insurance with their employer, and another 38.4 percent (8.6 percent in 2003) had a commercial insurance purchased for them by their employer.

Urban China's administrative system has been unable to cope with the consequences of the changes that have affected the urban landscape for providing public goods and services. The two most significant changes have been the shedding of social welfare and other obligations by the workplace and the influx of large numbers of migrants into the cities in search of work, as described in chapters 2 and 3. Employees of SOEs, and particularly workers laid off from SOEs in the process of restructuring, have lost many of their benefits and receive inadequate coverage from state institutions. Migrants, as noted in chapter 3, do not receive most benefits and are not effectively integrated into those urban services for which they are eligible.

Given that most services used to be provided through the workplace, the infrastructure of government was relatively weak at the local level, especially below the district. Street Offices and residents committees were not set up to deal with major welfare support or the provision of public goods and services.

Experiments have been conducted to create new organizational forms at the grassroots level that can provide better social infrastructure. The most important is the program of community construction (*shequ jianshe*), which the Ministry of Civil Affairs (MOCA) has been promoting since the mid-1990s (figure 8.5).[4] The need to develop a more universal and comprehensive welfare system to replace the fragmented workplace-based system led the ministry to put forward different models of communities for experimentation.[5] This need for experiment was put forward in November 2000 and was supported by a joint document of the Office of the Chinese Communist Party Central Committee and the Office of the State Council, which called on all government and party committees to set up these new structures. The call was a clear acknowledgment that the old administrative system could not meet the new demands.

The *shequ* were formed out of the residents committees that were under the Street Offices, but they are geographically larger than the old residents committees and have a wider scope of obligations. They are asked explicitly to take over the social welfare tasks that had previously been the domain of the workplace, the residents committees, or the Street Offices. The MOCA favored a model developed in Shenyang, a city that was home to many SOEs and was thus hard hit by the reforms of the mid- to late-1990s.[6] It was felt that the residents committees were too small to operate effectively and the Street Offices too large to function as effective grassroots organization. The MOCA referred to the new organizations as community residents committees (*shequ jumin weiyuanhui*).

The party has acted to replace one form of collectivity with another, as Bray (2005) notes. Rather than allowing people to interact individually with government and the market, the government has created new organizations to take over the collective aspects of work and service provision that had been provided by the workplace. These organizations, which fall under the authority of the Street Office, are responsible for implementing the state's guarantees to provide minimum support to those in need; taking care of vulnerable populations; managing urban sanitation and health care; enforcing party policy, such as family planning and the maintenance of social stability; and helping with public security work. They are also expected to liaise with other key organizations. While the *shequ* can raise some funds from services it provides, it is essentially dependent on budget appropriations from the Street Office.

---

4 This account draws on Derleth and Koldyk (2004) and Bray (2005).
5 Eleven communities were originally designated; another 15 were added in 2000.
6 Other models described by Derleth and Koldyk (2004) are the Shanghai, Wuhan, and Qingdao models. The degree of autonomy and control of government and party over the communities varies across models.

Figure 8.5. Organization of Urban Government

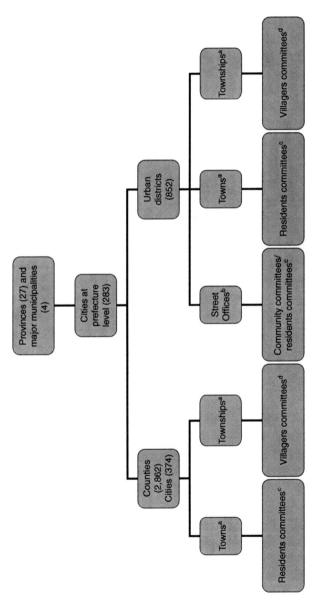

Source: NBS 2007.

a. There were 34,673 towns and townships at the end of 2005, comprising 19,522 towns (a decrease of 331 from 2004) and 15,151 townships (a decrease of 2,300). In 2004, 956 towns and townships were merged or cancelled.

b. There were 6,152 Street Offices in 2005, an increase of 248 over 2004.

c. There were 79,947 urban residents committees at the end of 2005, a decrease of 70 from 2004.

d. There were 629,079 villagers committees at the end of 2005, an increase of 3,932 from 2004.

The development of these new organizations has not taken off as planned, in part because the agenda is too ambitious for the staff involved. Most *shequ* have just three to six full-time workers, who are not particularly well paid, and the work is not considered prestigious. In addition, the government expects the organizations to undertake many functions but does not provide the budget for them to do so. In Qingdao, 160 functions of the Street Office are divided among the *shequ*, government-funded service centers, and charitable organizations (Derleth and Koldyk 2004). Bureaucratic inertia is also a factor: urban administrations have a complex set of organizations, which it is difficult to restructure to integrate the *shequ*. As a result, Derleth and Koldyk (2004) conclude that "active" *shequ* are the exception rather than the rule.

Conclusions and Policy Recommendations

With increased burdens inherited through decentralization and new vulnerable populations to deal with in urban areas, most local governments lack the financial capacity to provide the same level of public services provided in the past. Service provision can be maintained only by rethinking the role of the state and its relationship to the market and institutions of civil society. Government needs to move beyond simply raising more revenue, although raising revenue would clearly help. Four main areas of reform would improve local governments' capacity to deliver more effective public goods and services.

Rethink the Government's Role in Providing Public Services
Government needs to rethink its role in public service provision, eliminating remaining subsidies and distortions left over from the centrally planned system. Government at all levels needs to complete the transition from being the sole provider of services to being a regulator and coordinator—"steering" rather than "rowing" the boat, as the World Bank says. Government should be the provider of last resort of services for which there is no market or where the market disadvantages specific groups, such as migrant workers or the new urban poor (Moss 2002).

Incentives are needed to encourage local governments to pay greater attention to social development. Local finances should be strengthened at the district level in urban areas and the county level in rural areas to allow better investment decisions to be made and redistributive mechanisms to be developed. The strengthening of local finances would be aided by more rapid financial development and deepening, as proposed in chapter 5. Transparency of local government work should be increased, to allow better monitoring of performance and to combat the misuse and diversion of resources. Reforms of government functions should be accompanied by an enhanced role for the market in areas such as housing and pension management and an expansion of the not-for-profit sector as service providers.

The central government needs to provide a framework for the redistribution of resources within society and between different levels of government while ensuring equitable access to public goods and services for all. Currently, the financial system is distorted, with a strong bias toward urban, coastal, and other areas where SOEs are strongly represented. China's investment patterns and fiscal policies have favored the coastal regions at the expense of the interior; formal credit access is highly biased in favor of capital-intensive SOEs, as described in chapter 5; and rural net taxes are regressive.

Focus on a Limited Number of High-Priority Areas

To facilitate more effective resource flows and enhance equity, the central government needs to focus on a limited number of priority areas, as proposed in chapter 1, and then ensure that the financial resources are available to meet its policy objectives. Development practice shows that it is better to deliver results on a smaller number of key tasks than to pursue a long list of policy objectives. Pursuing too broad an agenda dilutes policy impact and makes it easier for local officials to procrastinate and deflect policy intent. Focusing on a few key objectives will make it easier to mobilize resources, set indicators for progress, and hold officials accountable.

Create New Partnerships with Society and the Market

Creating new partnerships will require strengthening the government's regulatory functions and accepting that the market or civil society institutions can perform many development tasks better than the government. Government officials need to recognize that the state is no longer, if it ever was, the sole development actor and that in some areas it may no longer be the most important actor. The emerging mixed economy model for delivering social welfare needs to be legitimized and regulated effectively. In this model, the role of government changes, with less emphasis on direct public financing through taxing and spending and more emphasis on enabling the development of private arrangements that are indirectly subsidized through tax expenditures and publicly regulated. Public funds can be used to support contracts with voluntary and for-profit organizations for the delivery of social services. Doing so would allow scarce government funds to be deployed on essential services and support that neither the market nor voluntary organizations can provide.

For local governments, reforms should be made in both the financial and administrative structures that would allow for more effective provision of services. Better-targeted central government subsidies should be combined with the restructuring of local government finance (for thoughtful analysis, see Wong 1997). Like many other countries, China has witnessed a de facto transfer of new responsibilities to lower-level authorities without the complementary transfer of the necessary financial resources to carry out these functions. Extrabudgetary and off-budget revenues should be incorporated in a unified transparent budget, with a realignment of expenditure and revenue assignments for the various levels of government.

Reducing the reliance on off-budgetary sources and achieving transparency are long-standing policy objectives; meeting them requires some fresh approaches. One option would be to allow local governments to retain a higher percentage of specific taxes collected to cover education, health, and public infrastructure. The burden of service provision should also be reduced for counties, districts, townships, and villages. For example, provision of social security and unemployment insurance should be shifted to provincial governments (if not the national level), so that the benefits of risk pooling can be attained (World Bank 2002).

Establish Basic Criteria for Evaluating Whether Tasks Should Be Performed by Government or Outsourced

In determining which services government should provide, two basic questions need to be answered (Kennedy School of Government 1995). First, does the task involve the making of public policy or the implementation of policy? Second, is the service a "core" one that must be provided by government (for example, the courts or public security), or could the service (for example, trash collection or providing utilities) easily be provided by the market? If a service does not involve policy making and is not a core function, contracting out to the market or civil society organizations should be considered.

The fiscal and administrative changes noted above would allow governments at all levels to play a more effective role in providing social welfare. However, better incentives have to be provided to encourage local officials to pay more attention to social development. These reforms should be supported by a better understanding of what kind of services citizens expect from government and how they prioritize them. Government cannot provide all services; it should allow an enhanced role for alternate providers. This process of restructuring would allow China to develop an enabling governing structure that would provide good guidance to further the impressive economic reforms achieved to date.

References

Bray, D. 2005. *Social Space and Governance in Urban China: The Danwei System from Origins to Reform.* Stanford, CA: Stanford University Press.

Center for Comparative Politics and Economics. 2006. *Innovation and Excellence in Chinese Local Governance (2005–2006).* Beijing:

China Daily. 2004. March 13–14.

Derleth, J., and D. Koldyk. 2004. "The Shequ Experiment: Grassroots Political Reform in Urban China." *Journal of Contemporary China* 13 (41): 747–77.

Edin, M. 2000. *Market Forces and Communist Power: Local Political Institutions and Economic Development in China.* Uppsala, Sweden: Uppsala University Press.

Flynn, N., I. Holliday, and L. Wong. 2001. "Introduction." In *The Market in Social Chinese Policy,* ed. L. Wong and N. Flynn. Basingstoke, United Kingdom: Palgrave.

Han, J. 2003. "Public Finance Crisis in Chinese Counties and Towns: Performance, Causes, Impact and Measures." Mimeo. World Bank, Beijing.

Kennedy School of Government. 1995. "Organizing Competition in Indianapolis: Mayor Stephen Goldsmith and the Quest for Lower Costs." Case Program C18–95–1270.1, Harvard University, Cambridge, MA.

Kish, L. 1949. "A Procedure for Objective Respondent Selection within the Household." *Journal of the American Statistical Association* 44 (247): 380–87.

Lin, J., R. Tao, and M. Liu. n.d. "Decentralization and Local Governance in the Context of China's Transition." CCAP Working Paper 03–E3, Center for Chinese Agricaltural Policy, Beijing.

Ministry of Civil Affairs. 2006. *Zhongguo minzheng tongji nianjian 2006 (China Civil Affairs' Statistical Yearbook).* Beijing: China Statistical Press.

Ministry of Civil Affairs. 2007. http://admin.mca.cn/news/content/recent/2007523122309.htm.

Moss, D. 2002. *When All Else Fails: Government as the Ultimate Risk Manager.* Cambridge, MA: Harvard University Press.

Mountfield, E., and C. Wong. 2005. "Public Expenditure on the Frontline: Toward Effective Management by Subnational Governments." In *East Asia Decentralizes: Making Local Government Work*. Washington, DC: World Bank.

NBS (National Bureau of Statistics). 2007. http://www.stats.gov.cn/english.

"NGOs Can Become Key Social Partner." 2004. *China Daily*, March 13.

OECD (Organisation for Economic Co-operation and Development). 2006. *Challenges for China's Public Spending. Toward Greater Effectiveness and Equity*. Paris: OECD.

Pew Research Center. 1998. "How Americans View Government: Deconstructing Destruct." Pew Research Center, Washington, DC.

Rong, Jingben, Z. Cui, S. Wang, X. Gao, Z. He, and X. Yang. 1998. "*Cong yalixing tizhi xiang minzhu hezuo tizhi de zhuanbian*" *(The Transformation from a Pressurized System to a Democratic Cooperative System)*. Beijing: Zhongyang bianyi chubanshe (Central Translation Bureau Publishing House).

Saich, T. 2000. "Negotiating the State: The Development of Social Organizations in China." *China Quarterly* 161 (March.): 124–41.

———. 2003. "Enhancing Economic Security in Transition: Pluralism in Service Delivery." Focus Programme on Socio-Economic Security Paper 35, International Labor Organization, Geneva.

———. 2006. "Social Policy Development in the Era of Economic Reform." In *HIV/AIDS in China*, ed. J. A. Kaufman, A. Kleinman, and T. Saich. Cambridge, MA: Harvard University Asia Center.

Su, M., and Q. Zhao. 2006. "The Fiscal Framework and Urban Infrastructure Finance in China." World Bank Policy Research Working Paper 4051, Washington, DC.

"33 Indexes Evaluate Government Performance." 2004. *People's Daily*. August 2.

White, R., and P. Smoke. 2005. "East Asia Decentralizes." In *East Asia Decentralizes: Making Local Government Work*. Washington, DC: World Bank.

Whiting, S. 2001. *Power and Wealth in Rural China: The Political Economy of Institutional Change*. New York: Cambridge University Press.

Wong, C., ed. 1997. *Financial Local Government in the People's Republic of China*. New York: Oxford University Press.

World Bank. 2002. *China: National Development and Sub-National Finance: A Review of Provincial Expenditures*. Report No. 22951–CHA. Washington, DC: World Bank.

Index

Lightning Source UK Ltd.
Milton Keynes UK
24 November 2010

163380UK00001B/135/P